Palgrave Studies in Literature, Science and Medicine

Series Editors
Sharon Ruston
Department of English and Creative Writing
Lancaster University
Lancaster, UK

Alice Jenkins
School of Critical Studies
University of Glasgow
Glasgow, UK

Catherine Belling
Feinberg School of Medicine
Northwestern University
Chicago, IL, USA

Palgrave Studies in Literature, Science and Medicine is an exciting new series that focuses on one of the most vibrant and interdisciplinary areas in literary studies: the intersection of literature, science and medicine. Comprised of academic monographs, essay collections, and Palgrave Pivot books, the series will emphasize a historical approach to its subjects, in conjunction with a range of other theoretical approaches. The series will cover all aspects of this rich and varied field and is open to new and emerging topics as well as established ones.

More information about this series at
http://www.palgrave.com/gp/series/14613

Kathleen Béres Rogers

Creating Romantic Obsession

Scorpions in the Mind

palgrave
macmillan

Kathleen Béres Rogers
College of Charleston
Charleston, SC, USA

Palgrave Studies in Literature, Science and Medicine
ISBN 978-3-030-13987-2 ISBN 978-3-030-13988-9 (eBook)
https://doi.org/10.1007/978-3-030-13988-9

Library of Congress Control Number: 2019933869

Cover illustration: Hunt William Holman - Isabella and the Pot of Basil Contributor: Painters/Alamy Stock Photo

This Palgrave Macmillan imprint is published by the registered company Springer Nature Switzerland AG
The registered company address is: Gewerbestrasse 11, 6330 Cham, Switzerland

Preface and Acknowledgements

Sometimes, ideas can be fleeting; we experience them, tuck them away, and return to our everyday lives. Often, however, they have immense power to change an individual or even a culture. When I was growing up in the 1980s, certain ideas took a hold of my young mind and would not let it go: I remember the Tylenol poisoning scare, after which I absolutely refused to ingest a pill for fear that it would result in my death. I remember a slew of kidnappings, a result of which was that I refused to sleep by the window lest someone snatch me from my loving family. Oftentimes, I could not sleep or eat because of how powerful these "ideas," these fears, were. I was originally told I had an "active imagination," which later translated to an anxiety "disorder."

At what point, though, do imagination and pathology intersect? And how can we avoid becoming obsessed by ideas in a culture that promotes obsession in marketing campaigns and the media at large? As a young woman, ideas perpetuated by the media formed my understanding of gender, sexuality, nationality, patriotism, and, of course, mental health. These ideas, I grew to realize, obsessed not only me but our entire culture, so much so that women binge or purge to achieve the perfect body, and, lately, people separate from family and friends over political ideals repeatedly perpetuated by the media. While the stigma of mental "illness" no longer connotes being "put" in a mental asylum, certain types like schizophrenia or OCD are still misunderstood and misrepresented.

The power of the imagination, of the idea, was central to the Romantic era, but I first became interested in obsession—and what it would have meant to the Romantics—in 2010, when I was teaching *Isabella, or the Pot of Basil* to a Keats class at the College of Charleston. With my students, we engaged in a lively discussion about the topic, and it has, for lack of a better word, obsessed me ever since. Around this same time, I taught a Literature and Medicine seminar with Joseph John at the Ralph V. Johnson VA Center in Charleston, and we watched *The Hurt Locker* together. Watching this, I thought about obsession with war, with violence, and with the sublime.

Many people have contributed to my thinking about the Romantic pathologization of obsession; I first presented my paper about *Isabella, or the Pot of Basil* at the 2013 International Conference on Romanticism, a conference that has seen many iterations of all of my book chapters with the exception of Chapter 2. Alan Vardy, the editor of *Essays in Romanticism*, suggested that I submit a longer version for publication, and he worked very patiently with me through the process; the essay, half of Chapter 4, was published in *EiR* as "Breeding Scorpions in the Brain: Obsession in Keats's Isabella, or the Pot of Basil," *Essays in Romanticism* 19, no. 4 (2014): 33–47. As I grew more interested in the topic of obsession (or, rather, the different kinds of Romantic obsession), I submitted part of Chapter 3 for publication in *Literature and Medicine* 36, no. 2 (Fall 2018): 356–371. Both Catherine Belling and, especially, Anna Fenton-Hathaway, were helpful with their constructive comments.

Since Romantic obsession is so very broad, I've had the pleasure of working with a variety of colleagues in many subspecialties. Jacob Steere-Williams, a historian of medicine, was helpful in helping me conceptualize my introduction and conclusion. Marjean Purinton, always a pleasure to talk to about both work and corgis, changed my thinking about curiosity and theater. Jane Calvert helped me unpack Charles Brockden Brown's Quaker influence. Diana Edelman suggested Mary Hays's *Memoirs of Emma Courtney* as an example of gendered intellectual monomania, and she also helped me access M. D. T. Bienville's *Nymphomania*. Terence Bowers read and commented on my Revolutiana chapter, and I gained valuable knowledge about Poe from James Hutchisson and Scott Peeples, both Poe scholars, as well as Amy Shore, my running partner and an expert on epilepsy. I also vetted the Coleridge part of the chapter to my fall 2015 FLASC (Faculty Liberal Arts and Sciences Colloquium) group, which included Richard Bodek,

Irina Erman, Nancy Nenno, Scott Poole, Michaela Ruppert-Smith, and Jacob Steere-Williams. The Department of English at the College of Charleston has been incredibly supportive, and we had a nice turnout for my sabbatical talk about the book. The book has gone through three department chairs, Patricia Ward, Scott Peeples, and Myra Seaman, all of whom have allowed for me to vet it in various ways. Timothy Carens read and commented on my proposal, and I spent a lot of time discussing it with a now-retired colleague, Cynthia Lowenthal. My colleagues at the Medical University of South Carolina have offered medical context; Lisa Kerr provided me some more background about Poe and also invited me to a 2018 *Frankenstein* panel, and Robert Sade invited me to give the Pitts Memorial Lecture about *Frankenstein* in 2018. And all of my chapters have been read and commented on my our virtual "coterie," namely Kellie Donovan Codron and Rebecca Nesvet. Rebecca has been incredibly patient and positive throughout this process, reading multiple drafts and making incredibly useful suggestions, including the addition of A. S. Byatt's *Possession* in the coda. She is the most well-read scholar I know, and she also approaches the study of literature with an eye toward social activism and change.

At the College of Charleston, we embrace a teacher-scholar model, so I'm especially grateful to the students who have helped me along the way, from that first Keats class to my graduate assistants, Emily Conheady Lee, Katie Molpus, and Mindy Buchanan King, the latter of whom spent a summer assisting me with the final book revisions. I also had a chance to teach a graduate class, entitled "Scorpions in the Mind," in Fall of 2016. I want to thank the participants of that class for informing my ideas about Romantic obsession.

This book has taken me a long time to write and has been funded by a variety of sources; I received a grant to attend Stephen Behrendt's 2010 NEH Seminar, "Romantic Aesthetics," where I was inspired by so many attendees, especially Jennifer Santos, Kristen Girten, Allison Dushane, and Soledad Caballero. In 2015, The College of Charleston awarded me a Research and Development Grant, combined with Dean Jerold Hale's Dean's Discretionary Fund, that allowed me to spend two weeks at the National Library of Medicine in Bethesda, Maryland. The librarians and scholars there were all helpful and collegial and added immensely to the primary materials in this book. I also participated in West Virginia

University's Literature and Science seminar, facilitated by Richard Sha in 2013. I want to thank the library staff at the College of Charleston, especially Brendan Lewter, and Susan Hoffius at the Waring Historical Library, who often helped me with some really egregious interlibrary loan requests.

My fascination with the Romantic era has been cultivated by two advisors: Alan Richardson, who advised my M.A. at Boston College and facilitated my interest in the brain/mind, and, especially, Jeanne Moskal, my Ph.D. advisor and friend. Jeanne has also taken time to read through drafts of my writing and mentor me in my publication process. She is the kind of mentor I hope to be someday, staying connected with and interested in her students, both academically and personally.

I have also been graced with a wonderful community of friends: I'd like to thank my Charleston friends, Susan Hoffius, Stephen Hoffius, Amy Shore, Colleen Glenn, Susan Divine, Cara Delay, Noelle Zeiner Carmichael, Sandra Slater, Beth Phillips, and David Parisi, all of whom have listened to my ideas ad nauseum. I'm grateful for my tight-knit group of graduate school friends: Elizabeth and Eric Brignac, Caroline and Alex Christman, Eliza and Mark Laskowski, and Sara and Michael Smith. Eliza and Mark have also graced me with my beautiful Goddaughter, Beatrice Laskowski, who always makes me smile. Sandra Neidhart and Pamela Foster have been my friends since second grade, and, even though I don't often talk to Jenny Ree, she is never far from my heart. Cynthia Darling has been like a sister to me for twenty-three years and has been by my side through so many phases of life.

And finally, I need to thank my family, all of whom have always believed in me. My extended family in Hungary took me in during my 1995 Fulbright Grant, and I especially treasure the friendship of my cousin, Fritschné Kenéz Judit, and her parents, Kenéz Attila and Vali; Kenéz László; and Kenéz Antal. I've lost some Hungarian family during this process, namely Kenéz Zsuzsa and both of my grandparents, Kenéz Antal and Etelka. My grandfather would have been (as he always was) proud. Patty and Jim Rogers have always encouraged me, watching my daughter so that I could travel to the National Library of Medicine, for one. Lee and Maggie Rogers have similarly been amazing cheerleaders.

My mother, Katalin Béres, always asked about the book, reads all of my writing (even if she doesn't understand it), and has been one of my intellectual role models. Through many long car trips, biking/running expeditions, and late nights, my husband, Ben Rogers, has listened to me talk through my ideas and added some different facets to my thinking. My daughter, Julia Rogers, is the light of my life, and she makes everything else worthwhile.

I dedicate this book to my father, Julius Béres, who always said his daughter would someday write a book. I wish he could read it.

Charleston, USA

Kathleen Béres Rogers

Contents

List of Figures

CHAPTER 1

Introduction: Scorpions in the Mind

> The Mind, that broods o'er guilty woes
> Is like the Scorpion girt by fire
> In circle narrowing as it glows
> The flames around their captive close
> Till inly search'd by thousand throes
> And maddening in her ire
> One sad and sole relief she knows,
> The sting she nourish'd for her foes
> Whose venom never yet was vain
> Gives but one pang, and cures all pain,
> And darts into her desperate brain. (Lord Byron, *The Giaour*, 422–452)

In both British and American Romanticisms, the "brooding" mind, the mind that obsessed over an idea, was, surprisingly often, connected to the image of the scorpion. In a still-debated myth dating from the time of Paracelsus, a scorpion will sting itself to death when surrounded by a ring of fire. This vivid image is woven through Romantic-era literature concerned with obsessive thinking, such as John Keats's *Isabella, or the Pot of Basil*, Lord Byron's *The Giaour*, and Percy Bysshe Shelley's *The Cenci*, and my book uses it as a central metaphor for sustained, destructive thinking about one central idea. Biologist J. L. Cloudsley-Thompson writes that "this [myth] must be nonsense, because no animal, other than man, could possibly have the imagination to realize that by self-destruction it might avoid unnecessary pain."[1] One might read

K. Béres Rogers, *Creating Romantic Obsession*,
Palgrave Studies in Literature, Science and Medicine,
https://doi.org/10.1007/978-3-030-13988-9_1

"self-destruction" here as suicide, but the mind also attempts to avoid "unnecessary pain," paradoxically, through self-destructive ideas.

The self-destructive imagination is a popular Romantic-era trope, especially after 1810, when Etienne Esquirol coined the term monomania. In his 1819 play *The Cenci*, Percy Bysshe Shelley refers to Orsino and Giacomo as "scorpions ringed with fire." "What," they ask, "should we do but strike ourselves to death?"[2] Here, as Stuart Curran argues, the scorpion becomes symbolic of self-defense in an evil society. While this self-defense does become obsessive, resulting in Beatrice's suicide, Byron's *The Giaour* (1813), quoted at the beginning of this introduction, refers more closely to obsessive thinking. Here, instead of the mind being besieged by "foes" or by Satan, the brain takes "the sting she nourish'd for her foes," its ideas, and uses them to cure its own "pain." Ideas become destructive and the imagination, far from being the celebrated object of Romanticism, becomes diseased.

Other scholars have extensively studied the pathologization of the imagination. The field of Romantic literary studies owes much to psychoanalytic literary theory; Julianne Buchsbaum, Thomas Frosch, and Charles Rzepka have contributed valuable readings of authors like William Blake, Percy Bysshe Shelley, and Samuel Taylor Coleridge.[3] Diane Hoeveler's work has particularly loomed large, exploring ideas ranging from the fetish to the uncanny to beating fantasies. However, I wish to diverge from a psychoanalytic approach as well as the approach taken by Joel Faflak in his 2009 *Romantic Psychoanalysis*, in which he positions the "discovery" of what we now call psychology in the Romantic era. While the Romantics were interested in the science of mind, this progressivist account does not accord enough attention to the Romantics' own, unique medical discourse. Most akin to my approach is that of William Brewer, who argues for a Romantic-era conception of psychology as opposed to our own.[4] I, too, argue that the Romantics viewed psychology, or what they might have called the "science of mind," differently than we do today. However, I wish to expand on Brewer's work by not writing about the "passions" writ large, but by focusing on the discourse of obsession.

In my use of the word obsession, I mean to use a modern-day term to gesture to a multiplicity of Romantic discourses, all centered around a sustained idea. The words they use, namely "frenzy" or "phrenzy," "mania," "melancholy," and, later, "monomania," all betray their own cultural and discursive contexts, but they point to what I argue is the Romantic pathologization of a common human condition. In this book, I argue that understanding what came to be known as a "condition" helps us reflect on some of the anxieties shaping Romantic-era England…and how some of these anxieties have shaped our modern construction of obsession.

Part I: Origins—Demonic Possession

The first use of the word obsession, in 1548, was as "the action of besieging a place" (OED), and this place most often related to a religiously constructed human soul, not the brain. "Obsessio," a term used by the exorcist Johann Joseph Gassner in 1774, was related to sorcery; witches and sorcerers could summon the devil to "obsess" an unwitting victim.[5] Even, according to Erik Midelfort's perceptive study, "long after witchcraft ceased to trouble the waking and sleeping hours of most Europeans, demons and the devil were taught to be independently active in this world."[6] If one's heart was "pure" and demons could not completely "possess" him, they could still "obsess" him (or her), the difference being that the victim would be aware of but unable to control disturbing thoughts and physical ailments.[7]

Historians of literature often view Romanticism itself as a shift: a shift from rational to imaginative or from religious to secular. Yet, as Diane Hoeveler argues in *Gothic Riffs* (2010), the supernatural did not immediately become secularized or even pathologized. Hoeveler convincingly asserts that, when "nature" displaces the supernatural, we are left with the uncanny, the inexplicable: the "demonic." "But," she writes,

> rather than force people to choose exclusive allegiance to either the immanent order or the transcendent, the rise of ambivalent secularization actually allowed modern Europeans to inhabit an imaginative space in which both the material (science and reason) and the supernatural (God and the devil) coexisted as equally powerful explanatory paradigms.[8]

Hoeveler's study of this interstitial space between "immanent order" and "the transcendent" works to explain the "uncanny," or, more specifically, the popularity of the Gothic. Like a monster, most often monstrous due to its hybridity, the Gothic exists in a neither-nor space: neither the Enlightenment nor the Romantic era, neither religion nor science.[9] This unresolvability characterizes not only the Gothic genre, but also the human mind, which nineteenth-century physicians attempted to control, to normalize, by pathologizing socially unacceptable thought patterns. It is precisely this evolving notion of the "norm" which, as Lennard Davis argues, was coined around 1840, that constructs the notion of "disability," here mental disability.[10] The Romantic era is of interest precisely because these notions were still evolving, because ordering, nosology, and "the transcendent" coexisted in an uneasy partnership.

We all know the obsessed scientist trope from Mary Shelley's *Frankenstein*, and the reader can only wonder at the Romantic-era proliferation (in prose as well as poetry) of lovers, readers, soldiers, and others consumed with a repeated, terrifying but magnetic, idea. This idea still has its room in the "transcendent" or spiritual; we see this in Mary Shelley's critique of "enthusiasm," John Keats's use of ghosts and supernatural tropes, and Samuel Taylor Coleridge's Christian references and footnotes. And nowhere do we see the old idea of demonic possession more clearly than in "actual" accounts, from Bedlam and other asylums, of female patients.[11] Because woman, especially in the nineteenth century, is often reduced to her body, even her obsessive thoughts are bodily, featuring fears of poisoning or death. Completing the circle of possession, women were then seen, in popular accounts, as witches or as aligned with the devil, retaining a connection to the supernatural.

Part II: Proto-Psychology

Even though demonic possession still finds its place in the discourse of obsession, we do see a Romantic-era move toward placing the "disorder" in the material body. As asylum keepers and medical practitioners interested in what Alan Richardson calls the "science of the mind" began to observe patients in mental asylums, a new nosology of symptoms, a creation of a disease-state, was born.[12] The late eighteenth-century and earlier nineteenth-century writers categorized patients broadly, pronouncing them frenetic or melancholic. As Joanna Baillie's 1798 *Plays on the Passions* attest, late eighteenth- and early nineteenth-century ideas about repetitive thinking also focused on the idea of the "passion," here the "ruling passion," a significant term in light of the "rule" of reason and the "rule" of the "mad" King George.

The conflation of the ruling passion and the overly passionate ruler could not have evaded British and American citizens. King George III had suffered "bilious" attacks in 1788 but seemingly recovered after "taking the waters" at Cheltenham Spa. This recovery was short-lived, and a series of doctors were called to diagnose the "raving" monarch: Sir George Baker, an eminent physician, was followed by William Heberden and Sir Richard Warren, the president of the Royal College of Physicians. As the king declined further and further, the court called in Francis Willis, a notorious mad-doctor who habitually relied on the straightjacket as a curative method.[13] Straightjackets and purges were habitual means of regulating the mad, but Willis was even more well-known for his uncanny ability to rule over his own patients through eye contact. Edmund Burke, a philosopher whose notions of the sublime inform much of this book, quizzed him about this power, to which he held his gaze for so long that the sheepish Burke looked away and "acknowled[ged] his basiliskon authority."[14] Here, the rule is transferred from the King to his passion and, perhaps most disturbingly, to his physician.

The notion of the ruling passion—and the degrees to which such a passion can be manipulated—weighed heavily on the British consciousness. Even after Thomas Arnold, in 1786, attempted a new nosology of insanity by mental symptoms this language is often used to illustrate one emotion or idea that holds sway, or "rules," over others.[15] For Arnold, ideal insanity meant a "total" loss of reason, due to the afflicted person's imagining of unreal things. "Notional" insanity, on the other hand, meant that the person was in charge of his or her senses, but some smaller part of the brain had gone awry. One of these forms of notional insanity was pathetic insanity, in which,

> One Passion is in full, and complete possession of the mind; triumphs in the slavery, or desolation, of reason, and even exercises a despotic authority over all the other affections ... all, or nearly all, the varieties of this species of Insanity, are accompanied with distress, dejection, anxiety, or restlessness of mind ...[16]

Here, passion, in a Kantian way, deposes reason; Emmanuel Kant had, in his *Critique of Judgement*, argued that, since the passions "abrogate" freedom, and since reason is necessary to freedom, the passions also impede or completely erase "reason."[17] In an era during which even the king could become subject to an overwhelming passion, the discourse of obsession easily became politicized, as one passion was seen as enslaving other parts of the mind and ruling with "despotic authority."

Thomas Cogan, writing *A Philosophical Treatise on the Passions* (1800), again alludes to the mind being "ruled" or having no agency. In fact, he stresses that the root word of "passion" is passiveness, and that, in medical language, the person being acted upon (by "insanity" as well as physical disease) is called a "patient." His ideologies mirror those of Edmund Burke; Burke writes about the importance of "novelty" in inspiring the sublime, and Cogan writes about "surprise." If, he argues, an idea is sudden and unexpected, it will affect the subject more vividly. If the idea or "object" is vast, then "astonishment" unites with this surprise. After time, this "astonishment" will undoubtedly result in "fatigue of the brain," which indicates itself through headaches, weariness, "prostration of strength," "loss of appetite, indigestions, and flatulencies, &c."[18] Here, Cogan attempts to diagnose "attention of mind," which he reads negatively, in physiological terms. For him, the idea results in physiological symptoms, but others, such as Philippe Pinel, view them as interconnected or, even, as reversed.

In his 1801 *Treatise on Insanity*, translated into English in 1806, Philippe Pinel argues that the both "melancholia" and "hypochondriasis" come from the stomach and radiate up to the brain.[19] As evidenced in the 1999 best-seller *The Second Brain*, and, as explored by critics like Paul Youngquist in terms of Romantic psychology, the stomach and its irritations have long been (and still are) linked to the brain.[20] In Romantic-era medical journals, the debate rages between the brain and the stomach; Villermay, for instance, argues that hypochondriasis has its seat in the stomach, but Falret and Georget both argue that it is located in the brain.[21] Sometimes, the cases do not necessarily originate in the stomach but in other parts of the body; in St. George's hospital, a patient had suffered from acute rheumatism. "Suddenly violent maniacal symptoms arose, attended with a prevailing fear that he was doomed to expiate, in prolonged tortures, crimes probably imaginary."[22] The doctor, Edward Seymour, clearly views the patient's suffering, pain in his joints, as having a sympathetic relationship with his suffering mind.

It is a bit difficult for the modern scholar to ascertain the division between melancholia and hypochondriasis, but it seems to be the relative level of anxiety; the melancholic can be obsessed with an idea, as can a hypochondriac, but the latter will experience more maniacal moods (what other scientists define as asthenic, depressive, versus sthenic, manic, insanity). George Nesse Hill, among others, utilizes these categories but links them to the brain, not the body. For Hill, sthenic insanity derives from "too great mobility of brainular action" and usually comes with fever.[23] Here, we might think about Victor Frankenstein literally working himself into a frenzy. In opposition, the aesthenic person's brain has "too great immobility," like Isabella's when she pines over the head of Lorenzo.

This notion of the active, mobile brain owes much to David Hartley (and others') notions of associationism. In *Hartley's Theory of the Human Mind, on the Principle of the Association of Ideas*, he explains that a sensation can produce an association, which can then produce a successive association (A → B → C). When associations derive from past associations, the effect becomes exponential.[24] Because, according to Hartley, every sensation produces a vibration of the mind, a complex series of associations revolving around the same object,

> affecting one and the same part of the brain, in nearly one and the same manner, must irritate it at last, so as to enter the limits of pain, and approach to the states peculiar to fear, anxiety, despondency, peevishness, jealousy, and the rest of the tribe of hypochondriacal passions.[25]

Therefore, if sensation causes vibration and association, then the obsessive association causes psychological "pain." Joseph Mason Cox repeats this idea in his *Practical Observations on Insanity*, writing that "Any train of thought or any line of conduct to which we are not accustomed, and the grounds of which we cannot comprehend, shocks our understanding."[26]

Cox reiterates the philosophical discourse of the incomprehensible and, by using the word "shock," also refers to his contemporaries' notions of electrotherapy. In 1743, Johann Gottlieb Krüger began urging his students to see electricity as therapeutic; "in response, they began applying charges to bodies in hopes of treating all manner of maladies."[27] This is evidenced by an outbreak of mass hysteria in Lancashire, in 1787, when a girl, playing a trick on her friend, dropped a mouse down her friend's dress. The friend understandably flew into a fit, but this fit seemed to spread to other girls and, later, men in the community. Dr. William St. Clare, a physician with an interest in electrotherapy, was called in; with his portable electrical machine, he "methodically shock[ed]" each patient, whereupon they were "universally" healed.[28]

Cox also references magnetism, most specifically Mesmer's original notion of animal magnetism, which depended on electrically charged particles traveling from one person to another.

In order for the imagination to remain healthy, association must be accompanied by some form of selection. Thomas Bakewell, in his published letter inquiring into the state of "mad-houses" (1815), writes that thoughts

> are the materials from which mind is made, but thoughts are involuntary, unchangeable, and uncertain; mind is, or should be, a permanent quality...and this quality...depends upon the selection we make from our thoughts.[29]

Here, "thoughts" seem to belong to the brain, but "mind" is something else entirely, something akin to a soul. Bakewell's published letter, addressed to the Chairman of the Select Committee of the House of Commons, also introduces an important point for Romantic-era readers and writers thinking about the obsessive thought. No longer are the Bedlamites, the "insane," comfortable Others. Because of the proliferation of print media, the increased clustering of people (and ideas) into confined spaces, and early nineteenth-century emergence of professions as well as disciplines, people have more and more reason to ruminate on an idea. Now "we," everyone, can experience any train of thought and, depending on our "selection"s, can be prone to insanity. Perhaps more than any other mental illness, obsession is democratic, available to the poet, the scientist, the tailor, the homemaker. As J. R. J. Dubuisson writes in 1816, Vesania (his term for the repeated thought) "anticipates the functions of the grave, which levels all mankind."[30] Lennard Davis comments on this leveling in his *Obsession: A History* when he argues that the notion that obsession led to (or even comprised) madness occasioned "a humanizing of the insane and an insanizing of the human."[31] If anyone can have a train of thought that goes awry in a state of astonishment or of "shock," then anyone can, to put it bluntly, become "mad." As the brain is viewed as more and more of a material entity, replete with organs and nerves, the notion of the "disabled" brain becomes more and more prominent.

By 1817, when Johann Gaspar Spurzheim wrote *Observations on the Deranged Manifestations of the Mind, or Insanity*, materialism, the notion that the physical brain determined the "mind," was clearly in ascendancy. Performing autopsies of inmates, Spurzheim attempted to classify their brains and determined that, in acute cases of insanity, the brain is hard; in chronic insanity, the brain is soft. Although Spurzheim does not mention gender here, one wonders if the weakness of the chronically insane, "soft" brain squares with his later assertion that "the female sex is the weakest."[32]

This notion—of ascertaining one's personality based on his or her physical brain—clearly informed Spurzheim's later research with Franz Joseph Gall. Their system of phrenology has been studied in great detail, and one can easily find maps of the "organs," manifested by bumps on the head, and their locations in the brain. Of interest to this book is the "organ of philapprobativeness," which would be larger in a character like Count Basil of Joanna Baillie's *Count Basil*, obsessed with the idea of military glory.[33] It is, of course, gendered, and it produces "ambition as in heroes, love or ornament as in many females…more men are proud and more women vain. And these characteristics are preserved in the mental insanities of male and of female maniacs."[34] Thus Basil pines over military glory and love (for him, these two are interchangeable), while Emma Courtney, in Mary Hays's *Memoirs of Emma Courtney*, assumes, vainly, that Augustus Harley will reciprocate her monstrous feelings.

For Gall and Spurzheim, feelings could also become monstrous, out of control, when one had an enlarged "organ of causativeness." A "morbid affection" of this particular organ produced "hypochondriasis," here defined as a fear of death, fear of hell, or any other fear.[35] Finally, the "organ of ideality" belongs to "poets and men of imagination in general."[36] This organ, when larger than the others, occasions a "recurrent train of early association of ideas."

This sense of "ideality" groups itself, for Esquirol, under the blanket term "melancholy," a term with long and varied associations. For him, "Melancholy consists in the permanent and exclusive impression of any object whatever, pursued with ardor, and almost always accompanied with fear, suspicion, etc."[37] When this fixed idea, the "permanent and exclusive impression" on the senses, is actively pursued but accompanied with negative emotions, it is classified under "melancholy."[38] When, in contrast, the repetitive thought causes excitement, he classifies it as "mania."

Within this wider rubric, Esquirol proposes subcategories. Lypemania, for instance, consists of any idea "contrary to reason" but, like melancholy, "fixed and sustained by a depressing passion."[39] Lypemania is, according to Esquirol, a type of delirium. Following Gall and Spurzheim, he reads emotions physiologically: "In person, the lypemaniac is lean and slender, his hair is black, and the hue of his countenance pale and sallow."[40] The pallor and slenderness correspond with Romantic notions of melancholy—more specifically, male Romantic notions of melancholy—but it also carries interesting resonances with Mary Shelley's descriptions of both Victor Frankenstein and his creature, as will be detailed in Chapter 3.[41]

The fixed ideas of lypemaniacs tend to be very vague but generally tied to the idea of death. In one case, a woman is constantly frightened by the idea of soldiers; another "fears poison, another, dishonor; the latter wishes to do penance, the former believes that if he eats, he shall compromise his relatives or friends…"[42] The notion of "penance" and honor seem crucial to this category of patient: the fear of eating, or consumption, is, in a vicious associative play, somehow related to dishonoring "relatives or friends." These people also need to tell their stories. Like Samuel Taylor Coleridge's ancient mariner, "they relate without ceasing, and to everyone, the story of their ills, their fears, and despair."[43]

Classed under Lypemania is "erotic melancholy," often termed by other writers as Erotomania or even Nymphomania. These categories tend to be gendered, and "girls, widows, and sometimes women at the critical period of life, are a prey to erotic melancholy."[44] Based on case studies that will be examined in Chapter 4, most of the people classified with erotic melancholy are either virgins in their late twenties or menopausal women. Unlike men, whose obsession with women tends to be based more on possession, women's fixation on the idea of either love or sex is mapped on to their bodies.

Although the idea of demonic possession is, as Esquirol states at the beginning of his treatise, obsolete, women still suffer from "demonomania," much more than men.[45] As will become clear in the chapter about erotomania, this particular mania is almost always a form of bodily possession. To provide just one example, Esquirol details a woman suffering from "Demonomania." "The devil," he writes, "has extended a cord from the sternum to the pubes, which prevents the patient from standing up. He is in her body, burning and pinching it. He also knows her heart, and rends her entrails."[46] This "cord" from the "sternum to the pubes," not coincidentally, would traverse not only the woman's stomach and intestinal tract but also her reproductive organs. The phrase "in her body" is not only sexualized, with the "burning and pinching," but also obviously recalls earlier instances of demonic possession. Often, the notion of rending entrails is connected, as in Dante and Shakespeare, with corpses, so the woman is effectively a corpse, a dead body, except for the fact that the devil, like a diabolical confessor, also "knows her heart." Like Lypemania, this type of mania is then associated with religion, guilt, and moral will.

Yet the type of mania most often connected to what we now call obsession is what Esquirol, in 1810, entitled "monomania."

> The patients seize upon a false principle, which they pursue without deviating from logical reasonings, and from which they deduce legitimate circumstances, which modify their affections, and the acts of their will… illusions, hallucinations, vicious associations of ideas, false and strange convictions, are at the basis of this delirium, which I would denominate, intellectual monomania.[47]

In many ways, monomania sounds like lypemania, with the "vicious associations," "delirium," "false…convictions," and even illusions. However, monomania is "intellectual," and the patients importantly do not "deviate[ ] from logical reasonings." The logic is there, the reason is there, but the associative chain is derived from a "false principle." The monomaniac, unlike the lypemaniac, who lives within himself, "lives without himself, and diffuses among others the excess of his emotions."[48] These patients write letters or tell their stories insistently, like the Ancient Mariner or Victor Frankenstein.

Unlike Lypemania, which for Esquirol derives from the abdomen, monomania is "formed in the brain" and then pervades the rest of the body. Thus monomania is the product of excessive ideation or, as we now call it, obsessed genius. One patient, "After being fatigued by reading, and even during the night…is seized with a passion for study, and at the same time persuades himself that his enemies are about to make an attempt upon his life."[49] Here, the "passion for study" and the irrational fear go hand in hand. Unlike the delusions caused by gastrointestinal distress, the overtaxed brain here makes false associations. In his *On the Illusions of the Insane*, in fact, Esquirol states that "This symptom [of hallucinations] is an intellectual phenomenon, totally independent of the organs of sense, and takes place although they may be inactive, or have even ceased to exist."[50] In monomaniacs, hallucinations, like the idea of the enemies attempting the patient's life, are not tied directly to initial sensations or, indeed, to the "organs of sense." Even if the person is blind or deaf or unable to feel, he or she, argues Esquirol, can experience monomania.

What, in 1810, caused obsessive thinking to merit its own pathological category? This question can best be answered through works of literature that introduce the problem of obsessive thinking and begin to examine many of the anxieties that generated "monomania." These anxieties are historical—they revolve around issues like the proliferation of print media and war—as well as medical—they also mirror the Romantic-era's interest in the brain and its inner workings.

Chapter 2 connects this interest in the brain, what was called the "science of the mind," with "vigilia," one of Erasmus Darwin's stages of erotomania. Vigilia, what he calls a "watchfulness [that] consists in the unceasing exertion of volition," forms the basis for both William Godwin's 1794 *Caleb Williams* and Charles Brockden Brown's 1799 *Edgar Huntly, or Memoirs of a Sleep-Walker*. In both of these texts, "vigilia" associates a growing interest in the "science of mind" with one of its pathologized conditions. Both Caleb Williams and Edgar Huntly are analysts, prying into another's "private" life, into another's selfhood, in order to satisfy their curiosity. While critics have read these secrets as illicit homosocial desire (both Edgar and Caleb pursue other men), I read them as representative of a late eighteenth-century desire to penetrate the human mind. Both, in the end, become obsessed with probing the other's secrets and demonstrate the very "frenzy" they initially set out to observe. Here, the mysterious trunk, full of secret documents, serves as a metaphor for the secrets embedded in the human mind. In this way, the very curiosity that drives scientific observation can, like any form of excessive curiosity, become a pathological condition.

Chapter 3 adds to curiosity and frenzy the idea of "enthusiasm," a notion initially grounded in religious discourse that was, as the eighteenth century wore on, appropriated by philosophers and connected to madness. This chapter examines one of Esquirol's categories, "intellectual monomania," or a madness arising from an "overstrained intellect," through the lens of two novels, Mary Hays's 1796 *Memoirs of Emma Courtney* and Mary Shelley's 1818 *Frankenstein*.[51] Hays's protagonist, Emma, reads so many novels that she begins to obsess over the *idea* of the romantic hero, whom she finds in Augustus Harley; Victor, too, obsesses over the *idea* of creating life and, later, over the appearance of the creature himself, seeing him everywhere and at all times. Both authors illustrate that this state of mind is a physiological one, replete with fevers, shuddering, and an inability to breathe. Both invoke David Hartley's notions of associationism to illustrate that a number of physiological and mental effects can be traced back to one original sensation or idea. Yet while Victor's mind is overpopulated, Emma's is eventually erased and melts into nothingness. The two novels illustrate the gendering of "intellectual monomania," with Victor reading books of—albeit disreputable—scientific inquiry while Emma reads indiscriminately from Gothic novels, most notably Jean-Jacques Rousseau's *Héloïse*. Thus male readers become associated with "overstrained intellect" while female readers from insatiable appetite, usually located somewhere in their bodies.

Chapter 4 furthers the discussion of gendered obsession by exploring the (themselves gendered) categories of erotomania and nymphomania. While these "diseases" were both present in the discourse of lovesickness, I argue that John Keats, in his 1809 *Isabella, or the Pot of Basil* and Charlotte Dacre, in her 1811 *The Passions*, use the notions of erotomania and nymphomania in order to complicate their gendering. In doing so, they illustrate the proto-psychological thinking of the time, which I describe here through works by Charles Bell, Esquirol, M. D. T. de Bienville's treatise *Nymphomania* (1775), and articles from archival journal sources. John Keats would have read and known many of these sources in his training as a surgeon-apothecary. He also studied herbal cures at the Chelsea Physic Garden. Basil, one of these cures, was thought to both cause and to cure "scorpions in the brain." He illustrates the "scorpion" of erotomania in *Isabella, or the Pot of Basil*. Here, Isabella cuts off the head of her murdered lover, brings it home, and plants it in a pot, out of which grows basil, more luxuriant because she waters it with her tears. This excess of emotion, which Keats also illustrates in the male characters of Lorenzo and his brothers, is absent from Charlotte Dacre's female protagonist, Apollonia. In *The Passions*, Apollonia is spurned by Wiemar and plots to facilitate a relationship between Wiemar's wife, Julia, and Darlowitz, who, also married, develops an obsessive attraction toward Julia that destroys both himself and her. While Dacre does present Apollonia as an irrational scorned woman, she illustrates the condition of nymphomania more prominently in her *male* character, Darlowitz. Thus these "monstrous" women are interchangeable with monstrous men, distorting a gendered divide that still exists today.

Another gendered notion for the Romantic era (and, still today) was a masculine obsession with possession, power, and conquest. This type of fixation finds its expression in what American doctor Benjamin Rush termed "Revolutiana," an "enthusiasm," to return to that word, in battle.[52] Again, it is the *idea* of war that occupies the mind, making civilian, ordinary life nearly impossible. In Chapter 5, I examine this notion through Thomas De Quincey's essays, "The English Mail-Coach" and "On War," both of which stress war as a sign of a nation's technological innovation. I then turn to Lord Byron's "The Siege of Corinth," which illustrates the obsessive nature of war (the sounds, sights, and smells of explosions) in a foreign land. This foreignness, this distance, introduces the Romantic concept of the sublime, a sense of fear and awe in the external landscape as well as in the subjects' minds. The sublimity of Byron's scene is replicated in Georg Gleig's *Subaltern*: Chronicle of the Peninsular War (1825). This, as well as other memoirs, emphasize the notion of war as spectacle, leading to my exploration of the panorama, most famously Robert Ker Porter's 1802 *Storming of Seringapatam*. Here, the obsession is with the viewers, men and women who crowd, often repeatedly, to view the panorama and feel as if they, too, were partaking in the foreign war. Not only was the audience surrounded by a painting of a battle scene, but the venues, linked to the London theaters, often also included sound effects. This theatrical, spectacular notion of war finds its ultimate expression in Joanna Baillie's 1798 *Count Basil: A Tragedy*, one of her plays on the passions. While this "passion" was ostensibly love, I argue that "love," in the form of conquest, only stands in for Basil's real obsession with war, spectacle, and the martial sublime: the military, he says, was his "mistress." Not only is the audience viewing a spectacle here, but Baillie also includes spectacles, pairing a martial procession with a "train" of women and ending with a masque including satyrs. This chapter also introduces aural elements of obsessive thinking—the repetition of sounds—and references a contemporary debate concerning the definition of "masculinity" in the Romantic era.

Chapter 6 turns my examination of obsession to Johann Spurzheim and Francis Gall's notion of "ideality." This notion, gleaned from phrenology, posits that a person's (most usually a poet's) "organ of ideality" can grow so large that his—and the gender is usually masculine here—ideas can become more *real* than external events. To pathologize this state, both physiognomy and phrenology looked to the large forehead, the arched eyebrows and, always, the "glittering eye." A person with this disorder can also communicate ideas, so that poets and writers, akin to mesmerists, will use ideas in order to situate them in the minds of their readers. In this way, writing or "telling" is both a compulsion that momentarily relieves one of the obsessive thought, and a way of spreading or communicating that very thought. I first examine this notion in Samuel Taylor Coleridge's 1797 and, later, 1817 (with the gloss) *Rime of the Ancient Mariner*, looking specifically at Coleridge's influence by Hartleian association as well as natural philosophers like Tom Wedgwood, Thomas Beddoes, and Erasmus Darwin. I argue that the mist, snow, solitude, and dream-like state that characterize the poem even before the albatross is shot produce a "swoon," a state in between dreaming and waking, wherein the mariner loses all volition. This nightmare is later replicated in the crew, the parching sun, and life-in-death until the mariner can replace it with another idea. Even so, he must retell his story, again and again, in order to gain even momentary relief from his initial feeling (in his *Biographia Literaria*, Coleridge had argued that one did not need sensation to produce an association, and that even feelings could produce a train of related ideas). By telling his story repeatedly, and having the narrator tell the story to us, he also compels readers into the obsessive circle.

Edgar Allan Poe, writing later than Coleridge, was nonetheless extremely influenced by his philosophical ideas, by phrenology and physiology, and also by the proto-psychological ideas of his time, namely those of Rush, Thomas Prichard, and his friend and asylum director, Pliny Earle. It is important to remember that medical ideas often traveled to the United States far after they had been popular in England, and that Spurzheim and Gall's notions of phrenology were extremely popular in 1830s America when Poe was writing "Beatrice" and "The Tell-Tale Heart." For Poe, the obsession—which he, writing after 1810, actually calls "monomania"—is almost always with the idea of death, but it manifests through an obsession with a *thing*, in Poe's case a body part. This form of fetishism simultaneously brings the idea to life (the idea "becomes" the teeth in "Berenice") and objectifies–and thereby feminizes–the person in question. His "Berenice" (1835) features a narrator obsessed with a woman's teeth, and his more famous "The Tell-Tale Heart" (1843) concerns an old man's eyes. In both cases, it is the "idea" of the teeth and the "idea" of the eye that obsess the narrators and occasion their gruesome acts; in both cases, the narrators feel that they must, defensively, confess. As they "write" their confessions, these ideas come to infect their readers: readers of miscellanies that, like mesmeric thoughts, circulated, much as medical ideas circulate circumatlantically.

It is important to note that "phrenzy," "mania," "enthusiasm," and "monomania" are not functional equivalents of what we now call obsession or pathologize as obsessive compulsive disorder, or OCD. Twenty-first-century media representations of OCD focus on the compulsions associated with obsession: hand washing, counting, compulsive cleaning, and so on. These are easier to represent visually and so understandable that they have become a cliché: "I am," people say, "a little OCD." Even taken in its medical context, the notion of OCD today is very different from what the Romantics called frenzy or ideality or monomania. The coda of this book examines the twenty-first-century (DSM V) discourse of OCD, noting both some similarities with Romantic obsession but, most often, differences (for instance, "workaholism" is no longer pathologized, and nymphomania has been removed to a different psychological category).

It is in popular depictions of obsession that we still see remnants of Romantic-era discourse. There are, of course, countless science fiction novels and films about scientists on a Frankenstein-like quest for new knowledge, for new life. There are also movies about nymphomania, a category that is now referred to as "hypersexuality" in the DSM V but remains gendered in popular culture. Lars Von Trier's 2013 *Nyphomaniac*, for instance, illustrates the protagonist's obsessive search for sex by paralleling her desires with the sport of fly-fishing. In terms of war, media representations like Kathryn Bigelow's 2008 *The Hurt Locker*, produced by a woman, emphasize the awe and sublimity of war, as well as the obsessive (male) need to reenlist and reexperience these emotions. Yet these emotions are also mixed with the trauma of war, making our societal image of the "good soldier" all but untenable. And perhaps ideality is best illustrated by an obsessive need to tell stories, no matter how true or untrue, as illustrated by Tim Burton's 2003 *Big Fish*. My coda ends with a close reading of A. S. Byatt's 1990 *Possession*, which illustrates the ways that the Romantic concept of intellectual monomania informs Byatt's portrayal of academic obsession; similarly, Romantic erotomania shades the various heterosexual relationships in the novel. What has changed is the gender norms associated with both intellectual monomania, gendered male in the Romantic era, and erotomania, often gendered female. In Byatt's postmodern novel, the categories are upended, causing the reader to question their very pathologization.

In the end, obsession is interesting because it is, as Lennard Davis puts it in his 2005 *Obsession: A History*, so democratic. We have all become enamored of a project (to the degree that we forget to eat or take showers), of a person, or of sexual pleasure. Some of us have been captivated by violence, by war, both pulled to and pushed from the scene of conflict. And while fewer of us become obsessed with irrational thoughts, we can all understand the desire to tell and retell a good "fish tale." The Romantic era presents us with a time when these common feelings become pathologized, categorized, and labeled as diseased, "abnormal" states. And since norms change with time periods and with cultures, what we obsess about today can tell us a lot about our culture's own anxieties.

Notes

1. J. L. Cloudsley-Thompson, "Scorpions in Mythology, Folklore, and History," in *The Biology of Scorpions*, ed. Gary A. Polis (Stanford: Stanford University Press, 1990), 475.
2. Stuart Curran, *Shelley's Cenci: Scorpions Ringed with Fire* (Princeton: Princeton University Press, 1970). Curran reads this passage as a metaphor for Beatrice's suicide, an act, he argues, of self-defense in the face of ubiquitous evil.
3. See Julianne Buchsbaum, "Abjection and the Melancholic Imagination: Towards a Poststructuralist Psychoanalytic Reading of Blake's the Book of Urizen," *Romanticism and Victorianism on the Net* 56 (2009); Thomas R. Frosch, *Shelley and the Romantic Imagination: A Psychological Study* (Newark, DE: University of Delaware Press, 2007); and Charles J. Rzepka, "Christabel's 'Wandering Mother' and the Discourse of the Self: A Lacanian Reading of Repressed Narration," *Nineteenth Century Contexts* 10, no. 1 (1986): 17–43.
4. William D. Brewer, *The Mental Anatomies of William Godwin and Mary Shelley* (Madison, NJ: Fairleigh Dickinson University Press; London, England: Associated University Press, 2001).
5. Henri F. Ellenberger, *The Discovery of the Unconscious: The History and Evolution of Dynamic Psychiatry* (New York: Basic Books, 1970), 55.
6. Erik H. C. Midelfort, *Exorcism and Enlightenment: Johann Joseph Gassner and the Demons of Eighteenth-Century Germany* (New Haven: Yale University Press, 2005), 7.
7. Hilaire Kallendorf, *Exorcism and Its Texts: Subjectivity in Early Modern Literature of England and Spain* (Toronto: University of Toronto Press, 2003), 109.
8. Diane Hoeveler, *Gothic Riffs: Secularizing the Uncanny in the European Imaginary, 1780–1820* (Columbus: Ohio State University Press, 2010), 6.
9. For more about the links between monstrosity and hybridity, see Paul Youngquist, *Monstrosities: Bodies and British Romanticism* (Minneapolis and London: University of Minnesota Press, 2003), in which he also compares the hybridity of the human monster with the hybridity of Wordsworth's poetic forms.

10. Lennard Davis, "Introduction: Disability, Normality, and Power," in *The Disability Studies Reader*, ed. Lennard J. Davis (Routledge, 2017), 3.
11. These accounts were, of course, transcribed by physicians or asylum proprietors, the so-called "alienists."
12. See Alan Richardson, *British Romanticism and the Science of the Mind* (Cambridge: Cambridge University Press, 2001).
13. John Wiltshire, "Frances Burney, the Court, and Pathography," *Women's Writing* 23, no. 3 (2016): 378–389.
14. Quoted in Roy Porter, *Medicine in the Enlightenment* (Amsterdam: Rodopi, 1995), 258.
15. Thomas Arnold, "Observations on the Nature, Kinds, Causes, and Prevention of Insanity, Lunacy, or Madness," in *Three Hundred Years of Psychiatry*, ed. Richard Hunter (Hartsdale, NY: Carlisle Publishing, 1982). While Hunter calls this "psychiatry," this too is an anachronistic term.
16. Ibid., 471.
17. Emmanuel Kant, *Critique of Judgement* (Oxford, UK: Oxford University Press, 2007). ProQuest ebrary. Web. June 7, 2015. 102.
18. Thomas Cogan, *A Philosophical Treatise on the Passions* (London, 1800), 295.
19. Philippe Pinel, *A Treatise on Insanity, in which Are Contained the Principles of a New and More Practical Nosology of Maniacal Disorders …*, trans. D. D. Davis (Sheffield, 1806), 41.
20. See Michael Gershon, *The Second Brain* (HarperCollins, 1999); Paul Youngquist, "De Quincey's Crazy Body," *Publications of the Modern Language Association of America* 114, no. 3 (1999): 346–358; and Paul Youngquist, "Rehabilitating Coleridge: Poetry, Philosophy, Excess," *ELH* 66, no. 4 (1999): 885–909, Project MUSE, the latter of which I write about in Chapter 6.
21. Roderick Macleod and John Bacot, eds., *London Medical and Physical Journal*, vol. 47 (London: J. Souter, 1823).
22. *London Medical and Physical Journal*, vol. 12 (London: J. Souter, 1804), 304.
23. *London Medical and Physical Journal*, vol. 35 (London: J. Souter, 1816), 493.
24. Joseph Priestley, *Hartley's Theory of the Human Mind, on the Principle of the Association of Ideas; with Essays Relating to the Subject of It* (London: J. Johnson, 1775), 16.
25. Ibid., 231.
26. *Edinburgh Medical and Surgical Journal*, vol. 1 (1805), 230.
27. David Parisi, *Archeologies of Touch: Interfacing with Haptics from Electricity to Computing* (Minneapolis: University of Minnesota Press, 2018), 77–78.

28. Lennard Davis, *Obsession: A History* (Chicago: University of Chicago Press, 2008), 34.
29. Thomas Bakewell, *A Letter to the Chairman of the Select Committee of the House of Commons, Appointed to Enquire into the State of Mad-Houses: To Which is Subjoined, Remarks on the Nature, Causes, and Cure of Mental Derangement* (Stafford, 1815), 36–37.
30. *London Medical and Physical Journal*, vol. 37 (London: J. Souter, 1817), 242.
31. Davis, *Obsession*, 100.
32. Johann Spurzheim, *Observations on the Deranged Manifestations of the Mind, or Insanity* (Boston, 1836), 102.
33. For recent research concerning phrenology as regards Romantic-era literature, see Alan Richardson, *British Romanticism and the Science of the Mind* (Cambridge: Cambridge University Press, 2001); María Isabel Jiménez González, "Phrenology and Mesmerism in Edgar Allan Poe," in *Studies in Philology: Linguistics, Literature and Cultural Studies in Modern Languages*, eds. Gema Alcaraz Mármol and Maria del Mar Jiménez-Cervantes Arnao (Newcastle upon Tyne: Cambridge Scholars Publishing, 2014), 305–314; Brett Zimmerman, "Phrenology," in *Edgar Allan Poe in Context*, ed. Kevin J. Hayes (Cambridge: Cambridge University Press, 2013), 301–312; and G. A. Starr, "The Bump Above Robert Wrighim's Ear: Phrenology in Hogg's *Confessions of a Justified Sinner*," *Studies in Hogg and His World* 19 (2008): 81–89.
34. Thomas F. L. S. Forster, *Sketch of the New Anatomy and Physiology of the Brain and Nervous System of Drs. Gall and Spurzheim* (London, 1815), 53.
35. Ibid., 91.
36. Ibid., 55.
37. Etienne Esquirol, *Mental Maladies: A Treatise on Insanity* (Philadelphia: Lea and Blanchard, 1845), 203.
38. Although I will use the term "fixed idea," and Esquirol also uses it, the term idée fixe was not coined until 1836 (OED).
39. Esquirol, *Mental Maladies*, 203.
40. Ibid., 203.
41. See Elizabeth A. Dolan, "British Romantic Melancholia: Charlotte Smith's Elegiac Sonnets, Medical Discourse and the Problem of Sensibility," *Journal of European Studies* 33, no. 3–4 (2003): 237–253.
42. Esquirol, *Mental Maladies*, 205.
43. Ibid., 206.
44. Ibid., 211.
45. Ibid., 243.
46. Ibid., 239.
47. Ibid., 320.
48. Ibid., 323.

49. Ibid., 326.
50. Etienne Esquirol, *Observations on the Illusions of the Insane, and on the Medico-Legal Question of Their Confinement*, trans. William Liddell (London: Renshaw and Rush, 1833), 1, accessed via archive.org and Medical Heritage Library.
51. Alexander Morison, *Lectures on Insanity, for the Use of Students* (Edinburgh, 1841), 670.
52. Although his term referred specifically to his work with soldiers during the American revolution, such ideas inform writers discussing the French Revolution and, later, the Napoleonic Wars.

Bibliography

Arnold, Thomas. "Observations on the Nature, Kinds, Causes, and Prevention of Insanity, Lunacy, or Madness." In *Three Hundred Years of Psychiatry*, edited by Richard Hunter. Hartsdale, NY: Carlisle Publishing, 1982.

Bakewell, Thomas. *A Letter to the Chairman of the Select Committee of the House of Commons, Appointed to Enquire into the State of Mad-Houses: To Which is Subjoined, Remarks on the Nature, Causes, and Cure of Mental Derangement.* Stafford, 1815.

Brewer, William D. *The Mental Anatomies of William Godwin and Mary Shelley.* Madison, NJ: Fairleigh Dickinson University Press; London, England: Associated University Press, 2001.

Cloudsley-Thompson, J. L. "Scorpions in Mythology, Folklore, and History." In *The Biology of Scorpions*, edited by Gary A. Polis. Stanford: Stanford University Press, 1990.

Cogan, Thomas. *A Philosophical Treatise on the Passions.* London, 1800.

Curran, Stuart. *Shelley's Cenci: Scorpions Ringed with Fire.* Princeton: Princeton University Press, 1970.

Davis, Lennard. "Introduction: Disability, Normality, and Power." In *The Disability Studies Reader*, edited by Lennard J. Davis. Routledge, 2017.

———. *Obsession: A History.* Chicago: University of Chicago Press, 2008.

Dolan, Elizabeth A. "British Romantic Melancholia: Charlotte Smith's Elegiac Sonnets, Medical Discourse and the Problem of Sensibility." *Journal of European Studies* 33, nos. 3–4 (2003): 237–253.

Edinburgh Medical and Surgical Journal, vol. 1. 1805.

Ellenberger, Henri F. *The Discovery of the Unconscious: The History and Evolution of Dynamic Psychiatry.* New York: Basic Books, 1970.

Esquirol, Etienne. *Mental Maladies: A Treatise on Insanity.* Philadelphia: Lea and Blanchard, 1845.

———. *Observations on the Illusions of the Insane, and on the Medico-Legal Question of Their Confinement*. Translated by William Liddell. London: Renshaw and Rush, 1833. Archive.org and the Medical Heritage Library.

Forster, Thomas F. L. S. *Sketch of the New Anatomy and Physiology of the Brain and Nervous System of Drs. Gall and Spurzheim*. London, 1815.

Hoeveler, Diane. *Gothic Riffs: Secularizing the Uncanny in the European Imaginary, 1780–1820*. Columbus: Ohio State University Press, 2010.

Kallendorf, Hilaire. *Exorcism and Its Texts: Subjectivity in Early Modern Literature of England and Spain*. Toronto: University of Toronto Press, 2003.

Kant, Immanuel. *Critique of Judgement*. Oxford, UK: Oxford University Press, 2007. ProQuest ebrary. Web. June 7, 2015.

London Medical and Physical Journal, vol. 12. London: J. Souter, 1804.

London Medical and Physical Journal, vol. 35. London: J. Souter, 1816.

London Medical and Physical Journal, vol. 37. London: J. Souter, 1817.

London Medical and Physical Journal, vol. 47. London: J. Souter, 1823.

Midelfort, Erik H. C. *Exorcism and Enlightenment: Johann Joseph Gassner and the Demons of Eighteenth-Century Germany*. New Haven: Yale University Press, 2005.

Morison, Alexander. *Lectures on Insanity, for the Use of Students*. Edinburgh, 1841.

Parisi, David. *Archeologies of Touch: Interfacing with Haptics from Electricity to Computing*. Minneapolis: University of Minnesota Press, 2018.

Pinel, Philippe. *A Treatise on Insanity, in Which Are Contained the Principles of a New and More Practical Nosology of Maniacal Disorders …* Translated by D. D. Davis. Sheffield, 1806.

Porter, Roy. *Medicine in the Enlightenment*. Amsterdam: Rodopi, 1995.

Priestley, Joseph. *Hartley's Theory of the Human Mind, on the Principle of the Association of Ideas; with Essays Relating to the Subject of It*. London: J. Johnson, 1775.

Richardson, Alan. *British Romanticism and the Science of the Mind*. Cambridge: Cambridge University Press, 2001.

Spurzheim, Johann. *Observations on the Deranged Manifestations of the Mind, or Insanity*. Boston, 1836.

Wiltshire, John. "Frances Burney, the Court, and Pathography." *Women's Writing* 23, no. 3 (2016): 378–389.

CHAPTER 2

Vigilia and the Science of the Mind in William Godwin's *Caleb Williams* and Charles Brockden Brown's *Edgar Huntly, or Memoirs of a Sleepwalker*

In his 1794 *Zoonomia*, Erasmus Darwin, a doctor and poet, not only categorized plants and animals, but also mental states, or what his contemporaries called "the passions." The stages Darwin details pertaining to erotomania, a fixation on a person, correspond exactly to the plots of both William Godwin's *Caleb Williams, or Things as They Are* (1794) and Charles Brockden Brown's *Edgar Huntly, or Memoirs of a Sleep-Walker* (1799). The sequence begins with "reverie," or "the visionary state that triggers somnambulism": Caleb Williams becomes overly curious about a chest belonging to his erratic employer Falkland, spending much of his mental energy on deciphering both Falkland (who he rightly suspects of being a murderer) and the chest's contents. Similarly, Edgar Huntly sees Clithero, a servant on his family's farm, sleepwalking; certain that Clithero murdered his best friend, he becomes lost in curiosity and, literally, in his own somnambulism.

Darwin's sequence then proceeds to a desire for solitude in mountains and forests—while neither character desires this solitude, Edgar Huntly wakes up in a cave and must traverse the rocky wilderness, and Caleb Williams spends time in the wilderness attempting to evade Falkland, who Williams, by this time, knows to be a murderer. Finally, "erotomania" ends with "furious or melancholy insanity; and suicide, or revenge."[1] The original ending of *Caleb Williams* features Caleb descending into insanity, partly spurred by his desire for revenge on Falkland. In *Edgar Huntly*, our protagonist goes on a killing spree, murdering Native Americans for seemingly little reason.

K. Béres Rogers, *Creating Romantic Obsession*,
Palgrave Studies in Literature, Science and Medicine,
https://doi.org/10.1007/978-3-030-13988-9_2

This chapter returns to the beginning of the cycle, focusing on a component of "reverie," what Darwin defined as "vigilia," or "watchfulness [that] consists in the unceasing exertion of volition."[2] Here, I argue that "vigilia" both connects with the religious roots of obsession and associates a growing interest in the "science of mind" with one of its pathologized conditions. In order to understand another's psyche (or, as the Romantics would have put it, the workings of another's mind), the observer needs to remain vigilant: to watch for details, to probe the person's secrets, and, as Joel Faflak argues, to discern a person's very selfhood. At what point, though, does this curiosity become pathological, manipulative and, as critics have argued of both *Caleb Williams* and *Edgar Huntly*, erotically charged? While both of these texts can be—and have been—read in multiple, equally productive ways, I propose that both critique a growing proto-psychology movement that leaves the observer obsessed with learning his subject's secrets.

The notion of learning a subject's secrets does tie to the growth of what we now call psychology. Scientists in general were often accused of undue curiosity. In his *History of Madness*, Michel Foucault writes that one of the prime causes of "frenzy" was, according to the Encyclopédie, "a love of science or a devotion to letters, both of which are increasingly widespread."[3] If the will, so important to philosophers like Kant and Descartes, allowed for attention, that will could easily become subsumed by "appetite."[4] French naturalist René Antoine Ferchalt de Réamur, for instance, looked so intently and diligently at maggots that they became "marvels" to "rival fairy tales and *The Thousand and One Nights*."[5] When critics wrote about these observational regimes, they "reproached [the scientists] for self-indulgence and a lack of moderation, for appetites run amok."[6] Here, the scientist, the observing subject, becomes the observed object.

Proto-psychologists often displayed what could be viewed as a voyeuristic desire to understand others' mental workings. When Adam Ferguson of Edinburgh became professor of moral philosophy and pneumatics in 1764, he answered to his title by making the "theory of mind" a proper part of his basic textbook, the *Institutes of Moral Philosophy*.[7] In order to cultivate a theory of mind—or to distinguish healthy from unhealthy minds—one had to observe subjects deemed insane. The number of these observations, recorded in asylums, hospitals, and by medical practitioners, is astounding…and telling. Medical practitioners like Thomas Forster and William Perfect write "scientific" texts detailing their theories, but these are undergirded by the more curious accounts of the "insane." In the *London Medical and Physical Journal*, readers could access articles like "reports on madhouses" as well as analyses of prominent asylum-keepers' observations. William Halloran, physician to the asylum at Cork, Ireland, writes *An Inquiry into the Causes Producing the Extraordinary Addition to the Number of Insane …*, and John Haslam, proprietor of the Bethlehem Hospital for the Insane (now known as Bedlam), writes *Sketches in Bedlam*. While insanity and its variants had been relegated to the "mad-house," readers were urged to themselves become ersatz psychologists and analyze those close to them, looking for signs of insanity, as indicated by the 1805 publication of Bakewell's *The Domestic Guide in Cases of Insanity*. In this text, Bakewell urges his readers to be vigilant and watch for signs of insanity, including an inability to "get something out of [a person's] head."[8] These readers, having purchased Bakewell's book, were advised to watch members of their households carefully; by watching vigilantly, they too could diagnose insanity.

Part I: The Vigil: Wakeful Curiosity

The very notion of "keeping a vigil" suggests a constant, almost suspicious watchfulness (one thinks here of the Biblical injunction to "be vigilant" against the Devil [1 Peter 5:8]). Of course, the vigil can also be a hopeful occasion; according to the OED, the Christian church defines a vigil as "The eve of (i.e. preceding) a festival or holy day, as an occasion of devotional watching or religious observance." The devotee is, here, watching and waiting for a joyous occasion, but watching, observance, and the lack of sleep remain—the vigil is, if nothing else, usually held at night. In fact, a definition contemporaneous with both Godwin and Brockden Brown would have been not religious, but physiological: "A wakefulness, or period of this, due to inability to sleep" (OED). Vigilia is paradoxical in that it can be both beneficial—one's vigilance protects against evil spirits and allows for intense devotion—and destructive: vigilance over someone's psyche, whether someone else's or one's own, can consume the mind to the exclusion of all else.

The introduction of this book has already explored the links between demonic possession and obsession, so I turn here to the notion of observation (of the self and of others) *as* obsession. In many ways, observation of others was endorsed by a culture that celebrated curiosity, nowhere better reflected than in the popularity of the curiosity cabinet. Even though these "cabinets of curiosity" were most often big rooms containing a vast collection of objects, they were often represented in literature as literal trunks to be opened. As such, argues Marjean Purinton, they invited viewers to take on the role of doctors and practice "speculation, observation, and prescription."[9] Physicians like James Graham encouraged viewers to indulge their curiosity about the mysteries of health and sexuality, showcasing objects like his Celestial Bed, meant to cure impotence and sterility and increase pleasure. Patrons of Graham's shows were even encouraged to observe fifteen-year-old Emma Lyon, dressed provocatively as Vestina, Goddess of Health.[10] Purinton adroitly compares these "medical" performances to two stage performances, namely George Colman the Younger's *The Iron Chest* (1796) and *Blue-Beard; or, Female Curiosity!* (1798). She argues that, "just as curiosity cabinets put crime and sexuality on display, these plays use chests and closets, in which pathological impulses are secreted, to engineer a meta-performance of cultural curiosity."[11] While these "chests and closets" do hide secrets, the desire to open them, the desire to *see*, is also, especially in the latter play, extremely problematic.

In *The Iron Chest*, the protagonist, Wilford, is a servant…much like William Godwin's Caleb Williams. Also like Caleb, he decides to peer at the documents inside his employer's iron chest and then proceeds to soliloquize about his uncontrollable desire:

> this unravels all, from the first day of my service—when a deep groan made me run into the library, and I found him locking up his papers, in the iron chest, as pale as ashes.—eh?—What can be in that chest!—Perhaps some proof of—no I shudder at the suggestion.—'tis not possible one so good can be guilty of—I know not what to think—nor what to resolve. But curiosity is roused, and, come what may, I'll have an eye upon him.[12]

Recall Darwin's definition of vigilia as "unceasing exertion of volition." Here, the aptly named "Will-ford" has a will that is seemingly not his own: a groan "made [him]" run into the library, and he narrates to us his thought process. While he "shudder[s] at the suggestion" of what Mortiner may have done, his curiosity is "roused," awakened, and he decides to keep observing him, to have "an eye" upon him. Much like Falkland, Caleb Williams' employer, Wilford extorts the overly curious boy to keep his secret, saying that "you have sought this secret: —Yes, / extorted it. I have not thrust it on you."[13] Again, the secret is not only actively "sought" but manipulatively "extorted." Finally, Wilford admits that his curiosity has indeed made his life more difficult, moralizing that "I have been / too curious, haply."[14]

In the latter play, *Blue Beard*, a villain who has beheaded six wives hides their corpses in a mysterious Blue Chamber, the contents of which are only known to (once again), his servant, Shacabac. However, Fatima, another of the play's many characters, seeks to discover the secret, which the audience of the play is also rewarded with when Shacabac turns the "charmed" key. In this scene, we see:

> …the Blue chamber appears streaked with vivid streams of Blood…The Pictures, and devices, of Love, change to subjects of Horror and death. The interior apartment (which the sinking of the door discovers), exhibits various tombs, in a sepulchral building; —in the midst of which ghastly and supernatural forms are seen; —some in motion, some fix'd—in the centre, is a large skeleton seated on a tomb, (with a dart in his hand) and, over his head, in characters of Blood, is written "the punishment of curiosity."[15]

As Purinton points out, such a scene would have fed the curiosity of theatergoers with its moving skeletons and its bleeding walls. Here, we have a meta-example of curiosity, with the theatergoers *and* Fatima sating their curiosity. Again, there is a doubled meaning in observation and curiosity, with curiosity being both positive (especially for Gothic writers and theater producers, for whom it is a source of income) and, here, literally negative.

To provide one more example, William Godwin had, in 1793—one year before the publication of *Caleb Williams*—read George De Lillo's *Fatal Curiosity: A Tragedy*.[16] This play also contains a "casket" given to Agnes to open. Like Wilford, Agnes debates opening the casket but cannot keep herself from acting:

> I'm strongly tempted
> To open it, and see—No, let it rest. Why should my curiosity excite me, To search and pry into th' affairs of others; Who have to employ my thoughts, so many cares
> And sorrows of my own!—With how much ease
> The spring gives way? Surprising ! most prodigious! My eyes are dazzled, and my ravish'd heart
> Leaps at the glorious sight. (III, I)[17]

Like Wilford, she attempts to contain her volition, telling the audience (and herself) that she should "let it rest," and that she should not "search" (a word that implies protracted action) or "pry" (a word used often by Godwin) into others' "affairs." Two lines later the spring passively "gives way" and her "ravished" heart is elevated by the sight of numerous valuable jewels. In an Oedipus-like twist, the treasures' deliverer, disguised and known to her only as a "stranger," turns out to be her own son, but, tempted by the thought of wealth, she murders the boy. In this way, her curiosity proves truly "fatal."

What might be the social anxiety behind curiosity, or the desire to know a secret? While, on one hand, the Enlightenment gloried in curiosity, uncovering the "secrets" of nature, this impulse, when applied to the human mind, collided with the culture's valuation of privacy. Reading the secrets of another's mind, what Patricia Spacks calls the "imagining of other people's privacies," was considered "dangerous."[18] How might this "imagining" be policed or regulated? Once someone started "reading" another's mind, who was to tell where his or her thoughts would go?

This anxiety was closely linked with novel reading. As the century wore on, novels were more and more focused on contemplating the "inner lives of their characters."[19] Not only did authors like Jane Austen and Anne Radcliffe focus on their characters' psychological states, but the readers themselves were encouraged to "read" characters based on the physiological symptoms:

> Weeping, blushing, fainting, "brain fever"—such evidence of psychic states might be read by any onlooker. Although ambiguity remained (did a father's illness occasion a young woman's tears, or did they attest to the existence of a lover?), the mythology of sensibility encouraged fantasies of accessibility. Not even a determined will to privacy, according to this mythology, could protect women in particular from offering inadvertent testimony to their inner states.[20]

Here, the language of sensibility—the weeping, blushing, fainting, and so on—also evinces a growing belief in a brain and body connection. As opposed to Descartes' mind–body divide, the mind here betrayed itself *in* the body, providing "inadvertent testimony" through physical gestures. In fact, as will be seen throughout this book, medical practitioners looked for these signs to read mental disease. The novel thus served as a psychological case study, encouraging readers to become amateur analysts.

Thus, readers peer into novels, arguably their own cabinets of curiosity, in order to learn about and understand characters who peer into other characters' minds. The two texts I analyze in this chapter also contain physical "cupboards" in the form of chests that the overly-curious characters seek out and open. Both chests contain documents to be read, further referring to the novels in which they are housed. In this way, gothic literature, British and American, both encourages the curiosity of its readers and expresses a cultural anxiety concerning the role that obsessive curiosity, *vigilia*, can take.

Part II: A "Restless Propensity": Curiosity in Caleb Williams

Although William Godwin disavowed himself of traditional religion later in life, his early education and influences are, I believe, important to his theories of the human mind. Brought up in a strict Calvinist environment, he was nonetheless educated at Hoxton Academy, a liberal, Presbyterian college. Even though he progressively drew away from his religious upbringing he, like many of the authors in this book, never espoused materialism, the belief that the human psyche is composed of the brain's "materials."[21] His beliefs were formed by reading the works of Samuel Clarke, James Beattie, and Andrew Baxter; Baxter's *Enquiry into the Nature of the Human Soul* (1745) had a profound effect on him. Baxter, using mathematical and philosophical reasoning and engaging with the work of Newton, eventually determines that "since matter cannot re-excite the motion in itself it follows that as an immaterial Power first impressed motion on matter, so it still reproduces the motion lost, and makes up the decays sustained."[22] In other words, Baxter firmly denies materialism, insisting that matter, here the human brain, needs an external force, an "immaterial power," to make it move and work.

Like Baxter, Godwin denied materialism, claiming that the focus on the physical brain "unnecessarily clogged" Hartley's more philosophical doctrine of association; to briefly paraphrase from the introduction, the notion that perceptions become associated with ideas, which are then associated with other ideas, and so on. And how better to observe this process of association than through a confessional novel? Here, Godwin relied on Rousseau's 1765 *Confessions*, in which Rousseau "investigat[es] the first traces of [his]sensible existence."[23] The Hartleian chain of ideas, a notion that recurs in all of the texts I analyze here, begins with "vigilia": with curiosity. Rousseau, writing about an encounter with Madam De Warrens, posits himself as:

> curious to know what she aimed at; and no sooner had I comprehended her design (which I could not easily do) than the novelty of the idea, which, during all the years I had passed with her, had never once entered my imagination, took such entire possession of me that I was no longer capable of minding what she said![24]

Here, Rousseau, using himself as test subject, illustrates a Hartleian chain of thought: it begins with curiosity, then difficulty in teasing out a "design," and finally an idea so "novel[ ]" that it takes "entire possession" of him.

This chain of thought can, when undertaken with reason, assist in achieving the perfectible society Godwin prophecies in *Political Justice* (1793). However, recall that the chain begins with an initial perception which, according to Godwin, can always be improved upon. Our first impression is often fallacious, an important point in *Caleb Williams*, a novel subtitled "Things as They Are." As Mark Philp notes in his introduction to *Political Justice*, Godwin argues that association only works well when we gain "clear and distinct ideas and combine these in propositions."[25] Otherwise, for Godwin, excessive curiosity can become obtrusive: a form of tyranny. To make this point, he argues that government regulation of human behavior stems from an excessive "inquisitorial spirit." "Who shall," he asks, "enter into my house, scrutinise my expenditure and count the dishes upon my table?"[26] Here, Godwin alludes back to the eighteenth-century (and modern day) concern over privacy, namely the government entering into our private spaces, intruding into the kitchen, the site of social communion.

It is impossible—and unwise—to overlook the political implications of Godwin's 1794 *Caleb Williams.* Many critics have read the book as a multilayered critique of tyranny, on the parts of both Falkland and Caleb.[27] To return to Godwin's religious upbringing, he would have known that, in the Bible, Caleb was one of the men sent to "spy out" the land of Canaan, and he uses the word "spy" repeatedly when discussing his protagonist. The treason trials of 1794, the year Godwin's text was published, resulted in the infamous "Gagging Acts"; governmental tyranny was clearly much on his mind. I agree with these readings (Godwin is nothing if not blunt) but wish to add that Godwin also critiques excessive curiosity and a *scientific* tyranny: a desire to intrude upon others' minds.

Both William Brewer and Joel Faflak have examined this element of Godwin's novel, and I hope to tie their readings back to the notion of curiosity and obsession. In *The Mental Anatomies of William Godwin and Mary Shelley*, William Brewer calls Caleb an "amateur mental anatomist...obsessed with both his master's states of mind and his own."[28] The "mental anatomist," like the physical version, "murders to dissect," probing all of the crevices of the human mind. Brewer views this character as an "ideal reader," but Faflak comments on what happens when the "reading" becomes intrusive and manipulative. For Faflak, Caleb's curiosity is "coercive, exorbitant": a form of "psychological violence."[29] Desiring to know Falkland's secrets, Caleb is, according to Faflak, a victim of "...A compulsive, coercive desire to see [Falkland's] inner life give up its secrets in the name of sociability."[30] In "The Romance of the Impossible," David Collings also agrees that both Caleb and Falkland worry that "their essential selfhood might become visible to the eyes of another."[31] Curiosity can unmask, make naked, the marker of one's individuality, one's "essential selfhood," until one is no longer a "self" but an object to be deciphered, a text to be read.

What none of these critics focus on is the obsessive nature of Caleb's curiosity and both men's paranoia. Peter Melville Logan does call the text a "nervous" narrative, tying Caleb and Falkland to the diagnosis of hysteria. In so doing, he feminizes Caleb, calling him the woman in the text, and the anxiety about nervous disorders as an anxiety about the "transformation of male bodies into female."[32] Caleb, alongside Edgar Huntly, the second protagonist to be studied in this chapter, is often described by scholars as delicate and overly sensitive. Logan argues that this anxiety over the effeminate male is replicated in Thomas Trotter's 1807 *View of the Nervous Temperament*. Here, Trotter compares the "rustic," who is strong, athletic, and muscular, to the modern-day man, who lives in a state of "effeminacy." As men move further and further away from agriculture, argues Trotter, they become more sensitive, delicate, and effeminate. This definitely fits with the description of Caleb Williams; when he dresses himself as a beggar, what gives him away is that his skin has all the "sleekness of a gentleman."[33] When Thomas, another of Falkland's servants, visits him in prison, he also remarks on how his skin is no longer "sleek." By sleek, Godwin would have meant "having a smooth skin, esp. as the result of being in good condition; plump" (OED), and this was certainly a marker of gentility and delicacy.

While Caleb comments that Falkland is “refined without foppery, elegant without effeminacy,” Caleb himself, like Edgar Huntly, possesses a number of “effeminate” attributes, one of which is his obsession with another man.[34] This serves to queer the conventional notion of “erotomania,” a heterosexual obsession with another person, to be explored in the fourth chapter. Scholars have examined *Caleb Williams* in light of what Eve Sedgwick calls “paranoid gothic”: when a man is not only “persecuted by, but considers himself transparent to and often under the compulsion of, another male.”[35] I argue here that this notion of transparency is, again, connected directly to an interest in the workings of the mind. In his reading of the novel as a commentary on late eighteenth-century court cases involving sodomy, Gary Dyer argues that a charge of sodomy was especially dangerous because it involved conjecture—active reading. In a number of late eighteenth-century court cases, blackmailing someone by accusing him of sodomy was akin to highway robbery. The “robbery” under consideration is not a robbery of physical assets but a “robbery” of something much more precious, namely someone’s reputation. Dyer, arguing that Falkland’s fear for his reputation reflects on these court cases, also connects the court cases to fear, for the only way to “prove” emotional blackmail was by determining how much fear or terror was instilled in the victim by such an accusation.[36] Often, these accusations rested on circumstantial evidence at best: one could “read” into a person’s facial expressions, understanding that the allegations were unsubstantial and based on fear or view the “unreadable” man as overly effeminate.

Caleb begins the novel by “reading” his master’s physiognomy. As he initially surveys Falkland, he reads him against a traditional masculine type:

> In place of the hard-favoured and inflexible visages I had been accustomed to observe, every muscle and petty line of his countenance seemed to be in an inconceivable degree pregnant with meaning.[37]

Instead of the more traditionally masculine, “hard-favoured” (which, according to the OED, means “coarse-featured” or having a “harsh” appearance) man that Caleb anticipates, Falkland is perhaps *too* flexible. In fact, his countenance, every little, “petty” line, is too easily readable, “pregnant” with meaning that he will invariably divulge.

Both Godwin and Brockden Brown lean heavily on the contemporaneous culture of sensibility, a culture that gave feelings "empirical origins" through the senses; the strength and comprehensiveness of one's sensory perceptions also, according to this discourse, determined the acuteness of one's feelings. These feelings could, conversely, be perceived through the senses, illustrated by the popular notion of physiognomy, which will be revisited, in terms of the eye, in Chapter 6.[38] In his 1783 *Essays on Physiognomy*, Lavater posited that one could "read" emotions and even mental states by simply viewing the lines of someone's face: for instance, the shape of her or his eyebrows, the shape of his or her nose. Figure 2.1 illustrates a number of mental states attributed to a variety of people.

Fig. 2.1 Johann Caspar Lavater, "Group of faces Set in a Circle" (*Source*: *Essays on Physiognomy*, vol. 1 [London: John Murray, 1789–1798], 96. Courtesy of the Wellcome Library, London)

Perhaps the face on the bottom right would most closely match Caleb's description of Falkland, whose "look bespoke the unquietness of his mind, and frequently wandered with an expression of disconsolateness and anxiety."[39] This type of reading rewards the viewer who, gazing at these expressions, can read and assign meaning to them at will; perhaps the gentleman in Fig. 2.1 is not anxious or disconsolate but frustrated and overwhelmed? The reader assigns the meaning but pieces together textual clues to do so.

Once Caleb's curiosity as to Falkland's psyche is aroused, he cannot stop his "speculation and conjecture" concerning his "character."[40] Falkland clearly expresses signs of "frenzy," one of the earlier terms used to describe monomania; using this word, Caleb tells us that Falkland would "strike his forehead, his brows became knit, his features distorted, and his teeth ground one against the other."[41] One of William Perfect's symptoms arising from too much study is, in fact, the "grinding of teeth."[42] While this is usually used to denote intellectual monomania, to be examined in the next chapter, one can "study" an idea too much, allowing it to attain psychic dominance. Caleb, ever the analyst, tries to unearth what this idea—what Romantics would have called a "ruling passion"—might be, but he, according to Falkland, oversteps his bounds and becomes intrusive, a "spy" upon Falkland's "privacies."[43] As I and other scholars have already argued, the word spy would have had great resonance in the 1790s; as the novel continues, we can see that Caleb is indeed being intrusive, unable to control his own curiosity.

This is where Caleb switches from "model analyst" to psychological subject, and his problem is that he cannot think of anything but Falkland and his secret. The idea of the secret is "fixed" in his mind:

> for ever. My thoughts fluctuated from conjecture to conjecture, but this was the centre about which they revolved. I determined to place myself as a watch upon my master.[44]

As is common in images of obsessive thought, ideas circulate, coming back to a common "center." Here, Godwin's character follows Darwin's pattern, illustrating reverie (living inside his head) and, more specifically, vigilia, keeping "a watch" upon Falkland. Caleb, at least in retrospect, knows that excessive curiosity is dangerous but sees it as a "restless propensity" that "hurries [him] forward the more irresistibly."[45] Again echoing the language of frenzy and of vigilia, Caleb labels curiosity as his "ruling passion," his "perpetual study."[46] It is here that we return to Godwin's notion, espoused in *Political Justice*, that association only works well with "clear" and "distinct" ideas. Since the initial stimulus is necessary, according to Hartley, for any association of ideas, it is the initial stimulus that determines the clarity and reason of any thought process. When Godwin has Caleb say that, in curiosity, the mind "is urged by a perpetual stimulus; it seems as if it were continually approaching to the end of its race...," he details the chain of ideas that can accompany a faulty perception.[47]

This initial perception, not of things "as they are" but of things as characters deem them to be, results in the tyranny of ideas over the mind. Here we return to the political nature of the "ruling" passion: the passion, like a king or a tyrant, "rules" over the rest of the body. Caleb says as much when he claims that the "vigilance even of a public and systematical despotism is poor, compared with a vigilance which is thus goaded by the most anxious passions of the soul."[48] Here, he uses the word "vigilance," a word used in *Zoonomia* by Darwin, to characterize both political, systematic oppression, and the oppression of the "anxious passions" that, in turn, intrudes upon and oppresses others. Ironically, though, the obsessive subject desires this type of oppression, needing the "ruling passion" in order to function. For Caleb, curiosity is stronger than "even the love of independence. To that," he tells his readers, "I would have sacrificed my liberty or my life; I would have submitted to the condition of a West Indian Negro, or to the tortures inflicted by North American savages."[49] The words "independence," "liberty," and "life" all recall Thomas Paine's 1776 *Common Sense* which, of course, argues for the "independence" of America from the tyranny of Great Britain. Yet Godwin goes further, comparing psychological tyranny (and, I argue, the tyranny of proto-psychology) to slavery and torture.

Caleb's curiosity—his desire to know Falkland's inner workings—is symbolized by the eroticized opening of, again, a chest. The incident occurs during a fire; instead of escaping the house, Caleb, finding his mind "already raised to its utmost pitch," decides to open the mysterious chest containing Falkland's secrets.[50] The diction in this passage is decidedly erotic: "I know not what *infatuation* instantaneously seized me.[51] The chest, he tells us "inclosed (sic) all for which my heart panted. After two or three efforts, in which the energy of uncontrolable passion was added to my bodily strength, the fastenings gave way..."[52] While Caleb has been read as hysterical or even, per Logan, the "woman" in the text, this passage is reminiscent of eroticized prints, such as Fig. 2.2, of natural philosophers (what we would now call scientists) uncovering the mysteries of nature.

Caleb is seized with "infatuation" for the chest that contains all "for which my heart *panted*" (emphasis mine). The last sentence signals his strength, his passionate efforts, and the final "giving way" of the chest to Caleb's probing eyes. Here, the chest becomes the secretive, well-covered female, and Caleb the prying, powerful (male) scientist who finally undoes its stays. His curiosity leads to a metaphorical rape of another person's private self.

Once Caleb does discover the secret, Falkland develops his own obsessive idea: that Caleb will, somehow, give him away. His obsession with controlling Caleb also turns into a form of tyranny. Although Godwin writes that "[Falkland] spared neither pains nor time in the gratification of the passion which choice had made his ruling one," one wonders how much "choice" Falkland has over his desire to keep vigil over Caleb. The two go back and forth, "irresistibly impelled" by ideas that they cannot "banish" from their minds: "associations" gone awry to such an extent that "imagination seems to refuse to obey the curb of judgment."[53] While this is, indeed, a novel about tyranny, it is more than a reaction to the Gagging Acts or to Edmund Burke's *Reflections*. Godwin probes deeper, showing how tyrannies, both governmental and psychological, influence all of our associations until we are led down dangerous paths. In the end, Caleb delineates this process clearly:

> The spring of action which, perhaps more than any other, characterised the whole train of my life, was curiosity. It was this that gave me my mechanical turn; I was desirous of tracing the variety of effects which might be produced from given causes. It was this that made me a sort of natural philosopher...[54]

Godwin provides us with the metaphor of a "spring" that works in an almost "mechanical" fashion, setting his life into action in a way reminiscent of Newton's theory of God as watchmaker or the Calvinist theory of predestination. Caleb's "mechanical turn" associates him with the scientist; the contemporary term "mechanical" meant "occupied with or skilled in the practical application of an art or science" (OED). What exactly is Caleb's "practical application of an art or science" if not studying others' motivations, attempting to unearth their motivations? He is,

Fig. 2.2 "The Secrets of Nature Displayed," frontisplate (*Source* Aristotle [pseud], *The Works of Aristotle*... [London: 1812]. Courtesy of the Wellcome Library, London)

as he himself says, a "sort of natural philosopher," but this "sort of" natural philosophy is something that Godwin, through his parallels to governmental tyranny, critiques.

The two endings of Godwin's novel reflect the paradox of the observer becoming the observed: the analyst becoming the analyzed. In the original ending, Caleb remains the analyzed: his words are not believed and he ends up in a madhouse, unable to coherently construct his own narrative. He does, however, leave his tale, his narrative, to Collins; as Logan argues, this "nervous narrative" does have power, and readers are left to decipher it. In the later ending, Caleb is the analyst, recognizing the humanity in Falkland and blaming himself for his death. Yet both are present in this character, this "natural philosopher" whose curiosity and supposed objectivity cannot coexist.

Part III: "A Mind Sorely Wounded": Somnambulism and *Edgar Huntly*

In a 1798 diary entry, Elihu Hubbard Smith, a doctor and friend of Charles Brockden Brown, wrote that Erasmus Darwin's *Zoonomia* was "slowly pervading the country."[55] Brown, arguably America's first gothic novelist, had read Darwin's work and was also influenced by William Godwin; in his diary, Smith also notes that Brown, in writing his 1793 *Arthur Mervyn*, was treading in the "profane steps" of "Caleb Williams."[56] While critics have examined similarities between these works, as well as *Caleb Williams* and Brockden Brown's 1798 *Wieland*, I argue here that his 1799 *Edgar Huntly, or Memoirs of a Sleep-Walker* perhaps best exemplifies Darwin's concepts of obsessive reverie, specifically vigilia. Both William Godwin and Charles Brockden Brown's novels concern men obsessed with their curiosity—and "truths"—about other men. In delineating these obsessions, Brown brings his Quaker background, with its focus on individual truth, or "inner light," to play.

While Brockden Brown was no longer an active member of the Quaker society, formally called the "Society of Friends of the Truth," when he wrote *Edgar Huntly*, his early religious influences influence his characters' beliefs in their own "truths." Brown's father grew up in Nottingham, where Quakers were persecuted, in large part due to their notion of the "inner Light," a form of "inward testimony" stronger than Biblical "truth."[57] John Churchman, an in-law of the Brown family, was one of the Quaker leaders in Pennsylvania. On December 19, 1756, Churchman visited Nottingham, where Brockden Brown's father, Elijah, lived, and wrote that "...a voice was uttered in me attended (I thought) with Divine authority thus, *I will bow the inhabitants of the earth, and particularly of this land, and I will make them fear and reverence me, either in mercy or in judgment.*"[58] The idea of a voice uttered "in" a person, "attended...with Divine authority," was understandably threatening to Biblical and legal authorities. How was one to know the truth of this authority? And if authority was "in" a person, how might that person be held to communal rules and standards?

One of the foremost concerns regarding the Quakers was that they emphasized the "Inner Light" more than they did scripture or even Christ. This was exemplified by the 1690 Keithian controversy. George Keith, who founded the town of Freehold and preached in Topanemus, began to have disagreements with his fellow believers. Some Quakers, according to Keith, had moved away from "orthodox Quakerism," believing that the "Light is sufficient without anything else," including the "Man Christ Jesus without us."[59] In other words, even the presence of Jesus would be insufficient without the Light. The problem with this, according to Keith, was that some ministers could then focus on their own understandings of the Light and "usurp" others' beliefs. He compared them to Papists, "tyrants" who imposed their beliefs upon others. They, too, practiced a form of psychological tyranny. The only solution to this was for people to realize that each individual only received a "measure" of the spirit, not a complete understanding. Instead, they had to come together as a group in order to fully understand; this concept, in the Quaker faith, is called the "Unity in the Light."

While anxieties about Quakers subsided after 1700, during a period labeled the "quietist" movement, the religion always had—and still does—privilege introspection, or the somewhat Keatsian emptying out of the self. In *The Quakers in America*, Thomas Hamm refers to this as a "crucifying and eradicating any evidence of human will."[60] We return here to the concept of "will," one also stressed in William Godwin's work; it is also no accident that Erotomania, which includes Vigilia, was classed by Darwin as a "disease of volition." The notion of the "human will" was, of course, central to the Romantics, who pondered to what degree inspiration came from outside or from within. One recalls Samuel Taylor Coleridge's "The Aeolian Harp," in which the reading begins with both internal and external—the breeze is compared to "some coy maid half yielding to her lover." Note that the "coy" maid, not giving up her subjectivity, only "half" yields to her lover, the external force of inspiration. As the poem proceeds, the maid/lute/poet's subjectivity recedes, to be replaced by the Coleridgean "One Life":

> ...within us and abroad,
> Which meets all motion and becomes its soul,
> A light in sound, a sound-like power in light,
> Rhythm in all thought, and joyance everywhere—
> Methinks, it should have been impossible
> Not to love all things in a world so filled;
> Where the breeze warbles, and the mute still air
> Is Music slumbering on her instrument.[61]

No longer a coy mistress, the motion, the harp, is met by the One Life, which "becomes" its soul, its selfhood. Yet this clearly happens through a material, sensory process of perception: Coleridge emphasizes sensory experiences, interchanging one for the other in a synaesthetic process. "Light" becomes "sound," sound becomes light, and thought becomes musical or, as it were, poetic. The air is "mute" and "still," but it paradoxically becomes "music," or at least the potential of music.

This question about the imagination, inspiration, and the limits of the self informed much of Romantic discourse about obsession. If imagination "obsessed" a person, how might that person's agency be reduced? Here we return to the concept of the inner light and the comparison of imagination, the One Life, with the Holy Spirit. Like the poet, the Quaker minister was, according to John Puncheon, a "flute for the Holy Spirit to play on." "If God," he wrote, "wanted the Bible quoted, God would put the appropriate verse in the minister's head."[62] This phrase recalls the Keithian controversy and its accompanying anxieties concerning the psychological tyranny that the Light could engender. Because Quaker beliefs relied so much on introspection and on personal interpretation, they were also equated, during the Romantic era, with mental illness. For instance, Spurzheim wrote that Quakers were more prone to insanity than the general population because they married within their group.[63] While intermarriage was definitely a factor, another fear was the focus on introspection, on self-study.

Perhaps for these reasons, William Tuke (1732–1822), a Quaker, founded his well-regarded, well-documented insane asylum named the Retreat, at York. While the Retreat, formerly for the "insane persons of the society of friends," was expanded to include all "insane persons," the description includes many cases involving obsession, or "apprehensions [of the] mind." One notable case involved a young man, who:

> ...appears to have been naturally of a timorous disposition, and the family in which he was an apprentice (21 y.o.) most inhumanly amused themselves in exciting dreadful apprehensions in his mind. One day, the servant maid, dressed herself in men's clothes and, armed with a pistol, entered the room in which he was alone. Pointing it at his head, she pretended to shoot him. The pistol, of course, was not loaded, but its effects were sufficiently injurious. He...remains in a state of hopeless imbecility! Surely, some punishment should await this intellectual murder![64]

This case is fascinating partly because of its focus on perception. The young apprentice perceives the servant maid as a man, perceives that the pistol was loaded, and undergoes genuine suffering due to his personal truths. Much medical writing of this time would have established imbecility or "idiocy" as the lowest form of "insanity"; a person might suffer from mania or melancholy and be eventually reduced to a state of selflessness. Tuke here alludes to the notion of psychological tyranny when he requests punishment for "intellectual murder." Again, a person's reason, like his reputation, is an asset, and destroying that asset is, here, akin to destroying the body.

Perhaps partly due to his Quaker heritage, the focus on the Inner Light, and this connection to insanity, Brockden Brown was fascinated by "stories of the abnormal"; although he considered himself a Gothic writer, he obtained much of his information from medical journals of his time (including the *Medical Repository*, edited by Elihu Hubbard Smith) and from the *Monthly Magazine*, which he edited.[65] In addition to the "abnormal," a category that was still markedly divided from the "normal," he was interested in more conventional "abnormal" tendencies, including obsession. In one of his fictional "Henrietta Letters," he analyzes himself, claiming that he was "formerly actuated by a boundless ardor for knowledge." His eyes, he writes,

> were so constantly and intently fixed upon my book that when I chanced at any time to look at objects around me, they wore an aspect of obscurity, and I felt the same sensations of which a man may be supposed to be susceptible on his rousing from a long and profound sleep…[66]

The constant, intent way in which the narrator "fixes" his eyes upon his book recalls Darwin's "vigilia," and, again, we see slippage between truth and perception. The ideas mentioned in his book become so clear that the outside world seems "obscure." Brown's comparison of reading a book to a "long and profound sleep" recalls the premise of *Edgar Huntly*, based on the notion of somnambulism.

Brown's novel begins and returns to the theme of sleepwalking. Edgar, visiting an elm tree where his brother Waldegrave was murdered, notices that someone, who seems to be sleepwalking, continually visits the site. The sleepwalker turns out to be a neighbor's Irish servant, Clithero Edny, whose story forms the first part of Brockden Brown's book. Edgar immediately becomes curious concerning the sleepwalker's motives, observing him again and again and musing that "The incapacity of sound sleep denotes a mind sorely wounded. It is thus that atrocious criminals denote the possession of some dreadful secret."[67] Here we might recall that an inability to sleep is part of Erasmus Darwin's diagnosis of Erotomania.

As in *Caleb Williams*, the notion of erotomania is queered in this text. At this point in his narrative, Huntly knows nothing about Clithero—not even his identity—but he, like Caleb Williams, attempts to penetrate his "dreadful secrets," assuming the man to be an "atrocious criminal." While the "secret" here turns out to be a supposed murder, one that Huntly believes is justified, the curiosity with which Huntly "hunts" his subject assumes homoerotic overtones. In his article about *Edgar Huntly* and "erotic pessimism," Shapiro argues, rightly, that the novel recalls the late eighteenth-century's "nascent ideal of male-male sexuality."[68] As in *Caleb Williams*, Edgar pursues Clithero a bit too relentlessly for the "secret" to be read literally. Yet, I argue, Shapiro takes his argument too far when he writes that, when Edgar traverses the caves and cliffs of Norwalk, a circular town, his "…sublime sense of deviation from the 'customary paths of men' anatomizes Norwalk's intestinal entryway as an anal terrain of male-male intercourse."[69] While homoeroticism plays a role in this novel, I believe that Brockden Brown, influenced by Darwin's work as well as contemporary medical accounts, is more interested in the psychological "deviation from the customary paths of men" provoked by the repeated idea. As in *Caleb Williams*, this repeated idea is expressed in both the psychological subject, Clithero, and in the analyst, here exemplified by Edgar Huntly.

Edgar Huntly is, in fact, a novel about another sort of penetration: a (to put it in Brown's words) "penetration into the recesses of [the] soul."[70] Edgar, intending to find his brother's murderer, becomes consumed by the need to understand the passions driving this mysterious sleepwalker. He decries his own feelings, telling his readers that curiosity is "vicious, if undisciplined by reason, and inconducive to benefit."[71] In this Lockean reading of the imagination, reason serves to contain and, in a book interested in criminality, "discipline" curiosity, which is otherwise "vicious." Curiosity, an essential element of scientific inquiry, has an element of the criminal or the "vicious," especially if it is, as Brown tells us, "inconducive to benefit." This phrase, too, bears exploring. Whose benefit? Is curiosity for the sake of curiosity—"mystery," in other words—potentially pathological?

This question is one that interested Brown's friends, placing Brown himself in the role of analyzand. Smith, in his letters to Brown, asks him why he:

> so much delight[s] in Mystery? Is it the disease of the Will? Or of Habit?... have you been so long accustomed to deal in visionary scenes, to intertwine the real with the imaginary, & to enwrap yourself in the mantle of ambiguous seeming, that your pen, involuntarily borrows the phraseology of fancy...[72]

The interest in "mystery," in secrets, is pathologized because the imagination must step in and attempt to provide a "visionary," a possible, solution. This "visionary," forward-looking solution must "intertwine the real," what is known, with the "imaginary," what can only be guessed at, and truth then becomes "fancy" or, as Smith puts it, "ambiguous seeming." Smith ascribes this pathological curiosity to a "disease of the Will," an inability, again, to discipline one's passions, or "Habit," a repetition of a similar idea.

Huntly's interest in Clithero becomes obsessive, and the mystery shrouding him dominates Huntly's life. His thoughts "perpetually revolved round a single point. These were scarcely more than a repetition, with slight variations, of a single idea."[73] This idea—that Clithero is a murderer—gains support in Huntly's reading of his physiognomy.

Like Falkland, Clithero evinces his secret in his face, the muscles of which "were distorted and tremulous."[74] Huntly also tells his readers that Clithero's "complexion varied from one degree of paleness to another. His brain appeared to suffer some severe constriction."[75] Edgar moves from analyzing Clithero's physiological features, the increasing paleness of his face, to probing into his material brain.[76]

In order to understand Clithero's "moral insanity," with which he is diagnosed at the end of the novel, we return here to Hartley's notion of association. Smith, writing about Brown, accuses him of conflating perception and reality, "truth" and imagination, he:

> began to fancy that these fictions were real; ...every subsequent event became tinctured with this conviction & accompanied by this diseased apprehension; the habit was formed; & you wandered in a world of your own creation.[77]

Not only does the "real" become intertwined with the "imaginary" in an attempt to penetrate a secret, but this thought, as we shall see with Clithero, begins to function, by association, to influence subsequent perceptions. In this way, one "diseased" perception or understanding forms others until this chain of thought forms a "habit." To provide a brief summary of a convoluted plot: Clithero, a poor Irish boy, is adopted and taken into the home of Mrs. Lorimer, who he reveres. Mrs. Lorimer, in turn, has a literal "evil twin" in her brother Arthur Wiatte, who was sent to prison on ship for committing a heinous crime, and was believed to have died in a mutiny. Arthur's daughter, Clarisse, is taken in by Mrs. Lorimer, and Clithero develops feelings for her. As one might guess, Wiatte is not dead, and he returns to London. One night, Arthur attacks Clithero on the street, and Clithero, in an act of self-defense, kills him. However, Mrs. Lorimer had, in the past, said that she would not be able to live knowing her brother had died. This irrational thought, repeated in Clithero's head, spurs the novel's sequence of events.

Mrs. Lorimer's exact words—"The stroke that deprives [Arthur] of life will not only have the same effect upon me, but will set my portion in everlasting misery"—gain prominence in Clithero's mind, forming associations that propel him to his later actions.[78] Clithero takes this idea, that the "stroke" that takes Arthur's life will take her own, quite literally. He becomes obsessed with the fact that, by killing Arthur, he has killed his benefactress. "My fancy," he tells Edgar in his confession, "began to be infected with the errors of my understanding. The mood into which my mind was plunged was incapable of any propitious intermission."[79] Clithero's false perception, the "errors of [his] understanding," "infect" the rest of his thoughts until this perception plagues him without ceasing. His mind, he says, was "harassed by the repetition of one idea."[80] This one idea, by process of association, "infects" all others until Clithero's perception becomes his reality.

Clithero's idea does indeed (he thinks) become his reality. Nothing, he says, can "modify my predominant idea" as he makes his way to Mrs. Lorimer's room, certain that she is dead. "The impulse," he tells Huntly, "was not to be resisted."[81] His idea has now become so controlling that he compares it to a "demon that possessed me."[82] This "demon," Clithero's ruling passion, controls his body, and he tells Edgar that he "had been defrauded, for a moment, of the empire of my muscles."[83] He attempts to perpetuate the murder and would do so except that he is stopped by Mrs. Lorimer. The woman in the bed is, of course, Clarisse. Yet Clithero confesses the murder to Mrs. Lorimer and spends the novel assured that she has died...because of him.

After Clithero "confesses" to Edgar, the latter spends the rest of the novel attempting to find and "cure" him. Convinced that Clithero is mistaken in his assumptions, he believes that his behavior indicates "frenzy rather than prejudice; but frenzy, like prejudice, was curable. Reason was no less an antidote to the illusions of insanity like his, than to the illusions of error."[84] As opposed to "prejudice," an error of judgment, Edgar diagnoses Clithero with "frenzy," a form of mania often tied to what was later called monomania. Yet even when Clithero is informed that Lorimer lives and has also moved to America, he cannot forgive himself and ends up committing suicide.

Clithero is deemed insane, while Edgar remains alive to tell his tale in these "memoirs." Yet the question of Edgar's sanity is itself suspect. While Edgar hunts Clithero in order to help him, he himself ends up in a cave because he, too, has been sleepwalking. In a much-commented upon section of the book, Edgar faces down and then devours a wild leopard and then, upon seeing Native Americans, recalls what he thinks are memories of these "savages" killing his parents. He goes on a killing spree, returning in order to murder more and more of the tribe.

What separates these murders from those committed by Clithero? Here, too, a predominant idea, the idea of revenge, dominates Edgar until he seemingly forgets his journey's purpose.

As opposed to Clithero, analyzed by our narrator and deemed insane by the novel's end, Edgar justifies his actions to Mary Waldegrave, his betrothed (and Waldegrave's sister). "You," he writes to Mary,

> will not be surprised that the fate of my parents, and the sight of the body of one of this savage band, who, in the pursuit that was made after them, was overtaken and killed, should produce lasting and terrific images in my fancy. I never looked upon or called up the image of a savage without shuddering.[85]

Edgar assumes that Mary will "not be surprised" that he experiences "lasting and terrific images," yet little separates these "lasting… images" from the repeated thoughts of Clithero. He continues that he not only shudders when he "look[s] upon" the image of a "savage," but also when he "call[s] up" such an image in his head. This, too, evokes the idea of association that Edgar has already explored in his own psychoanalysis of Clithero: like Clithero, he sees an image (of a Native American) and associates that sensation with a variety of "terrific," irrational images.

As Edgar proceeds with his narrative, he attempts to explain his killing of a number of Native Americans. At first, he believes that, as an essentially nonviolent person, his first murder must be mentally abnormal; he believed, he tells Mary, that he "suffered from delirium." Dana Luciano smartly connects Edgar's actions here to the "contagion" of hearing Clithero's story, which Edgar's clearly mimics, and to the similar contagion of savagery, exemplified by his ingesting a wild panther.[86] This convincing argument, grounded in anxieties surrounding the early American republic, gains more credence when paired with Brown's own "diagnosis" of Edgar. As Kate Ward Sugar argues and I have also attempted to prove, Edgar evidences the stages of Darwinian erotomania, the last of which is "furious or melancholy insanity; and suicide, or revenge." The furor and animalism with which Huntly disposes of five "Indians" attest to the fact that he has reached the final stage of a psychological disorder: one that began with obsessive curiosity.

In light of this diagnosis, Mary Waldegrave, Edgar's implied reader, serves an interesting role. If she, too, reads the story vigilantly, might she also be psychologically affected? Edgar attempts to clarify his post-cave mindset when he explains to Mary, using the language of reason, why he kills his fifth Native American, who he had originally only injured. "To kill him outright," he tells Mary, "was the dictate of compassion and of duty."[87] Sugar argues that this moment is part of Edgar's return to rationality, and that "compassion" and "duty" allow for him to return to a rational space from which Clithero is forever barred. Instead, I read this moment as Edgar's attempt to convince Mary, the vigilant reader, of his own sanity by justifying his irrational actions.

As Sugar has argued, Mary here serves as an overly sympathetic reader, always in a state of "reverie." Sugar ultimately argues that it is this "excessive sympathy" in Mary as well as Edgar that contributes to a "one-sided" manifestation of erotomania.[88] I agree that Edgar reads Mary as overly sympathetic, inscribing what he views as her responses to his actions, but argue that Edgar's feelings toward Clithero are more rooted in intense, obsessive curiosity: a need to know and to understand another's psyche. This is manifested when Edgar analyzes Clithero's motives and his somnambulism, eventually coming to the conclusion that he suffers from "frenzy."

Like Caleb Williams, Edgar Huntly begins by attempting to penetrate another person's secrets. Like Caleb, he analyzes, "reads" Clithero, both through his physiognomy and even by linking his supposed thoughts to the state of his nervous system, the "constriction" of his brain. Again like Caleb, though, Edgar, the psycho-analyst, becomes a victim to his own curiosity. Brockden Brown takes this one step further, illustrating that one man's insanity is another's justified violence. While Brockden Brown's form of violence is literal—the killing of Native Americans—and William Godwin's is metaphorical—psychological tyranny—both comment on the dangers of curiosity, of what Erasmus Darwin calls Vigilia, and of a newly developing field that will later be called psychology.

Notes

1. Stephen Shapiro, "'Man to Man I Needed Not to Dread His Encounter': Edgar Huntley's End of Erotic Pessimism," in *Revising Charles Brockden Brown: Culture, Politics, and Sexuality in the Early Republic*, eds. Philip Barnard, Mark L. Kamrath, and Stephen Shapiro (Knoxville: University of Tennessee Press, 2004), 217.

2. Erasmus Darwin, *Zoonomia* (London: J. Johnson, 1794), 362.
3. Michel Foucault, *The History of Madness*, ed. Jean Khalfa, trans. Jonathan Murphy and JeanKhalfa (New York: Routledge, 2006), 213.
4. Quoted in Lorraine Daston and Peter Gallison, *Objectivity* (Brooklyn, NY: Zone Books, 2007), 229.
5. Quoted in ibid., 241.
6. Ibid., 241.
7. Gary Hatfield, "Psychology as a Natural Science in the Eighteenth Century," *IRCS Technical Reports Series*, no. 153 (1994): 11. http://repository.upenn.edu/ircs_reports/153.
8. Thomas Bakewell, *The Domestic Guide in Cases of Insanity* (T. Allbut, 1805), 32.
9. Marjean D. Purinton, "George Colman's *The Iron Chest* and *Blue-Beard* and the Pseudoscience of Curiosity Cabinets," *Victorian Studies* (2007): 250–257.
10. Ibid., 251.
11. Ibid., 252.
12. George Colman, *The Iron Chest: A Play; in Three Acts.* Written by George Colman, the Younger. With a Preface. First Represented at the Theatre-Royal, Drury-Lane, on Saturday, March 12, 1796 (Dublin: Printed by Thomas Burnside, for P. Wogan, J. Rice, and G. Folingsby, 1796), 21. http://name.umdl.umich.edu/004804664.0001.000.
13. Colman, *Iron Chest*, 49.
14. Colman, *Iron Chest*, 51.
15. George Colman, *Blue Beard; or, Female Curiosity: A Dramatic Romance* (London: 1808), 22.
16. "William Godwin's Diary," Diary entry for April 28, 1793. http://godwindiary.bodleian.ox.ac.uk/diary/1793-04-28.html.
17. George Lillo, "Fatal Curiosity: A Tragedy," in *Lillo's Dramatic Works*, Thomas Davies (London, 1810).
18. Patricia Meyer Spacks, *Privacy: Concealing the Eighteenth-Century Self* (Chicago: University of Chicago Press, 2014), 10. ProQuest ebrary.
19. Ibid., 10.
20. Ibid., 56.
21. For extensive explorations of materialism during the early Romantic era, see Yasmin Solomonescu, *John Thelwall and the Materialist Imagination* (New York: Palgrave, 2014); Lisa Ann Robertson, "'Swallowed Up in Impression': Humphry Davy's Materialist Theory of Embodied Transcendence and William Wordsworth's 'Tintern Abbey,'" *European Romantic Review* 26, no. 5 (2015): 591–614; Allison Dushane, "Reverie and the Life of Things: Rousseau, Darwin, and Romantic Visionary Materialism," in *Wordsworth and the Green Romantics: Affect and Ecology*

in the Nineteenth Century, ed. Lisa Ottum, Seth T. Reno, and James C. McCusick (Becoming Modern: New Nineteenth-Century Studies. Durham, NH: University of New Hampshire Press, 2016), 127–145; and Rebecca Knell, "Re-Evaluating Science and Romanticism: The Case of Erasmus Darwin's the Loves of the Plants," in *Restoring the Mystery of the Rainbow: Literature's Refraction of Science*, ed. Valeria Tinkler-Villani and C. C. Barfoot (Amsterdam: Rodopi, 2011), 111–131.

22. Andrew Baxter, *An Enquiry into the Nature of the Human Soul* (London, 1745), 85, accessed via Google Books.
23. Jean-Jacques Rousseau, *The Confessions of Jean-Jacques Rousseau—Classic Illustrated Edition* (Heritage Illustrated Publishing, 2014), Kindle Edition, 337.
24. Ibid., 3046.
25. William Godwin, *An Enquiry Concerning Political Justice* (Oxford University Press, 2013), Kindle Edition, xvii.
26. Ibid., 309.
27. For more sociopolitical readings of *Caleb Williams*, see Casie Legette, "Remaking Caleb Williams in the Nineteenth Century," *Romanticism: The Journal of Romantic Culture and Criticism* 18, no. 2 (2012): 43–154; Daniela Garofalo, "'A Left-Handed Way': Modern Masters in William Godwin's Caleb Williams," *European Romantic Review* 17, no. 2 (2006): 237–244; and David S. Hogsette, "Textual Surveillance, Social Codes, and Sublime Voices: The Tyranny of Narrative in *Caleb Williams* and *Wieland*," *Romanticism on the Net: An Electronic Journal Devoted to Romantic Studies* (2005): 38–39.
28. Brewer, *The Mental Anatomies*, 40.
29. Joel Faflak, "Speaking of Godwin's *Caleb Williams*: The Talking Cure and the Psychopathology of Enlightenment," *ESC* 31, nos. 2–3 (2005): 102.
30. Ibid., 103.
31. David Collings, "The Romance of the Impossible: William Godwin in the Empty Place of Reason," *ELH* 70, no. 3 (2003): 863.
32. Peter Melville Logan, "Narrating Hysteria: 'Caleb Williams' and the Cultural History of Nerves," *Novel: A Forum on Fiction* 29, no. 2 (1996): 210.
33. William Godwin, *Caleb Williams* (Oxford World's Classics, Oxford University Press), Kindle Edition, 236.
34. Godwin, 19.
35. Eve Sedgwick, *Between Men: English Literature and Male Homosocial Desire* (Columbia University Press, 1985), 91.
36. Gary Dyer, "The Arrest of Caleb Williams: Unnatural Crime, Constructive Violence, and Overwhelming Terror in Late Eighteenth-Century England," *Eighteenth-Century Life* 36, no. 3 (2012): 40.

37. William Godwin, *Caleb Williams* (Oxford World's Classics, Oxford University Press), Kindle Edition, 4.
38. For more about the notion of sensibility and its medical [connections], see Adela Pinch, *Strange Fits of Passion: Epistemologies of Emotion, Hume to Austen* (Stanford University Press, 1996).
39. Godwin, *Caleb Williams*, 4.
40. Ibid., 5.
41. Ibid., 6.
42. William Perfect, *Cases of Insanity, the Epilepsy, Hypochondriacal Affection, Hysteric Passion, and Nervous Disorders, Successfully Treated*, 2nd ed. (Rochester: T. Fisher), 6 (with many additional cases). Eighteenth Century Collections Online.
43. Godwin, *Caleb Williams*, 7.
44. Ibid., 7.
45. Ibid., 109.
46. Ibid., 115.
47. Ibid., 115.
48. Ibid., 135.
49. Ibid., 139–140.
50. Ibid., 128.
51. Ibid., 128.
52. Ibid., 128–129.
53. Ibid., 252, 280–281, 308.
54. Ibid., 314.
55. James E. Cronin, ed., *The Diary of Elihu Hubbard Smith* (Philadelphia: American Philosophical Society, 1973), 420. In addition to being a physician, Smith was a student of Benjamin Rush and founder of *The Medical Repository*, the first American medical/scientific journal.
56. Ibid., 243.
57. Peter Kafer, *Charles Brockden Brown's Revolution and the Birth of American Gothic* (Philadelphia: University of Pennsylvania Press, 2004), 22.
58. Quoted in ibid., 25.
59. Quoted in Jane E. Calvert, *Quaker Constitutionalism and the Political Thought of John Dickinson* (Cambridge: Cambridge University Press, 2009), 124.
60. Thomas D. Hamm, *The Quakers in America* (New York: Columbia University Press, 2003), 30.
61. Samuel Taylor Coleridge, *The Major Works*, ed. H. J. Jackson (Oxford: Oxford University Press, 1985), 28.
62. Ibid., 72.
63. Johann Christoph Spurzheim, *Observations on the Deranged Manifestations of the Mind, or Insanity* (Boston, 1836), 102.

64. Samuel Tuke, *Description of the Retreat, an Institution Near York for Insane Persons of the Society of Friends* (London: Dawsons of Pall Mall, 1964), 198.
65. David Lee Clark, *Charles Brockden Brown: Pioneer Voice of America* (New York: AMS Press, 1966), 191.
66. Quoted in ibid., 191.
67. Charles Brockden Brown, *Edgar Huntly, or Memoirs of a Sleep-Walker* (Kent: Kent State University Press, 1984), 13.
68. Shapiro, "Man to Man," 216.
69. Ibid., 228–229.
70. Brown, *Edgar Huntly*, 14.
71. Ibid., 16.
72. Cronin, *The Diary*, 164.
73. Brown, *Edgar Huntly*, 32.
74. Ibid., 27.
75. Ibid., 64.
76. In 1709, Herman Booerhave had made popular the notion of "relaxed" and "constricted" fibers; based on a hydraulic model, these fibers either allowed too much or too little fluid into, in this case, the brain (explaining Clithero's extreme pallor).
77. Cronin, *The Diary*, 171.
78. Brown, *Edgar Huntly*, 76.
79. Ibid., 78.
80. Ibid., 78.
81. Ibid., 83.
82. Ibid., 83.
83. Ibid., 83.
84. Ibid., 95.
85. Ibid., 132.
86. Dana Luciano, "'Perverse Nature': Edgar Huntly and the Novel's Reproductive Disorders," *American Literature* 70, no. 1 (1998): 1–27.
87. Brown, *Edgar Huntly*, 154.
88. Kate Ward Sugar, "'A Wonderful Disease': *Edgar Huntly*, Erasmus Darwin, and Revolutionary American Masculinity," *James Dickey Review* 29 (2012): 35.

Bibliography

Aristotle (pseud). *The Works of Aristotle: In Four Parts.* London: 1812. Courtesy of the Wellcome Library, London.

Bakewell, Thomas. *The Domestic Guide in Cases of Insanity.* T. Allbut, 1805.

———. *The Iron Chest: A Play; in Three Acts.* Written by George Colman, the Younger. With a preface. First represented at the Theatre-Royal, Drury-Lane, on Saturday, March 12, 1796. Dublin: Printed by Thomas Burnside, for P. Wogan, J. Rice, and G. Folingsby, 1796. http://name.umdl.umich.edu/004804664.0001.000.

Baxter, Andrew. *An Enquiry into the Nature of the Human Soul.* London, 1745. Google Books.

Brewer, William D. *The Mental Anatomies of William Godwin and Mary Shelley.* Madison, NJ: Fairleigh Dickinson University Press; London: Associated University Press, 2001.

Brown, Charles Brockden. *Edgar Huntly, or Memoirs of a Sleep-Walker.* Kent: Kent State University Press, 1984.

Calvert, Jane E. *Quaker Constitutionalism and the Political Thought of John Dickinson.* Cambridge: Cambridge University Press, 2009.

Clark, David Lee. *Charles Brockden Brown: Pioneer Voice of America.* New York: AMS Press, 1966.

Coleridge, Samuel Taylor. *The Major Works.* Edited by H. J. Jackson. Oxford: Oxford University Press, 2008.

Collings, David. "The Romance of the Impossible: William Godwin in the Empty Place of Reason." *ELH* 70, no. 3 (2003): 863.

Colman, George. *Blue Beard; or, Female Curiosity: A Dramatic Romance.* London: 1808. Accessed via Google Books.

Cronin, James E., ed. *The Diary of Elihu Hubbard Smith.* Philadelphia: American Philosophical Society, 1973.

Daston, Lorraine, and Peter Gallison. *Objectivity.* Brooklyn, NY: Zone Books, 2007.

Faflak, Joel. "Speaking of Godwin's *Caleb Williams:* The Talking Cure and the Psychopathology of Enlightenment." *ESC* 31, nos. 2–3 (2005): 102.

Foucault, Michel. *The History of Madness.* Edited by Jean Khalfa. Translated by Jonathan Murphy and Jean Khalfa. New York: Routledge, 2006.

Godwin, William. *An Enquiry Concerning Political Justice.* Oxford World's Classics, 2013. Kindle Edition.

———. *Caleb Williams.* Oxford World's Classics, Oxford University Press, 2009. Kindle Edition.

Hamm, Thomas D. *The Quakers in America.* New York: Columbia University Press, 2003.

Hatfield, Gary. "Psychology as a Natural Science in the Eighteenth Century." *IRCS Technical Reports Series*, no. 153 (1994), 11. http://repository.upenn.edu/ircs_reports/153.

Kafer, Peter. *Charles Brockden Brown's Revolution and the Birth of American Gothic.* Philadelphia: University of Pennsylvania Press, 2004.

Lavater, Johann Caspar. *Essays on Physiognomy*, vol. 1. London: John Murray, 1789–1798. Google Books.

Lillo, George. "Fatal Curiosity: A Tragedy." In *Lillo's Dramatic Works*, Thomas Davies. London, 1810.

Logan, Peter Melville. "Narrating Hysteria: 'Caleb Williams' and the Cultural History of Nerves." *Novel: A Forum on Fiction* 29, no. 2 (1996): 210.

Luciano, Dana. "'Perverse Nature': Edgar Huntly and the Novel's Reproductive Disorders." *American Literature* 70, no. 1 (1998): 1–27.

Perfect, William. *Cases of Insanity, the Epilepsy, Hypochondriacal Affection, Hysteric Passion, and Nervous Disorders, Successfully Treated*, 2nd ed. Rochester: T. Fisher, with many additional cases. Eighteenth Century Collections Online.

Purinton, Marjean D. "George Colman's *The Iron Chest* and *Blue-Beard* and the Pseudoscience of Curiosity Cabinets." *Victorian Studies* (2007): 250–257.

Rousseau, Jean-Jacques. *The Confessions of Jean-Jacques Rousseau—Classic Illustrated Edition*. Heritage Illustrated Publishing, 2014. Kindle Edition.

Sedgwick, Eve. *Between Men: English Literature and Male Homosocial Desire*. Columbia University Press, 1985.

Shapiro, Stephen. "'Man to Man I Needed Not to Dread His Encounter': Edgar Huntley's End of Erotic Pessimism." In *Revising Charles Brockden Brown: Culture, Politics, and Sexuality in the Early Republic*, edited by Philip Barnard, Mark L. Kamrath, and Stephen Shapiro, 217. Knoxville: University of Tennessee Press, 2004.

Spacks, Patricia Meyer. *Privacy: Concealing the Eighteenth-Century Self*. Chicago: University of Chicago Press, 2014. ProQuest ebrary.

Spurzheim, Johann. *Observations on the Deranged Manifestations of the Mind, or Insanity*. Boston, 1836.

Sugar, Kate Ward. "'A Wonderful Disease': *Edgar Huntly*, Erasmus Darwin, and Revolutionary American Masculinity." *James Dickey Review* 29 (2012): 35.

Tuke, Samuel. *Description of the Retreat, an Institution Near York for Insane Persons of the Society of Friends*. London: Dawsons of Pall Mall, 1964.

"William Godwin's Diary." Diary entry for April 28, 1793. http://godwindiary.bodleian.ox.ac.uk/diary/1793-04-28.html.

CHAPTER 3

Intellectual Monomania and Enthusiasm in Mary Shelley's *Frankenstein* and Mary Hays's *Memoirs of Emma Courtney*

Étienne Esquirol, working with inhabitants of French mental asylums, was especially interested in the intersection between study and obsession. In one memorable case he observed "idiocy arising from an overstrained intellect. The understanding had been broken down, in consequence of having been overloaded."[1] Overloaded and "broken down," understanding or study paves the way for "idiocy," an interesting word choice considering its later conflation with intellectual disability.[2] This sense of an "overstrained intellect" is reminiscent of Victor Frankenstein, who reads Paracelsus, Agrippa, and a host of other writers, combined with modern chemistry, until he too becomes intellectually overstrained. Feverish and pale, he eventually ends up in a madhouse.[3]

Esquirol goes on to provide a metaphor of an overcrowded pawn shop to parallel the overstrained imagination, comparing the mind of the patient to a shop "which is furnished principally with other people's goods; a repository merely for ideas, not a soil out of which an idea ever grew."[4] For Mary Hays's characters in *The Memoirs of Emma Courtney* (1796), the mind seems to function in this way; the more Emma reads, the more "overstrained" and crowded her intellect becomes. Emma reads mostly novels: trash that would, metaphorically, find its way to a pawn shop (or, literally, to a circulating library). She, too, ends up feverish and pale, but her enthusiasm is, I argue, gendered. While intellectual monomania in male characters engages with the discourse of genius, female characters become less original, even more emptied of thought, by virtue of their indiscriminate reading.

K. Béres Rogers, *Creating Romantic Obsession*,
Palgrave Studies in Literature, Science and Medicine,
https://doi.org/10.1007/978-3-030-13988-9_3

Women seem to read novels, most prominently Rousseau's *Héloïse*, and become enchanted by them, responding in a predictably obsessive way, one often connected to the female body. On the other hand, male enthusiasm, less common in literary texts, resembles William Wordsworth's "spots of time": mired in loneliness and influenced by associative thinking, the enthusiast can become carried away, trapped inside himself. This chapter argues that, while women's intellectual monomania remains tied to the body and to the notion of obsession as possession *by* the body, male intellectual monomania becomes associated with the brain and with the original, albeit destructive, idea.

Part I: Enthusiasm

Both in describing Victor Frankenstein's unhealthy pursuit of knowledge and Emma Courtney's pursuit of Augustus Harley, Mary Shelley and Mary Hays often employ the word "enthusiasm." Clearly, this concept is important to Romantic-era obsession, so the word and its historical construction bear some close examination. Almost from the beginning, when Victor begins reading Agrippa, Shelley connects this word to his obsessive pursuit, writing that he opens the book "with apathy; the theory which he attempts to demonstrate, and the wonderful facts which he relates, soon changed this feeling into *enthusiasm*."[5] Mary Hays connects the concept with her protagonist by introducing it through her guardian, Mrs. Melmoth, who

> had great sensibility, quickness of perception, some anxiety of temper, and a refined and romantic manner of thinking acquired from the perusal of the old romances, a large quantity of which, belonging to a relation, had, in the early periods of her youth, been accidentally deposited in a spare room in her father's house. These qualities were mingled with a devotional spirit, a little bordering on fanaticism.[6]

Mrs. Melmoth, Emma's only mother figure, becomes the avenue through which her own enthusiasm awakens, and Hays's diction here parallels much of the discourse of both religious and medical enthusiasm. Her word choices—"great sensibility," "devotional spirit," and "fanaticism"—illustrate how enthusiasm can be both medical and religious, but always outside the bounds of social propriety. Like the "spare room" in which the books are "accidentally deposited," female enthusiasm remains outside, yet irreducibly related to, the temple of the body.

Since Shelley and Hays use the word so often, and in somewhat different contexts, it is worthwhile to pause and consider its Romantic-era connotations. "Enthusiasm" first, in 1579, meant "possession by a god, supernatural inspiration, prophetic or poetic frenzy; an occasion or manifestation of these" (OED). Two of these words—possession and frenzy—recur especially in pre-1810 medical texts that will be explored later in this chapter. Here, the conflation of "prophetic" and "poetic" are of note; while the latter would have had positive connotations, the former carried hints of extreme religiosity: of apocalyptic thinking gone awry.[7] These religious connotations are only strengthened by the idea of "supernatural" inspiration or possession "by a god."

In eighteenth-century England, Methodism and other dissenting sects that privileged divine inspiration—and, indeed, possession—led to the word gaining a more negative connotation as "ill-regulated or misdirected religious emotion." In other words, while enthusiasm may be characterized as generalized "madness," "mania," or "frenzy"—these words are used interchangeably in Romantic-era psychological and medical texts—it is always viewed as a "ruling passion." It is the lack of "regulation," of control, that problematizes enthusiasm. It was the "contagious enthusiasm" of Methodism that simultaneously allowed laypeople to make voluntary religious commitments and swept them away in its emotional currents.[8]

Mary Shelley and Mary Hays would also have read about "madness" in relation to enthusiasm, and "enthusiasm" would invariably have been linked to Methodism. Unlike Anglicans and rational dissenters (a group to which Mary Hays and Mary Shelley's father, William Godwin, belonged), Methodists often practiced extemporaneous preaching, allowing their emotions to guide their words. While Methodism itself emphasized discipline and hard work, these Puritanical tenets were alleviated by what E. P. Thomson calls "sabbath orgasms": "attempts to reproduce the emotional convulsions of conversion, conviction of sin, penitence, and visitation by grace."[9] 1817 and 1818, the years in which Mary Shelley was writing *Frankenstein*, marked the "great Primitive Methodist Revival"; this time period was one in which the "relationship between revivalism and political radicalism appears to have been especially close."[10] Clearly, the "artificial" nature of the Methodists' claims was reinforced by a class discourse: one that alleviated social anxieties by effectively Othering them as "mad." Enthusiasm implied a lack of control, a lack of reason, that posed a distinct threat to rule-based hierarchies.

Writing only two years after the initial publication of *Frankenstein*, Robert Southey reiterates many of these ideas in his *Life of Wesley*. In one case, Southey jestingly writes about a "complaint…made to the bishop that fifteen persons had been driven mad by the sermon." He continues by writing "The good man replied, he wished the madness might not be forgotten before the next Sunday."[11] Even this humorous pre-Methodist anecdote reinforces the importance of Anglican hierarchy, with the Bishop's good-natured comment serving to vitiate accusations of insanity.

As Southey proceeds in his history to the point at which Wesley popularizes Methodism, his diction becomes more and more pathologizing. For instance, in "The Case of Thomas Walsh," which he scientifically labels a "case," Southey writes that Walsh "caught the fever of Methodism," and it "went through its regular course with all the accustomed symptoms."[12] Not only does Southey use the common metaphor of a "fevered" imagination, but he also describes the religion as a disease with a "course" and "symptoms." He later makes it even more clear that this disease, this madness, relates to the new discipline of psychology. Describing an enthusiastic fit, he writes that it

> was brought on at a meeting, where, [the man] says, "the power of the Lord came down in the midst of them; the windows of heaven were opened, and the skies poured down righteousness, and his heart melted like wax before the fire." To the psychologist it may be interesting to know, by what words this state of mind was induced.[13]

As he relates his "history," Southey's narrator, like the authors examined in Chapter 2, takes a step back to help the hypothetical "psychologist," his reader, diagnose his patient.

Influenced by and influencing religious discourse, the notion of enthusiasm as pathological—as madness—also played its part in philosophical circles of the time. One can trace the notion of enthusiasm back to Plato's *Ion*, in which Ion himself is described using the term. Specifically—and this also nods to the connection between enthusiasm and insanity—"Ion is *ekphron*, 'out of his mind,' whenever he comes into contact with the Homeric poems."[14] Longinus, a classical writer who specifically writes a treatise entitled *On the Sublime*, then connects enthusiasm with his idea of the sublime.

The sublime has been defined in a variety of ways, mostly involving grandeur, awe, and, as Edmund Burke famously states, "astonishment." Longinus's sublime focuses on the rhetorical effects necessary to produce what the Romantics would later label sublimity. In *Peri Hupsous*, in which Longinus names "five most productive sources of the sublime in literature," he lists (1) grand conceptions, (2) inspiration of vehement emotion [enthousiastikon pathos], (3) figures, (4) elevated diction, and (5) overall arrangement.[15] Summaries of Longinus tend to focus on elevated diction, but the "enthousiastikon pathos" becomes more and more linked to proto-psychology through philosophy. David Hume, in "Of Superstition and Enthusiasm," writes that, when led by enthusiasm, a person's "reason, and even morality are rejected as fallacious guides: And the *fanatic madman* delivers himself over, blindly, and without reserve, to the supposed lapses of the spirit, and to inspiration from above."[16] Enthusiasm, like superstition (the two are often connected) results in a rejection of the Enlightenment concepts of "reason" and, importantly to Mary Shelley, "morality."

Similarly, John Locke's seminal *An Essay Concerning Human Understanding*, which Mary Shelley read in 1816, contrasts enthusiasm, which Locke calls "ungrounded fancies of a man's own brain," with Reason, that gift that Locke views as true divine revelation.[17] The lack of "regulation," this "ungroundedness", allows the "fancies of [the] brain," the imagination, to govern uncontrolled. Yet not all philosophers see enthusiasm as an essentially negative quality. In an early text, "Versuch über die Krankheiten des Kopfes," (Essay on the Sicknesses of the Head), Kant distinguishes enthusiasm from "*Schwärmerei*" (a swarm of thoughts assailing one's brain) based on the idea that true enthusiasm elicits action, whereas the latter "remains within the inactive sphere of imagined intimacy." "[The schwärmer] is actually a lunatic with a supposed immediate inspiration and great intimacy with the powers of heaven."[18] If enthusiasm can force action, like the writing of poetry or the painting of art, then it exists for a positive moral good. If not, it becomes like an avenging swarm and is only characteristic of the "lunatic."

As Kant posits, Romantic enthusiasm was not necessarily a negative quality; indeed, many of Mary Shelley's heroines exhibit an enthusiasm that becomes ultimately liberating. Lisa Vargo, writing about Shelley's later novels, links Shelley's notions of female enthusiasm to William Godwin's notion of perfectibility and political liberation. She cites the

Shelleys's contact with Italian improvisatore, performers moved by inspiration and enthusiasm to produce extemporary poems, as an influence on Mary Shelley's notion of the creative process. Yet Vargo—and, I would argue, Shelley—clearly distinguishes between the type of enthusiasm that "dissolve[s] the self," allowing for sympathy and community, and "egocentric" enthusiasm.[19] I would argue that it is this type of enthusiasm, typically male in Mary Shelley's world, that Victor Frankenstein embodies. This type of egocentric, self-absorbed enthusiasm echoes, again, Kant's notion of the *schwärmerei*.

As Mary Shelley's novel progresses, the word "enthusiasm" becomes more and more reminiscent of Kantian *schwärmerei*. When he begins to create the creature, Victor muses that unless he "had been animated by an almost supernatural *enthusiasm*, my application to this study would have been irksome, and almost intolerable."[20] Here, Shelley not only describes Victor's "application," the "object of assiduous attention," but she connects it to spirituality, calling it a "supernatural," or otherworldly, "enthusiasm." Later, looking back on his experiment, Victor associates his enthusiasm with "frenzy," or madness: "During my first experiment, a kind of enthusiastic frenzy had blinded me to the horror of my employment."[21] Later "medical" writer William Cullen would define frenzy as "an inflammation of the parts contained in the cavity of the cranium, and may affect either the membranes of the brain, or the substance of the brain tissues."[22] The line between social and mental regulation is a fine one: when the "parts" of the cranial cavity become "inflam[ed]," the worry is that the local inflammation will affect the entire brain...or, in anti-Methodist discourse, the body politic. Thus enthusiasm becomes pathologized—mapped onto the brain—and, in many Romantic-era documents, is used interchangeably with "madness" or, at least, "mania."

Part II: Intellectual Monomania

Mary Shelley plays not only with the notion of enthusiasm as a form of madness, but also with the idea that, until the eighteenth century, "fanaticism" or "madness" was not usually possession by God, but by the devil. If the word "enthusiasm" would have immediately conjured the notion of Methodism—and madness—to Mary Shelley's and Mary Hays's readers, these notions would also have been connected with a belief in demonic possession.

As I've argued in the introduction—and as Diane Hoeveler has compellingly argued in *Gothic Riffs*—this deeply religious understanding of the world exists, during the Romantic era, in tandem with an increasingly "scientific," materialistic one. Janis Caldwell also nods to this "dialogue between naturalism and theology."[23] It is this back-and-forth that attempts to, in Locke's words, "regulate" the modern subject, and that subject is contingent upon "control of the body with its concomitant issues—fertility, wellness, aging, and death."[24] I would add that, as the Romantic mind becomes embodied, philosophers, medical men, and priests attempt to "control" it by deciphering it. Yet, at the same time, they often maintain supernatural belief systems, existing in an uneasy, uncanny limbo.[25]

During the eighteenth century, many publications attempted to negotiate this limbo by combining a belief in demonic possession with a brain-based interpretation of mental illness. Dispensing advice for spiritual counselors, priest John Baptist Scaramelli wrote about the importance of restraining and controlling the intellectual appetite, writing that the overwrought appetite

> obeys the imagination rather than the will; nor does the imagination pay ready obedience to the commands of the will when this forbids it to dally with unlawful objects, or when it employs all due diligence in turning away the imagination ...[26]

This is what we would expect from religious discourse: a focus on the will as a means to retrain the imagination, to "turn [it] away" before it became subsumed with "unlawful" objects. It is edifying to reflect on what Scaramelli might mean by "unlawful." As a priest, he would have conceived of the word as tinged with implications of immorality and sin, but it also implies that "lawful" thoughts need to be communal, understood by a social body. In a society more and more interested in individualism and in religious enthusiasm, the soul needed to be reframed as "the object of study called the mind."[27]

Yet, writing about what we would now call obsession, Scaramelli appears much more sympathetic to the idea of "unlawful" thoughts being the product of a mental disorder. He writes that there are people so

> timorous, and of so delicate a conscience, that they feel great abhorrence to all impurity, and of every action in which a grievous sin may lurk. When an image or a feeling contrary to purity presents itself to such as these, they fall into great fear and feel intense pain …And what is the result? The more these thoughts are driven away the more they return to the mind.[28]

Scaramelli recognized the great paradox: the more a person tries to drive out obsessive thoughts, the more they, like Frankenstein's creature, become a haunting presence.

This presence is not only, in many ways, akin to demonic possession, but it is embodied, in the sense that obsession causes bodily pain and, in the Romantic era, bodily pain, most commonly a fever, could cause, or, paradoxically, relieve obsession. Mary Shelley goes to great lengths to illustrate the physiological results of a mental disorder. Perhaps most famous is the passage in which Victor describes his physiognomy as he undertakes his famous experiment. His cheek, he recalls, had

> grown pale with study, and my person had become emaciated with confinement…with unrelaxed and breathless eagerness, I pursued nature to her hiding places…my limbs now tremble, and my eyes swim with remembrance, but then a resistless, and almost frantic impulse, led me forward.[29]

Almost every clause here connects a feeling with a body part: the cheek "grow[s] pale," his limbs "tremble," his eyes "swim" with tears, and his entire body feels "unrelaxed," "breathless," and "frantic." Here, we see Victor's "enthusiasm" manifesting itself in a bodily manner. In this way, religion becomes reexplained as physiology and, later, psychology.

Thus enthusiasm weaves itself into the discourses of religion, philosophy, and now popular culture, where it becomes increasingly associated with madness. William Black, a London physician, reported that ten percent of those admitted to Bethlem Hospital (Bedlam) suffered from "Religion and Methodism."[30] In the 1767 mock epic, *Methodism Triumphant*, the poet invokes two muses, "Mania" and "Phantasia."[31] Thus it comes as no surprise that popular illustrators also made links between overenthusiastic religions, whether they be Methodism or Catholicism, and madness. Figure 3.1, for instance, is William Hogarth's 1762 engraving from *Credulity, Superstition, and Fanaticism*.

Here, the minister holds up two puppets, one a witch and one a devil. People throughout the congregation motion with their hands or gape in amazement, and a woman gives birth to rabbits.[32] Under the minister,

Fig. 3.1 William Hogarth, *Credulity, superstition, and fanaticism* (1762) (Scanned from *The Genius of William Hogarth*. Eds. Stuart Barton and Tony Curtis (Lyle Publications, 1972))

a man and a woman engage in an amorous encounter; Hogarth here mocks the "superstitious" nature of Methodism by having the man put an icon of the Blessed Virgin—clearly a barb at Catholicism—in the woman's breast. By doing so, he conflates two passionate, and anathemized, dissenting faiths. Next to the couple is a scroll that reads: "madness/ ConvulsionFits/ EXTACY/ LUST/ Love/ Heat." In the popular mind, then, the "heat" of enthusiasm, especially that expressed outside of mainstream Anglicanism, could produce convulsions, fits, and "madness."

In both Shelley's and Hays's novels, these convulsions and fits recur, associated with an idea (later, in 1815, called an "idée fixe" by J. G. Spurzheim), that consumes the character. Even if the idea is a "false" idea, it could be, according to Spurzheim and to Esquirol, followed by "logical reasonings," which was why intellectual monomania was so difficult to observe and pathologize. By the time this type of mania took hold, patients would suffer from the symptoms that Mary Shelley bestows upon her protagonist.

Not only was a "false principle" necessary for intellectual monomania, but that principle had to be excessively repeated. Physician Samuel Tissot wrote that the most affected were those who

> dwell too long upon one and the same thought; for thus one part of the sensorium being longer stretch'd than the rest, without ever being reliev'd by the others in their turn, is the sooner broke.[33]

French neurologist Jules Bernard Luys also suggests that, "since ideas, emotions, and actions had separate cortical localization, nervous excitation might give rise to bizarre ideas, involuntary emotions, or compulsive acts."[34] This "tightness" or "stretching" was importantly not confined to the "insane," those who were considered less than human. Instead, anyone, especially authors, could "dwell too long upon one" thought. In *Practical Observations on Insanity*, Cox writes that excessive study

> exhausts both body and mind. It has been supposed, and perhaps justly, that all our thoughts, sensations, and intellectual excursions, are accompanied with correspondent motions; close, severe, and exclusive thinking has a direct tendency to weaken, confuse, and destroy the intellect.[35]

Cox's notion of the exhausted mind depleting the rest of the body is one that returns, again and again, in Mary Shelley's fever-wracked novel. A materialist, Cox believes that all of our intellectual "moves" correspond to physical moves within the brain, and that too much of this "motion," if exclusive and severe, can literally destroy the mind. Esquirol's cases of intellectual monomania involve both reading and, of interest to prolific writers like Hays and Shelley, writing. He cites Andrew McKenot, who was "a man of great cleverness, a good scholar, versed in learned languages..."[36] This man, a patient at the Salpêtrière, suffers from the compulsion of always writing. Another of Esquirol's patients, "after being fatigued by reading, and even during the night, [] is seized with a passion for study, and at the same time persuades himself that his enemies are about to make an attempt upon his life."[37] Not only is the body depleted and the mind overcome by study, but that same "fatigue" results in obsessively paranoid fears.

This case can be directly paralleled with Shelley's Victor Frankenstein, who has become associated with this pattern, earning the moniker of the "obsessed scientist." When he reads Paracelsus and Agrippa, he tells us that "natural philosophy...became nearly my sole occupation."[38] In fact, Victor critiques his brother Ernest, who doesn't have his "habits of application" and is always "in the open air, climbing the hills, or rowing on the lake."[39] Over and over again, Shelley uses the word "application" to imply study and work, the "object of assiduous attention." Later, Shelley would write about a similarly obsessed scientist: the astronomer Merrival in her 1826 *The Last Man*. Shelley again puts her character within a scientific context, calling him "learned as" the French mathematician and astronomer Pierre-Simon LaPlace (1749–1827). Yet, aside from his learning, the rest of his being is "guileless" like a "child." His wife is "pale," they live in a "garrett," he himself feels no "hunger" or "distress." Like Victor, he ignores the needs of those around him, here his children's cries and his wife's hunger, all for the sake of his obsession, observing a "celestial phenomenon."[40] As he prophesies the end of the world, this character also links millenarianist religious movements with growing psychological curiosity.

"Application" also has its place in the discourses of Romantic natural philosophy. In his *History of Madness*, Michel Foucault also writes that one of the prime causes of "frenzy" was, according to the *Encyclopédie*, "a love of science or a devotion to letters, both of which are increasingly widespread."[41] This "love," this "devotion," results in an uncontrolled appetite or imagination that affects both the mind and the body. Johann Christian Heinroth foreshadows Shelley's novel when he writes that "misdirected research into the deepest mysteries of nature" results in lack of sleep, appetite, and tiredness.[42] In William Black's 1810 *Dissertation on Insanity*, illustrated with 3000 cases from Bedlam, "study" was one of the causes of monomania.[43] William Perfect also treated a man who had "long applied to intense study, and rigidly denied himself those relaxations, which a mind like his so greatly stood in need of, as a temporary relief and refreshment from the immoderate fatigue of intellectual researches"; his complaints include "anxiety [and] watchfulness,"[44] similar to Victor's "unrelaxed eagerness." Perfect goes on to describe

> excessive difficulty of breathing ensuing, constrictions of the external parts, with slight shiverings, and a stupor … which ended in a confirmed delirium; his mouth was distorted, he raved, was confined, and my advice thought necessary; I found the pulse full, great and quick; the countenance flushed and inflated, and the eyes wild and protuberant.[45]

Here, psychological anxiety caused by "intense study" results in difficulty breathing, shivering, a distorted mouth, a quick, full pulse, a flushed face, and "protuberant" eyes.

These physical connections were elaborated upon by Charles Bell, who wrote about "folly" and connected it with the par vagum, the respiratory nerve. "Why, at intervals," he writes, "is there a long drawn sigh; why are the neck and throat convulsed, and whence the quivering and swelling of the lip; why the deadly paleness, and the surface earthly cold; or why does convulsion spread over the frame like a paroxysm of suffocation?"[46] This discourse seems eerily familiar as we see Victor's body change throughout the book. Not only does he not realize the passage of seasons, but every night he feels a "slow fever," and calls himself "anxious to a most painful degree."[47] On the night of the creature's creation, this anxiety "almost amounted to agony."[48] During his nightmare on the eve of his creation, "a cold dew covered my forehead, my teeth chattered, and every limb became convulsed."[49] Again, Shelley refers to the feverish quality and spasmodic movements (the word "convulsion" is common) often assigned to frenzy. She pays especial attention to Victor's pulse; he says that it "beat so quickly and hardly, that I felt the palpitation of every artery"[50]; that his "heart palpitated in the sickness of fear"; and that he "felt my flesh tingle with excess of sensitiveness, and my pulse beat rapidly."[51] The tingling flesh, the beating pulse, the slow fever, and the chattering teeth all illustrate the feverish, overdrawn qualities associated, by writers like Heinroth and Bell, with what we would now call obsession.

These physiological markers of obsession are also present in Hays's Emma Courtney; once Augustus Harley rejects her after many frantic letters, she simply cannot stop thinking about him and becomes:

> Sad, vacant—inactive ...This was gradually succeeded by disease of body:—an inactivity, so contrary to all the habits of my past life, generated morbid humours, and brought on a slow, remitting, fever.[52]

Much of this passage resembles Mary Shelley's description of Victor: the slow fever, for instance, occurs in both novels. However, instead of "frenzy," shallow breathing, anxiety, and spasmodic movements, we have here an obsession that, instead of multiplying sublime effects in the mind, almost cancels out the mind itself. Words like "vacant" attest to a gendered "lack" (the woman as passive, a hole waiting to be made whole) and the faculties, instead of stretching taut like Tissot's string, are here "suspended." Weakness, enervation—literally a removal of nervous energy—and lethargy accompany Emma's fevered state. While both protagonists become obsessed with an idea (the idea of the creature and the idea of Harley, respectively), the different reactions stem from the very different, gendered, effects of study and "reading."

Jacqueline Pearson puts it well when she writes that, "While men's reading was shown to facilitate intellectual development, women's tended to be located in the female body, represented as a physical not an intellectual act."[53] While Agrippa and Paracelsus might be "bad" models, they do represent fields of intellectual inquiry. Pearson's statement becomes especially apt when Victor Frankenstein is paired with Emma Courtney, who reads indiscriminately. Hays hints at her reading choices by having her subscribe "to a circulating library, and frequently read, or rather devoured—little careful in the selection—from ten to fourteen novels in a week."[54] The image of consumption, of "devouring" books, implies a bodily connection; the books, in many ways, become part, not only of the mind, but also of the woman's body. While the notion of "appetite," as explored by Scaramelli and others, often connects with obsession, this metaphor is especially prominent in regards to women's reading choices.[55] To give one example, Hannah More, in *Strictures on Female Education*, refers to the woman reader's "glutted" imagination, again equating knowledge with (unhealthy) foods.[56]

These metaphors of (over)consumption which, as Barbara Benedict points out, colocate obsession in the woman's brain as well as her body, occur in protopsychological discourse as well. Perfect offers an example of a woman whose "appetite [was] so much depraved, that she would eat papers, cinders, bits of wall, anything that lay in her way," and John Haslam, the proprietor of Bedlam, gives an account of a 27-year-old Bedlamite who "conceived her inside full of the most loathsome vermin"[57] In these accounts from lunatic asylums, "vermin" often become "serpents," which then circle back to the initial, demonic component of obsession. In Bedlam, for instance, one of the residents is described as a thirty-year-old woman who "took the sacrament sacreligeously" and now believes she has serpents in her body.[58] The bodily nature of female obsession is directly referenced by Rush who writes that the

> distressing impressions made upon the minds of women frequently vent themselves in tears, or in hysterical commotions in the nervous system, and bowels, while the same impressions upon minds of men pass by their more compact nervous and muscular fibres, and descend into the brain…[59]

Tears, "hysterical commotions"—like envisioning serpents in one's body—and gastrointestinal stress, while they also exist in males, become, as opposed to the "brain," the exclusive domain of women's obsessive thinking.

In addition to literary and medical references, legal documents also reinforce this notion of the possessed obsessed woman. One details a "Mrs. Clerke" whose family claims her unable to control her finances. In this account, Mrs. Clerke is prescribed medicines for "lethargy" but begins to suspect poisoning. Then, her maid drops a vial of medicine and she takes some that "still had a piece of glass in it." Although the medicine is itself ostensibly poison, she also becomes obsessed with the idea that this piece of glass will kill her. She first asks her maid to "pull it out of her Throat with her Fingers," and, later, to thoroughly inspect the chamber pot.[60] Again, in this construction of obsession, the woman, instead of becoming obsessed with an external idea, becomes obsessed with something bodily, whether the poison or the shard of glass. And again, this document ties female obsession back to a religious discourse. When she visits her brother, Mrs. Clerke extols "her Purity, and [talks] of her being as unspotted, and as far from the Knowledge of Man, as the Virgin Mary." When her brother objects that she had been married for ten years and lay with her husband, she drops to her knees and "prayed aloud for some Time."[61] If her ostensible purity aligns her with the Virgin Mary, then her actual lack of purity aligns her with the opposite: the whore or, worse, the devil. We have, then, returned to Hogarth's enthusiasm, but this enthusiasm, engendered by sinful thoughts (which often come from leisurely reading), possesses the woman's body in addition to her mind.

By becoming even more physiological, female enthusiasm is easily mapped onto the discourse of addiction. In Coleridge's *Biographia Literaria* (1815), he writes: "For as to the devotees of the circulating libraries, I dare not compliment their pass-time, or rather kill-time with the name of reading."[62] Instead of "pass"ing time, these readers, who are not even *real* readers, actually "kill" or destroy time. Coleridge then continues on to parallel the circulating libraries with (typically male) addictions such as "gaming, swinging or swaying on a chair or gate; spitting over a bridge; smoking; snuff-taking, [and] conning word by word all the advertisements of the daily advertiser in a public house on a rainy day."[63] While gaming and memorizing are repetitive behaviors and could be characterized as obsessive, Coleridge's other examples are curiously bodily. "Swinging or swaying on a chair or gate" is a repetitive motion intended to stimulate the vestibular system; this desperate need for sensory input aligns women's reading or study with pure tactile stimulation, as do "spitting," "smoking," and "snuff-taking," curiously pejorative male parallels to women's reading.

When Emma is a little girl, one of the "day-boarders" at her school brings her books "from [such] a neighboring library," "which at every interval of leisure I perused with inconceivable avidity."[64] As opposed to Victor's study, validated by his later university education, this feminine reading is a "leisure" time activity. In fact, her father mocks her reading choices by critiquing the reading of Gothic novels:

> Your studies, for the future, must be of a soberer nature, or I shall have you mistake my valet for a prince in disguise, my house for a haunted castle, and my rational care for your future welfare for barbarous tyranny.[65]

The prince in disguise, the haunted castle, and the notion of "barbarous" (male) "tyranny" are all standard Gothic tropes. They also clearly point to a woman's lack of agency during this period; when she dreams about a prince to grant her financial security, she walks through many physical and psychological "haunted castles," and she experiences multiple forms of "barbarous tyranny." Hays's word choices illustrate that it is not only women's reading that betokens mental illness, but also—and, for her, mostly—the society on which that reading reflects.

In the Romantic era (and to this day) femininity is equated with passivity, so the passivity of reading becomes central to female enthusiasm.[66] A passive reader simply consumed books like luscious desserts; this is why these types of readers are often associated with circulating libraries, from which readers could rent and then return materials. Rereading, as Lee Erickson argues, was not necessary. In this context, reading becomes a form of escape, "a withdrawal from a woman's proper social concerns."[67] Ironically, women, isolated from the public sphere, can nonetheless not become *too* private, living within their own minds.

It is this type of reading—again, reading that fosters and is fostered by solitude—that becomes equated with obsession. Unable to participate as valued members of their society, women remain trapped, forced to reiterate thoughts and images in what Hays has Emma call the "magic circle":

> Hemmed in on every side by the constitutions of society, and not less so, it may be, by my own prejudices—I perceive, indignantly perceive, the magic circle, without knowing how to dissolve the powerful spell. While men pursue interest, honor, pleasure, as accords with their several dispositions, women, who have too much delicacy, sense and spirit, to degrade themselves by the vilest of all interchanges, remain insulated beings, and must be content tamely to look on, without taking any part in the great, though often absurd and tragical, drama of life.[68]

The "magic circle" might keep women out of the "constitutions of society"—and, as Hays perceptively argues, patriarchal constructions of gender are reinforced by women themselves—the metaphor of the circle, with its repetitive nature, is telling. Women "remain insulated beings," but this insulation also traps them within recurring, gendered, patterns and thoughts. The woman reader is possessed by the "magic," "powerful," sublime thought. Yet instead of the "powerful" thought overwhelming the brain, it possesses it in a way reminiscent of witchcraft (again, demonic possession), enchantment, and passivity.

As Katherine Binhammer argues, the woman becomes a sort of cipher onto whom her reading is inscribed. "The model of a passive reader," she writes, "equates the self with the text (you are what you read); thus, the world of the text becomes her world."[69] This notion of the passive reader is famously satirized in Charlotte Lennox's 1752

The Female Quixote and by Jane Austen in her 1817 *Northanger Abbey*, when Catherine Morland misreads materials from gothic novels as truth and, "instead of instantly conceiving, as any rational creature would have done, that such words could relate only to a circulating library, she immediately pictured to herself a mob of three thousand men assembling in St. George's Fields..."[70] For Emma Courtney, Augustus Harley becomes "the St. Preux, the Emilius of my sleeping and waking reveries."[71] These names are significant, as St. Preux stems from Rousseau's *Julie, ou La Nouvelle Héloïse* (1761), a novel widely credited with "seducing" women and exposing them to dangerous sexuality. When Emma first reads the book, she exclaims that she pursued the "dangerous," "enchanting" book with "enthusiasm" and "transport."[72] Instead of becoming an obsession, the book "enchants" her, possesses her, and transports her to another (perhaps more sexually progressive) reality.

Therefore, as Claire Grogan argues, Emma here seduces *herself*.[73] The images presented to her by Rousseau become her realities, to the degree that Harley is an empty signifier, to be filled with Emma's obsessive thoughts. It is at this point that Emma becomes a more active reader, reading (like Victor when he fears the creature's appearance) her thoughts into the world around her. The metaphor of reading is central to this novel/autonarration/memoir; tellingly, Mrs. Harley first tells Emma stories about Augustus.[74] Later, she reads his portrait, which hangs, naturally, in the library. When Harley first appears, the two form an acquaintance by reading novels. Emma reads—or reads into—Harley's letters, attempting to decipher their purport and, finally, her adopted son, Augustus Jr., will read her letters. Clearly, reading and misreading are central to the story, but again, the magic circle allows for very little deviation. For women, with a patriarchally inscribed story, the narratives they construct, the endings they write, often repeat the same, socially acceptable, formula.

Part III: Monstrous Associationism and the Science of the Mind

This very formula is one that depends on the (mis)association of thoughts, quickly followed by the remediation of the female protagonist. One can easily understand the social anxiety concerning David Hartley's doctrine of association. The key to healthy association, according to philosophers and writers, was what Samuel Taylor Coleridge, himself heavily influenced by Hartley, calls "the imagination's synthesizing influence."

Without it, he writes, "….[association] becomes free-associationism, in which the mind fires away at will."[75] Coleridge writes that, without this synthesis, "the fairest part of the most beautiful body will appear deformed and monstrous, if dissevered from its place in the organic Whole."[76] If, as Hume posited, the mind consists of a canvas on which various sensations, which build upon one another, form the "soul," these sensations can only be synthesized, made "organic," through the imagination. What happens, though, when the imagination, instead of synthesizing, merely adds to the cacophony of sensation? Significantly, Coleridge anthropomorphizes the imagination as a "body." He calls the unsynthesized mind "deformed" and "monstrous," much like Victor's thoughts. They run away from him, ironically uncontrolled because they are so centered on one object.

Emma Courtney's imagination overtakes her as well, but Mary Hays's notion of associationism is, here, a bit different. Instead of "runn[ing] away" uncontrolled, Emma Courtney's brain, formed throughout childhood by her reading and experiences, returns again and again to the same place. Scott Nowka's important article makes clear that Hays, too, was influenced by Hartley's theories. Nowka argues that Hartley's work was very influential in the thinking of Joseph Priestley and Helvétius, both of whom shaped Hays's philosophy.[77] For Hays, instead of becoming monstrous and unruly, association results in what Nowka calls a kind of "psychological determinism" and what Hays herself called her theory of materialism. In other words, if early experiences and associations form the brain in a certain manner, they, for Hays, predict the eventual outcome.

In a letter to Godwin, Hays elaborates on her notion of the material brain:

> I have said that I was a materialist…man appears to me to be but of one substance, capable of receiving from external impressions sensible ideas, successively formed into various combinations and trains, carried on by means of sympathy and association with mechanical exactness, in an infinite series of causes and effects.[78]

Hays's explanation of "materialism" pairs with her notion of association to posit the reader or observer as a blank slate or, at least, a Humean canvas of impressions. For Hays, as for Harley, the "external impressions" coalesce into "sensible ideas" which are then associated with other ideas in "various combinations and trains." Therefore, cause and effect informs Hays's psychology; initial impressions, like those gained through childhood reading, must become the basis for later thoughts and ideas.

In her preface, Hays describes her novel/memoir as a form of psychological experimentation:

> The most interesting, and the most useful, fictions, are, perhaps, such, as delineating the progress, and tracing the consequences, of one strong, indulged, passion, or prejudice, afford materials, by which the philosopher may calculate the powers of the human mind, and learn the springs which set it in motion—.[79]

While certain "springs" set Victor Frankenstein's ideas "in motion," the point is that, without the synthesizing function of the imagination, one cannot clearly "delineate" their progress or trace them through the novel. In other words, one can see obsession take varied, tangentially related forms. Emma Courtney's imagination, on the other hand, seems to play little role in her condition. Her images are deposited in her brain, like items in a pawn shop, and she returns to them, again and again, using the ideas of Rousseau and Helvetius in order to inscribe meaning onto her own story. Continuing her preface, Hays writes that "Every possible incident, in works of this nature, might, perhaps, be rendered probable, were a sufficient regard paid to the more minute, delicate, and connecting links of the chain."[80] In order to understand Emma's mind, we must understand links that bring us, the readers, back to the beginning of the chain.

Hays's novel, then, is firmly entrenched in Hartley's notion of association, Hume's theories of perception, and, it seems, Coleridge's idea of reading as "habit"; she makes it a point to tell her (female) readers that "associations and habits which make us what we are; for without outward impressions we should be nothing."[81] In the "memoir" itself, Francis takes this point further, comparing the human mind to a piece of paper, telling Mr. Courtney that, while "any inlet to perception remains, your paper will infallibly contract characters of some kind, or be blotted and scrawled!"[82] The paper, like the woman reader, remains passive, "contracting" characters like a disease; taking the metaphor even further, one might consider the idea of misleading original impressions as a "blot" or "scrawl" on the psychological text: an apt metaphor for a train of thought that is, for one reason or another, derailed.

Emma Courtney's original impression is, importantly, the *idea* of Harley; when the reader stops to examine their conversations, it is clear that Emma cannot know Harley himself. Again, the idea of "leisure," curiously gendered as the feminine form of "solitude," allows for association outside of a social context. "To what purpose," Emma writes her son,

> should I trouble you with a thousand wayward, contradictory, ideas and emotions, that I am, myself, unable to disentangle— which have, perhaps, floated in every mind, that has had leisure for reflection—.[83]

With too much "leisure for reflection," the ideas and emotions become entangled, "floated" in the mind like an unmoored kite.

The ideas in Emma's mind are only exacerbated by her intellectual pursuit of reading philosophy:

> Philosophy, it is said, should regulate the feelings, but it has added fervor to mine! What are passions, but another name for powers? The mind capable of receiving the most forcible impressions is the sublimely improveable mind![84]

Here, "passion" is directly associated with "power"; these impressions are "forcible," strong, and only the mind capable of receiving them is "improveable." Otherwise, Hays suggests, the mind will receive forcible impressions and become further inflamed by them.

It is this inflammation, this "fervor," that Hays associates with obscurity. Burke famously connected the obscure with the sublime, arguing that obscurity only furthers the sense of sublimity. For Hays, when the brain itself becomes "obscured" by the power of the passions, it descends into fancy and pain. Writing to Harley about his vague letters, Emma states that this "obscurity" is part of the problem:

> Objects seen through obscurity, imperfectly discerned, allow to the fancy but too free a scope; the mind grows debilitated, by brooding over its apprehensions; and those apprehensions, whether real or imaginary, are carried with accumulated pain to the heart.[85]

Like a painting, Harley's words, in their lack of clarity, allow for Emma's "fancy" to reign unimpeded, which, in turn, affect her bodily, causing her "pain." This notion of obscurity recurs multiple times in Hays's text, tying Emma's obsession with Harley to the notion of sublimity. She writes to her son that it was "obscurity and mystery" that turned her feelings into "frenzy," here tying the uncertainty of the sublime to mental illness.[86]

Emma Courtney's obsession turns her inward; by the end of the novel, Emma is (somewhat) happily married to Montague, has a child, but cannot free herself from her damaging obsession. When Harley comes to her house, dying, she immediately spends all of her time nursing him, despite the way it appears to the surgeon, Mr. Lucas, or to Montague himself. "My thoughts," she writes, "with fatal mechanism, ran back into their old and accustomed channels.— For a moment, conjugal, maternal, duties, every consideration but for one object faded from before me!"[87] Again, Hays references her belief in association which, for her, works in a fatalistic, "mechanistic" way. Because of Emma's earliest impressions—her readings from the circulating library—her thoughts and emotions can only function in this way. She compares her feelings to a pernicious, though "sublime" enthusiasm, and exclaims that "its ravages are scarcely to be remembered without shuddering— all the strength, the dignity, the powers, of my mind, melted before it!"[88] Enthusiasm acts upon the passive, female mind, "ravaging" it, until, overcome by that sublime heat, the mind "melts" into nothingness.

The uncertainty of the sublime, carried to an irrational excess by association, is also well illustrated by Shelley's novel. After the creature's creation, his image overwhelms Victor's imagination: "I issued into the streets, pacing them with quick steps, as if I sought to avoid the wretch whom I feared every turning of the street would present to my view."[89] Victor here tells Walton not that he did seek to avoid the "wretch," but that he paces *as if* he sought to avoid the wretch. This seemingly slight semantic difference moves the scene from the realm of the gothic to the realm of the imagination, specifically to many of the fears associated with associationism. Mary Shelley's textual hints lead us to wonder how much of Victor's fear of the creature is due to the deformity of the creature himself, and how much of it spawns from an irrationally obsessive, uncontrolled imagination.

Shelley furthers this emphasis on obsession and the unsynthesized imagination by, in this same part of the text, having Victor quote from Coleridge's "Rime of the Ancient Mariner." Like the mariner, Victor sees himself as

> one who, on a lonely road
> Doth walk in fear and dread,
> And, having once turn'd round, walks on,
> And turns no more his head;
> Because he knows a frightful fiend
> Doth close behind him tread.[90]

This poem is its own tale of obsession, and it informs the Chapter 6 of this book. Clearly, the trope of the mariner repeating his tale because of "fear and dread" explores what happens when an obsessive fear becomes replaced by a compulsion, here the repetition of the tale, without, as Faflak argues, "working through the past."[91] The obsession gains power over the sufferer, much as Victor's obsessive fear of the creature does. Shelley's reference not only harkens back to the equally obsessed mariner Walton but also parallels the "frightful fiend" in Coleridge's poem and the "fiend" Victor continuously imagines until, without any knowledge of him, he is convinced of his monstrosity.

Shelley's language emphasizes this point. Even before the murder of William, Victor alludes to the creature as a "spectre." Though a "spectre" is an apparition, a phantom, or a ghost, it also meant, at this time, "an object or source of dread or terror" or "a phantasm of the brain" (OED). The latter is fascinating, as it situates the "phantasm" inside the brain, not outside in the creature himself. Again, this is "obsessio": like an act of sorcery, the form of the creature has infiltrated Victor's sensations, including his sight: "the form of the monster on whom I had bestowed existence was for ever before my eyes." Lest Shelley's readers think that this is a natural response to an unnatural creative act, Victor makes it a point to use the language of madness, telling Walton that he "raved incessantly concerning him."[92]

Victor's creation of a mate for the creature, grounded in the creature's rational argument, quickly also spirals out of control. When he attempts to create a mate for his creature, he compares the collection of his materials to "the torture of single drops of water continually falling on the head."[93] In this splendidly physiological comparison, Shelley details the reality of obsession—it is not the "single drops of water" that break the delicate "strings of the mind" that Tissot referenced, but their continuous nature. Through the very repetition of ideas or images, they become too overwhelming.

Mary Shelley also links obscurity to obsession. Once he has made the creature, Victor's ideas about him gain such power that they require no logical synthesis or proof. When he sees the creature highlighted by the lighting at Mont Blanc, he immediately "knows" that he murdered William, giving as proof the fact that "the mere presence of the idea was an irresistible proof."[94] Like the "idea" of the creature, this idea (although eventually proven true) gains power merely through its presence. Later, when Kirwin, the magistrate, tells him that a "friend" has come to visit, Victor immediately responds: "I know not by what chain of thought the idea presented itself, but it instantly darted into my mind that the murderer had come to mock at my misery."[95] Here we have a clear description of the associative process: the "chain of thought," prompted by a chain of sensations, leads to an idea which "instantly darted into" Victor's mind. This idea gains so much power over Victor that he shudders to see his visitor, who turns out to be his own father. Again, we have a Romantic disconnect between what should be reasonable and what the uncontrolled imagination can do. Scaramelli, writing about "scruples," contrasts "reasons" with "appearances, fancies, and frivolous motives." "Far from leaving our assent suspended," he writes, "[scrupulosity] inclines us to judge that there is grievous sin where in fact there is not the slightest fault. Besides which, scruples fill the mind with fears, anxiety, disquiet, harassing disturbance; none of which effects follow upon reasonable doubt."[96] These phrases, "reasonable doubt" (Scaramelli) and "reasonable proof" (Shelley), imply an almost legalistic method of policing or controlling the monstrous imagination.

While outside the immediate context of this book, this legalistic discourse makes its appearance again and again in novels concerning what Foucault calls "abnormal" mental states. *Frankenstein* clearly evinces Mary Shelley's interest in the concept of legal justice—the case of Justine Moritz was, as scholars have argued, based on the case of Eliza Fenning—, but Shelley more broadly alludes to the social need to circumscribe the imagination gone awry.[97] In this way, the Gothic novel is, as Sue Chaplin has argued, a symbolic representation of burgeoning literary, ethical, and moral laws.[98]

In addition to showing us that Victor's response to the creature is irrational and indicates a diseased imagination, Shelley also illustrates that Romantic obsession turns the sufferer inward. After Victor receives the letter from Alphonse detailing William's death, he never once thinks about Alphonse's fatherly grief. Instead, he only views events from his own perspective, looking at the beauty of the mountains, lake, and sky and asking if they "prognosticate peace, or…mock at [his] unhappiness?"[99] Even more disturbing is the fact that, after Victor destroys the creature's mate and the creature says "I will be with you on your wedding night" (a phrase that resounds in Shelley's text), Victor thinks "In that hour I should die, and at once satisfy and extinguish his malice."[100] Immediately, "I will be with you" becomes "I should die," and again, this idea assumes such force that Victor cannot think differently. The same idea—that the creature plans to kill him on his wedding night—occupies Victor's waking thoughts as well as his dreams. In one scene, he experiences a "kind of night-mare; I felt the fiend's grasp in my neck, and could not free myself from it; groans and cries rung in my ears."[101] Again, to use a Romantic-era term, his sensorium has been so overwhelmed by this idea that he hears, feels, and sees only this repetitive idea. Victor's obsessive vision of his own death keeps him from seeing other alternatives, including the death of Elizabeth. He even states that death "was no evil to me, if the loss of Elizabeth were balanced with it," but he does not—he cannot—consider that it is exactly the "loss of Elizabeth" that the creature has planned.[102] Victor's obsession, here with the idea of the creature killing him, has become a process of associationism gone awry, to the exclusion and damage of those around him.

Victor's obsessive vision of his own death, what Deanna Koretsky calls a "suicide wish," also parallels the frequent mention of suicide in medical accounts of obsessive thinking.[103] Cox's 1813 text not only connects what he terms "hypochondriasis" ("close, severe, and exclusive thinking") to suicide, but it also reinforces the earlier religious connotations of enthusiasm. "Many an unhappy instance has occurred in my own practice," he writes, "where the ignorant or injudicious zeal of preachers has induced hypochondriasis, insanity of the most incurable species, and moping melancholy, often terminated by suicide."[104] Later, in 1822, J. P. Falret wrote *De l'Hypochondrie et du Suicide*, which was subsequently reviewed by the *London Medical and Physical Journal*.[105] Why did people commit suicide? It could, as Cox argues, be caused by an "injudicious zeal," or, as Falret argues, be caused by a material defect in the brain. These two medical examples illustrate that the Romantics simultaneously embraced religious enthusiasm and materialism, shifting, as Caldwell argues, comfortably between the two.

By closely observing Mary Shelley and Mary Hays's word choices, one can decipher the discourses of both religious enthusiasm and materialist proto-psychology in their novels. Furthermore, both Victor and Emma's character development leaves no question in the reader's mind that associationism gone awry produces enthusiasm, whether religious or scholarly, which overwhelms the sufferer until it controls him or her. By the time Walton sees Victor, he claims to never have seen

> A more interesting creature: his eyes have generally an expression of wildness, and even madness ... he is generally melancholy and despairing; and sometimes he gnashes his teeth, as if impatient of the weight of woes that oppresses him.[106]

Shelley's word choice is telling. Victor is, significantly, called a "creature" and described in an animalistic fashion. Much like his own creation, Victor "gnashes his teeth."[107] Perfect, writing about madness caused by too much study, details the symptoms as "grinding of the teeth, quickness of hearing, incredible strength, insensibility of cold."[108] While the first symptom connects Victor to his creature, it would be productive to read the creature as symbolic of Victor's obsession. Not only does he exhibit Perfect's other symptoms, but, according to Esquirol, the lypemaniac, who entertains ideas "contrary to reason," is "lean and slender, his hair is black, and the hue of his countenance pale and sallow."[109] The black hair, the sallow countenance, and the insensibility to cold are all evinced in the creature, who becomes the physical type of Victor's intellectual monomania.

Emma, too, has a double, one who not only entertains similar passions to hers but has the agency to act on them: Montague. The male enthusiast in Hays's text, Montague is obsessed by Emma and responds physically to his emotions. When he, hardly knowing Emma, first proposes to her, his actions seem an extension of his emotions: "starting as if from a reverie, [he] seized my hand, while his own trembled with a visible agitation."[110] Much like Victor, Montague cannot prevent the power of his emotions from manifesting in bodily ways. He suffers from "starts of passion," "restlessness," and is, over and over again, referred to as "impetuous."[111] The idea of "starts" implies a lack of control, as does "impetuous," which Hays uses to describe both Montague and Emma.

Hays blatantly compares the two characters in a dialogue that diagnoses them with the same condition. Emma, talking to Montague about her refusal to marry him because of her love for Harley, tells him not to reproach her because

> "my situation is far more pitiable than yours. I am, indeed, unhappy?" —added I, after a pause; "I, like you, am the victim of a raised, I fear, a distempered imagination."[112]

Both Montague and Emma suffered from what she initially refers to as a "raised" imagination, meaning that their passions are merely heightened. On second thought, Emma diagnoses both herself and Montague with "distemper" of the imagination, indicating disease on account of excessive passion. Later, when Montague's obsessions overwhelm his reason, he is described as a madman: " —[Emma] held him with a strenuous grasp — he raved—he stamped — he tore his hair — his passion became frenzy."[113] The "rav[ing]" and Hays's use of the word "frenzy" informs her readers that we are, here, to conflate Montague with inhabitants of insane asylums.

Montague's excessive passion, paired with his training as a physician, produce deadly consequences. When he finds out about Emma's continued feelings for Augustus, he retaliates against her by forming an attachment to their child's young nurse, Rachel. This liaison results in a pregnancy, and Montague attempts to abort the child with "abortifacients," but he only succeeds in stimulating a premature birth. As he gazes upon the child, he realizes

> that the vital flame played but feebly —that life was but as a quivering, uncertain, spark —a sudden and terrible thought darted through my mind. I know not whether my emotion betrayed me to the ear of Rachel —but, suddenly throwing back the curtain of the bed, she beheld me grasp —with savage ferocity —with murderous hands![114]

Montague's "sudden" thought, his idea, assumes a life of its own; this form of obsessive ideation will be explored in Chapter 6. The idea of the "savage" grasp and the "ferocity" indicates that we are to read Montague's obsessive mind as "monstrous."

For the Romantics, who pathologized intellectual monomania, ideas gained from reading could be monstrous, creating a circular pattern of obsessive thinking that, like the scorpion, destroyed the thinker. While modern-day popular culture continues to portray this anxiety concerning *science*, Mary Shelley and Mary Hays both illustrate Romantic-era anxieties about *reading*. As William St. Clair's 2002 *The Reading Nation in the Romantic Period* compellingly argues, the Romantics experienced a veritable explosion of print media; copyright restrictions made older texts available as magazines, journals, and annuals proliferated. With this increase in print came an increase in knowledge which, as the creature states in *Frankenstein*, can function in the "mind" like a "lichen on a rock," possessing the mind in a dangerous (so argued Esquirol and others) manner.[115] This chapter has illustrated the anxieties around knowledge: anxieties equated with the discourse of "enthusiasm" and complicated by David Hartley's theory of association. By exploring Mary Hays's *Memoirs of Emma Courtney*, which features a woman whose obsessive thoughts, garnered from promiscuous novel reading, locate in her body, I have shown that female obsessive thinking was conceived of differently than the obsessive thinking associated with the man of science, Victor Frankenstein.

Although both characters end up feverish and mad, there is an important difference between Victor's experiment and Emma's love for Hartley. Both characters are passive, prone to possession by enthusiasm over an obsessive idea, but Victor's brand of femininity, not co-opted by a female body, can coexist with the concept of genius. As Christine Battersby puts it, "Biological femaleness mimics the psychological femininity of true genius."[116] Thus Victor can, through reading, create life—what Mary Shelley critiques is his inability to care for and sympathize with his creature. Emma, on the other hand, can only draw from real life to imitate characters in novels. Both Shelley and Hays thus set up recognizably gendered models of obsessive thinking, only to critique and pathologize them. The next chapter will examine the pathologization and gendering of what used to be "lovesickness," erotomania.

Notes

1. Esquirol, *Mental Maladies*, 470.
2. Idiocy and madness were, for most of the nineteenth century, interchangeable ideas, and people with intellectual disabilities were often institutionalized with the mentally ill. For more, see Patrick McDonagh, *Idiocy: A Cultural History* (Liverpool: Liverpool University Press, 2008).
3. This is not to say that Shelley's character is only influenced by his obsession; his guilt concerning the creature's actions and his friends' deaths also forces the deterioration of his mental health. Yet Mary Shelley saw fit to detail his (and, later, the creature's) reading list, and she was herself obsessed with detailing her reading lists. See Michele Turner Sharp, "If It Be a Monster Birth: Reading and Literary Property in Mary Shelley's 'Frankenstein,'" *South Atlantic Review* 66, no. 4 (2001): 70–93.
4. Esquirol, *Mental Maladies*, 470.
5. Mary Shelley, *Frankenstein*, ed. D. L. Macdonald and Kathleen Scherf (Peterborough: Broadview Press, 2012), 67–68.
6. Mary Hays, *Memoirs of Emma Courtney*, ed. Marilyn Brooks (Peterborough, ON: Broadview Press, 2000), 45.
7. James Hogg satirizes this type of extreme enthusiasm through the character of Robert in his 1824 *Confessions of a Justified Sinner*, who views a religious doctrine (the Calvinist doctrine of justification) as carte blanche for a variety of misdeeds.
8. Michael J. Crawford, "Origins of the Eighteenth-Century Evangelical Revival: England and New England Compared," *Journal of British Studies* 26, no. 4 (1987): 374. JSTOR. While enthusiasm, in the context of my book, refers mostly to psychological control, the word's pathologization also refers to the lack of state control over dissenters; as my colleague, Dr. Rebecca Nesvet, has pointed out, the word does not seem to apply to the religious experience of Anglicanism.
9. E. P. Thompson, *The Making of the English Working Class* (London: Pelican, 1968), 428.
10. According to Clement Hawes, "the enthusiastic subject, as it comes down to us in British texts—must be understood as taking its modern impetus and meaning from the class-based rhetoric of seventeenth-century radical Puritan conflict" (28). See *Mania and Literary Style: The Rhetoric of Enthusiasm from the Ranters to Christopher Smart* (Cambridge: Cambridge University Press, 1996). While the term "primitive" does seem pejorative, the Primitive Methodist church still exists today and is characterized by a desire to return to the roots of the Methodist movement, see http://www.primitivemethodistchurch.org/history.html.
11. Robert Southey, *The Life of Wesley: And the Rise and Progress of Methodism*, vol. 1 (New York, 1820), 141, accessed via archive.org.

12. Ibid., 202.
13. Ibid., 203.
14. Peter Fenves, "The Scale of Enthusiasm," in *Huntington Library Quarterly: Enthusiasm and Enlightenment in Europe, 1650–1850*, eds. Lawrence E. Klein and Anthony J. La Vopa (San Marino, CA: Huntington Library, 1998), 117.
15. Robert Doran, *The Theory of the Sublime from Longinus to Kant* (Cambridge: Cambridge University Press, 2018), 59.
16. David Hume, "Essay X: Of Superstition and Enthusiasm," in *Essays Moral, Political, and Literary (1742–1754)*, http://www.english.upenn.edu/~mgamer/Etexts/hume.superstition.html. (Emphasis mine.)
17. John Locke, *An Essay Concerning Human Understanding* (Kitchener, ON: Batoche Books, 2001), 584. For Mary Shelley's reading list, see Paula R. Feldman and Diana Scott-Kilvert, eds., *The Journals of Mary Shelley: 1814–1844* (Oxford: Clarendon Press, 1989), 659.
18. Quoted in Fenves, "The Scale of Enthusiasm," 123.
19. Lisa Vargo, "Mary Shelley, Corinne, and 'The Mantle of Enthusiasmm,'" *European Romantic Review* 19, no. 2 (2008): 171–177.
20. Shelley, *Frankenstein*, 78.
21. Ibid., 173.
22. William Cullen, *First Lines of the Practice of Physic* (Edinburgh, 1816), 128.
23. Janis McLarren Caldwell, *Literature and Medicine in Nineteenth-Century Britain* (Cambridge: Cambridge University Press, 2005), 10.
24. Hoeveler, *Gothic Riffs*, 31.
25. According to Sigmund Freud's "original" definition, "An uncanny experience occurs either when repressed infantile complexes have been revived by some impression, or when the primitive beliefs we have surmounted seem once more to be confirmed" ("The Uncanny," first published in Imago, Bd. V., 1919; reprinted in Sammlung, Fünfte Folge, trans. Alix Strachey, accessed http://web.mit.edu/allanmc/www/freud1.pdf). It is in the context of these "primitive" religious beliefs that Hoeveler and I use the term.
26. John Baptist Scaramelli, *Directorium Asceticum: Or, Guide to the Spiritual Life*, vol. 2 (London, 1917), 363, accessed via archive.org.
27. Michelle Faubert, *Rhyming Reason: The Poetry of Romantic-Era Psychologists* (London: Pickering and Chatto, 2009), 41.
28. Scaramelli, *Directorium*, 326.
29. Shelley, *Frankenstein*, 82.
30. Brett C. McInelly, "Method or Madness: Methodist Devotion and the Anti-methodist Response," in *Religion in the Age of Reason*, ed. Kathryn Duncan (New York: AMS Press, 2009), 200.
31. Ibid., 204.

32. This is a not-so-subtle allusion to the 1726 hoax perpetuated by Mary Toft. The story was that, frightened by a rabbit (and clearly lacking emotional restraint), she gave birth first to a pig and then to a litter of rabbits ("Archæologica Medica. XIX. Mary Toft, The Rabbit Breeder," *The British Medical Journal* 2, no. 1856 [July 25, 1896], 209–210).
33. Samuel Auguste Tissot, *An Essay on Diseases Incidental to Literary and Sedentary Persons: With Proper Rule for Preventing Their Fatal Consequences and Instructions for Their Cure* (London, 1768), 43, accessed via Google Books. The sensorium is the sensory apparatus (eyes, ears, taste buds, etc.) considered as a whole.
34. Quoted in Davis, *Obsession*, 14.
35. Joseph Mason Cox, *Practical Observations on Insanity: In Which Some Suggestions Are Offered Towards an Improved Mode of Treating Diseases of the Mind…* (London, 1813) 23.
36. Esquirol, *Mental Maladies*, 58.
37. Esquirol, *Mental Maladies*, 326.
38. Shelley, *Frankenstein*, 77.
39. Shelley, *Frankenstein*, 89.
40. Mary Shelley, *The Last Man*, ed. Anne McWhir (Peterborough: Broadview Press, 1996), 226.
41. Foucault, *The History of Madness*, 213.
42. Johann Christian Heinroth, *Textbook of Disturbances of Mental Life: Or Disturbances of the Soul and Their Treatment*, ed. George Mora (Baltimore: Johns Hopkins University Press, 1975), 225.
43. William Black, "A Dissertation on Insanity: Illustrated with Tables, and Extracted from Between Two and Three Thousand Cases in Bedlam, 1810," in *Three Hundred Years of Psychiatry*, 646.
44. William Perfect, *Methods of Cure in Some Particular Cases of Insanity* (1779), 209–210, microfilm, National Library of Medicine, USA.
45. Ibid., 211.
46. Charles Bell, *The Nervous System of the Human Body* (London, 1830), 171.
47. Shelley, *Frankenstein*, 84.
48. Ibid., 84.
49. Ibid., 85.
50. Ibid., 86.
51. Ibid., 87.
52. Hays, *Emma Courtney*, 178.
53. Jacqueline Pearson, *Women's Reading in Britain, 1750–1835* (Manchester: University of Manchester Press, 2005), 4.
54. Hays, *Emma Courtney*, 53.
55. Barbara M. Benedict, "Jane Austen and the Culture of Circulating Libraries: The Construction of Female Literacy," in *Revising Women:*

Eighteenth-Century 'Women's Fiction' and the Social Engagement, ed. Paula R. Backscheider (Baltimore: Johns Hopkins University Press, 2000), 167.
56. Hannah More, *Strictures on the Modern System of Female Education* (London: Cadell and Davies, 1799), 189, accessed via Google Books.
57. Perfect, *Cases of Insanity*, 204; John Haslam, *Observations on Insanity: With Practical Remarks on the Disease, and an Account of the Morbid Appearances on Dissection* (London: J. Hatchard, 1798), 48, accessed via Medical Heritage Library.
58. *Constant Observer* (London, 1823), 283.
59. Benjamin Rush, *Medical Inquiries and Observations Upon the Diseases of Mind* (Philadelphia, 1812), 61.
60. Sir Edward Clerke, *The True Case of Mrs. Clerke: Set Forth by Her Brothers, Sir Edwardand Mr. Arthur Turnor—To Which Are Added, All the Depositions on That Occasion. In Answer to a Scandalous Pamphlet Lately Publish'd, Call'd, Mrs. Clerke's Case* (London, 1718), 8, Eighteenth Century Collections Online.
61. Ibid., 20.
62. Samuel Taylor Coleridge, *The Major Works*, ed. H. J. Jackson (Oxford: Oxford University Press, 2008), 182.
63. Ibid., 183.
64. Hays, *Emma Courtney*, 54.
65. Ibid., 55.
66. For a thorough philosophical examination of this often-accepted conflation, see Kelly Oliver, *Womanizing Nietzsche: Philosophy's Relation to the "Feminine"* (Routledge, 2016).
67. Lee Erickson, "The Economy of Novel Reading: Jane Austen and the Circulating Library," *Studies in English Literature 1500–1900* 30, no. 4 (1990): 584.
68. Hays, *Emma Courtney*, 116.
69. Katherine Binhammer, "The Persistence of Reading: Governing Female Novel-Reading in *Memoirs of Emma Courtney* and *Memoirs of Modern Philosophers*," *Eighteenth-Century Life* 27, no. 2 (2003): 5.
70. Jane Austen, *Northanger Abbey*, ed. Marilyn Butler (New York: Penguin Classics, 1995), 108.
71. Hays, *Emma Courtney*, 91.
72. Ibid., 60.
73. Claire Grogan, "The Politics of Seduction in British Fiction of the 1790s: The Female Reader and Julie, ou La Nouvelle Héloïse," *Eighteenth Century Fiction* 11, no. 4 (1999): 459–476.
74. For more about the generic debate concerning Hays's text, see Tilottama Rajan, "Autonarration and Genotext in Mary Hays' 'Memoirs of Emma

Courtney,'" in *Romanticism, History and the Possibilities of Genre: Re-forming Literature, 1789–1837*, eds. Tilottama Rajan and Julia M. Wright (Cambridge: Cambridge University Press, 1998), 213–239.

75. Quoted in Joel Faflak, *Romantic Psychoanalysis: The Burden of the Mystery* (Albany: SUNY Press, 2008), 57.
76. Ibid.
77. Scott A. Nowka, "Materialism and Feminism in Mary Hays's *Memoirs of Emma Courtney*," *European Romantic Review* 18, no. 4 (2007): 529.
78. Marilyn Brooks, ed., *The Correspondence of Mary Hays, 1779–1843, British Novelist* (Lewiston: Edwin Mellen Press, 2004), 400.
79. Hays, *Emma Courtney*, 35.
80. Ibid., 37.
81. Ibid., 44.
82. Ibid., 58.
83. Ibid., 115.
84. Ibid., 16.
85. Ibid., 135.
86. Ibid., 151.
87. Ibid., 202.
88. Ibid., 197.
89. Shelley, *Frankenstein*, 86.
90. Quoted in ibid., 85.
91. Faflak, *Romantic Psychoanalysis*, 147.
92. Shelley, *Frankenstein*, 88–89.
93. Ibid., 183.
94. Ibid., 103.
95. Shelley, *Frankenstein*, 204.
96. Scaramelli, *Directorium*, 336.
97. Tim Marshall, "Not Forgotten: Eliza Fenning, Frankenstein, and Victorian Chivalry," *Critical Survey* 13, no. 2 (2001): 98–114.
98. For more on the case of Eliza Fenning, see Tim Marshall, "Not Forgotten." For Chaplin's excellent analysis of the Gothic and its connections to law, see Sue Chaplin, *The Gothic and the Rule of Law, 1764–1820* (New York: Palgrave, 2007).
99. Shelley, *Frankenstein*, 101.
100. Ibid., 193.
101. Ibid., 207.
102. Ibid., 214.
103. Deanna P. Koretsky, "'Unhallowed Arts': Frankenstein and the Poetics of Suicide," *European Romantic Review* 26, no. 2 (2015): 252.
104. Cox, *Practical Observations on Insanity*, 23, 27.
105. *London Medical and Physical Journal* 47, 73.

106. Shelley, *Frankenstein*, 58.
107. Ibid., 119.
108. Perfect, *Cases of Insanity*, 6.
109. Esquirol, *Mental Maladies*, 203.
110. Hays, *Emma Courtney*, 94.
111. Ibid., 197.
112. Ibid., 107.
113. Ibid., 211.
114. Ibid., 217.
115. Shelley, *Frankenstein*, 136.
116. Christine Battersby, *Gender and Genius: Towards a Feminist Aesthetics* (London: The Women's Press, 1989), 3.

Bibliography

Austen, Jane. *Northanger Abbey*. Edited by Marilyn Butler. New York: Penguin Classics, 1995.

Battersby, Christine. *Gender and Genius: Towards a Feminist Aesthetics*. London: The Women's Press, 1989.

Bell, Charles. *The Nervous System of the Human Body*. London, 1830.

Black, William. "A Dissertation on Insanity: Illustrated with Tables, and Extracted from Between Two and Three Thousand Cases in Bedlam, 1810." In *Three Hundred Years of Psychiatry*, edited by Richard Hunter. Hartsdale, NY: Carlisle Publishing, 1982.

Brooks, Marilyn, ed. *The Correspondence of Mary Hays, 1779–1843, British Novelist*. Lewiston: Edwin Mellen Press, 2004.

Caldwell, Janis McLarren. *Literature and Medicine in Nineteenth-Century Britain*. Cambridge: Cambridge University Press, 2005.

Chaplin, Sue. *The Gothic and the Rule of Law, 1764–1820*. Basingstoke, UK: Palgrave Macmillan, 2007.

Clerke, Sir Edward. *The True Case of Mrs. Clerke: Set Forth by Her Brothers, Sir Edward and Mr. Arthur Turnor—To Which Are Added, All the Depositions on That Occasion. In Answer to a Scandalous Pamphlet Lately Publish'd, Call'd, Mrs. Clerke's Case*. London, 1718. Eighteenth Century Collections Online.

Coleridge, Samuel Taylor. *The Major Works*. Edited by H. J. Jackson. Oxford: Oxford University Press, 2008.

"Constant Observer." *Sketches in Bedlam*. London, 1823.

Cox, Joseph Mason. *Practical Observations on Insanity: In Which Some Suggestions Are Offered Towards an Improved Mode of Treating Diseases of the Mind*... London, 1813.

Crawford, Michael J. "Origins of the Eighteenth-Century Evangelical Revival: England and New England Compared." *Journal of British Studies* 26, no. 4 (1987): 374. JSTOR.

Cullen, William. *First Lines of the Practice of Physic*. Edinburgh, 1816.
Davis, Lennard. *Obsession: A History*. Chicago: University of Chicago Press, 2008.
Doran, Robert. *The Theory of the Sublime from Longinus to Kant*. Cambridge: Cambridge University Press, 2018.
Erickson, Lee. "The Economy of Novel Reading: Jane Austen and the Circulating Library." *SEL* 30, no. 4 (1990): 573–590.
Esquirol, Etienne. *Mental Maladies: A Treatise on Insanity*. Philadelphia: Lea and Blanchard, 1845.
Faflak, Joel. *Romantic Psychoanalysis: The Burden of the Mystery*. Albany: SUNY Press, 2008.
Fenves, Peter. "The Scale of Enthusiasm." In *Huntington Library Quarterly: Enthusiasm and Enlightenment in Europe, 1650–1850*, edited by Lawrence E. Klein and Anthony J. La Vopa. San Marino, CA: Huntington Library, 1998.
Grogan, Claire. "The Politics of Seduction in British Fiction of the 1790s: The Female Reader and Julie, ou La Nouvelle Héloïse." *Eighteenth Century Fiction* 11, no. 4 (1999): 459–476.
Haslam, John. *Observations on Insanity: With Practical Remarks on the Disease, and an Account of the Morbid Appearances on Dissection*. London: John Hatchard, 1798. Medical Heritage Library.
Hays, Mary. *Memoirs of Emma Courtney*. Edited by Marilyn Brooks. Peterborough, ON: Broadview Press, 2000.
Heinroth, Johann Christian. *Textbook of Disturbances of Mental Life: Or Disturbances of the Soul and Their Treatment*. Edited by George Mora. Baltimore: Johns Hopkins University Press, 1975.
Hoeveler, Diane. *Gothic Riffs: Secularizing the Uncanny in the European Imaginary, 1780–1820*. Columbus: Ohio State University Press, 2010.
Hume, David. "Essay X: Of Superstition and Enthusiasm." In *Essays Moral, Political, and Literary (1742–1754)*. http://www.english.upenn.edu/~mgamer/Etexts/hume.superstition.html.
Koretsky, Deanna P. "'Unhallowed Arts': Frankenstein and the Poetics of Suicide." *European Romantic Review* 26, no. 2 (2015): 241–260.
Locke, John. *An Essay Concerning Human Understanding*. Kitchener, ON: Batoche Books, 2001.
London Medical and Physical Journal, vol. 47. London: J. Souter, 1823.
Marshall, Tim. "Not Forgotten: Eliza Fenning, Frankenstein, and Victorian Chivalry." *Critical Survey* 13, no. 2 (2001): 98–114.
McDonagh, Patrick. *Idiocy: A Cultural History*. Liverpool: Liverpool University Press, 2008.
McInelly, Brett C. "Method or Madness: Methodist Devotion and the Anti-Methodist Response." In *Religion in the Age of Reason*, edited by Kathryn Duncan. New York: AMS Press, 2009.

More, Hannah. *Strictures on the Modern System of Female Education*. London: Cadell and Davies, 1799. Google Books.

Nowka, Scott A. "Materialism and Feminism in Mary Hays's *Memoirs of Emma Courtney*." *European Romantic Review* 18, no. 4 (2007): 521–540.

Pearson, Jacqueline. *Women's Reading in Britain 1750–1835*. Manchester: University of Manchester Press, 2005.

Perfect, William. *Cases of Insanity, the Epilepsy, Hypochondriacal Affection, Hysteric Passion, and Nervous Disorders, Successfully Treated*, 2nd ed. Rochester: T. Fisher, 1785, with many additional cases. Eighteenth Century Collections Online.

———. *Methods of Cure in Some Particular Cases of Insanity*. 1779. Microfilm. National Library of Medicine, USA.

Rush, Benjamin. *Medical Inquiries and Observations Upon the Diseases of Mind*. Philadelphia, 1812.

Russell, D. A. ed. *"Longinus" on Sublimity*. Oxford: Clarendon Press, 1964.

Scaramelli, John Baptist. *Directorium Asceticum: Or, Guide to the Spiritual Life*, Vol. 2. London, 1917. Archive.org.

Shelley, Mary. *The Last Man*. Edited by Anne McWhir. Peterborough: Broadview Press, 1996.

———. *Frankenstein*. Edited by D. L. Macdonald and Kathleen Scherf. Peterborough: Broadview Press, 2012.

Southey, Robert. *The Life of Wesley: And the Rise and Progress of Methodism*, vol. 1. New York, 1820. Archive.org.

Thompson, E. P. *The Making of the English Working Class*. London: Pelican, 1968.

Tissot, Samuel Auguste. *An Essay on Diseases Incidental to Literary and Sedentary Persons: With Proper Rule for Preventing Their Fatal Consequences and Instructions for Their Cure*. London, 1768. Google Books.

Vargo, Lisa. "Mary Shelley, Corinne, and 'The Mantle of Enthusiasm.'" *European Romantic Review* 19, no. 2 (2008): 171–177.

CHAPTER 4

The Stings of Love: Erotomania and Nymphomania in John Keats's *Isabella, or the Pot of Basil* and Charlotte Dacre's *The Passions*

> "I've done just about everything there is. Except a couple of things that are illegal. I'm a nymphomaniac."
> "Isn't nymphomania a sexual myth?"
> "It's a state of mind."
> —*The Breakfast Club*, 1985

Literature has often equated love with the mind and lust with the body, but what happens when the mind is embodied: when the repetitive thought of someone results in bodily manifestations? This chapter examines Charlotte Dacre's *The Passions* (1811) alongside John Keats's *Isabella, or the Pot of Basil* (1819), ultimately arguing that both authors update the ancient notion of "lovesickness" in order to account not only for Romantic-era medical notions of obsession and association but also to question the gendering of erotomania and nymphomania. Erotomania, formerly conceived of as "lovesickness," is such a literary cliché that both Keats and Dacre pay homage to their literary forebears, Dacre with her mentions of Virgil, Petrarch, and Shakespeare, and Keats by patterning *Isabella* upon a story from Boccaccio's *Decameron*; later, they will expand upon and complicate these older notions.

Dacre mentions her literary predecessors throughout her 1811 four-volume novel, *The Passions*. The novel begins with Apollonia, whose romantic advances Count Weimar spurns. Determined to avenge her

K. Béres Rogers, *Creating Romantic Obsession*,
Palgrave Studies in Literature, Science and Medicine,
https://doi.org/10.1007/978-3-030-13988-9_4

bruised pride, Apollonia finds a route when Weimar's young, naive wife, Julia, comes to Vienna, where Apollonia resides. The cunning woman gives young Julia various texts, including Rousseau's *Héloïse*—a text consistently, as in *Emma Courtney*, tied to the destructive nature of novel reading—in order to weaken her virtue and predispose her to an extramarital affair. Ironically, it is when Julia leaves Vienna (and Apollonia) to go to Italy—to stay with Weimar's best friend Darlowitz and his angelic wife Amelia—that she and Darlowitz fall in love with one another. Julia, unable to bear the guilt associated with her feelings, runs away, Darlowitz commits suicide, and Amelia dies.

In one scene, when Darlowitz hopes to catch Julia's eye, Dacre evokes what Christopher Warley argues is a well-known sonnet conceit: that of the speaker, a man, hunting an elusive woman, figured as a deer.[1] The Petrarchan conceit of a man "hunting" a woman is adapted in Sir Thomas Wyatt's "Whoso list to hounte," where the "hind" is unattainable because she belongs to the King: "for Cesars I ame/ and wyld for to hold, though I seme tame."[2] In Edmund Spenser's Sonnet 67, the deer only approaches the hunter once he stops hunting, and the "beast so wyld" is only "begyld" by her own "goodwill."[3] In both instances, the woman, the love object, is literally hunted. Dacre strengthens the gendered implications of this conceit when she not only figures Julia as a deer, but as an exotic, Arabian one. Darlowitz hopes to catch "bright beam of that lucid eye, tender and sweetly indignant as that of the timid gazelle of the mountains of Arabia."[4] While there is some sense of wildness—the "indignant" quality of the gaze—Julia is here depicted as a "timid gazelle," a slender, delicate, exotic creature, from the "mountains of Arabia," nonetheless known for its soft, attractive eyes.

Yet Dacre's literary allusions explicitly question Julia's passivity. She refers specifically to the elusive Laura of Petrarch's 366 sonnets, having Darlowitz write that, "If I could, [I] would immortalize thee, as Petrarch hath done his Laura."[5] In fact, this excess grows violent, more and more akin to madness, as Dacre references Dido's self-immolation in *The Aeneid* as well as Ophelia's suicide, occasioned by the loss of Hamlet.[6] Julia, driven to a nunnery by Darlowitz's extreme feelings,

> held in her hand a withered branch of the forest which she was waving to and fro. Her wretched attire hung in tatters, yet fantastic and wild, still betrayed in its disposition the disorder of her mind.[7]

This passage directly parallels Shakespeare's description of Ophelia, "larded with sweet flowers" (IV.5. 37–39). Here, the woman is no longer passive but uncontained, taking on a traditionally masculine role.

Keats, too, models himself on literary forbears, only to complicate gendered notions of erotomania. Scholars of Keats know that he derived his 1818 work from Boccaccio's (c. 1352) *Decameron*, which deals, in many ways, with lovesickness. In Boccaccio's text, Lorenzo's love is "fixed" on Isabella:

> Lorenzo...gave over all beauties in the city which might allure any affection from him, and only fixed his heart on her, so that their love grew to a mutual embracing, both equally respecting one another and entertaining kindnesses as occasion gave leave.[8]

When Isabella's brothers murder Lorenzo, she digs up the head and "fell into an extreme sickness, occasioned only by her ceaseless weeping."[9]

In Keats's version, Isabella and Lorenzo, her family's servant, fall in love with one another. Isabella's brothers, unable to bear the shame that this class difference would bring upon the family, contrive to have Lorenzo murdered and buried. Yet Lorenzo's ghost appears to Isabella, telling her exactly where his body lies. Isabella then digs up the body, chops off the head, and plants it in a pot, out of which luxuriant basil grows. She waters the basil with her tears until, wasting away, she dies.

Clearly, lovesickness is an ancient trope recognized by both Keats and Dacre, but why rewrite this hackneyed text? I argue that both authors use the notion of erotomania and nymphomania to explore the ways in which they are gendered.

Part I: Nymphomania and Erotomania

As early as Robert Burton's 1621 *The Anatomy of Melancholy*, "lovesickness" has been associated with the physiology of the brain. Burton classes this "sickness" under the category of "melancholy," a category that had, by the Romantic era, taken on additional meaning associated with the brain. Burton cites Galen when he classifies melancholy as a "privation or infection of the middle cell of the head," and he himself adds that "Now this humour ... is sometimes in the substance of the Brain, sometimes in the passages of the Ventricles of the Brain, or veins of those Ventricles." [10] Even in Burton's text, we have an association of melancholy with the "substance of the Brain," specifically with its "middle cell." The notion of a "middle cell" is intriguing, especially when paired with the contemporary meaning of "ventricle," defined as "[o] ne or other of a series of cavities in the brain (normally numbering four in the adult human being) formed by enlargements of the neural canal" (OED). An 1800 medical dictionary cites "vapour or water" in these ventricles, and Keats's own medical notebook mentions the moist, generative climate of the brain.[11] Such a climate could encourage growth, but, as with any other moist environment, this growth could quickly overwhelm its surroundings.

This sense of lovesickness as connected to the brain's nervous structure was only strengthened by the work of Charles Bell, who wrote his *Idea of a New Anatomy of the Brain* in the same year that Dacre published *The Passions* (1811). In this text, he hypothesized that the "nerves which we trace in the body are not single nerves possessing various powers, but bundles of different nerves, whose filaments are united for convenience of distribution, but which are distinct in office, as they are in origin from the brain."[12] Thus the nerves, like the roots of a basil plant, begin in bundles and then separate as they serve their various functions.[13] If the bundled nerves are materially deranged, the entire body will be affected.

Nymphomania, too, was suspected of beginning in the body, but it was most often confined to the uterus (called the "matrix") or the clitoris. When Esquirol presented the foremost causes of lypemania, defined as any idea "contrary to reason" but, like melancholy, "fixed and sustained by a depressing passion," the top two, after "hereditary predisposition," were "suppression of the menses" and "critical period."[14] While the Romantics' sense of heredity and mental illness seems prescient, what interests me here are the other items in the list, the "suppression of the menses" and what Esquirol calls the "critical period," which, based on contemporary journal accounts, seems to correspond with menopause.[15] In *Mental Maladies*, he asserts that "girls, widows, and sometimes women at the *critical period* of life, are a prey to erotic melancholy."[16] The "consequences of confinements" are most often, as in Wollstonecraft's *Maria*, due to pregnancy.

Whether due to puberty, pregnancy, or menopause, the origins of nymphomania were located in the body. According to De Bienville's 1775 treatise, "[nymphomania] begins by a melancholy delirium, the cause of which is in the vice of the matrix; it, then, turns to a maniacal delirium, the principle of which is in the disorder of the brain."[17] It thus seems that, as opposed to erotomania, nymphomania begins in the uterus and is later located "in the brain," in the imagination. Yet these divides between mind and body are hazy at best. Shortly after he writes of the "vice in the matrix," De Bienville shifts to the notion of "seminal fluid," which circulates through the body along with the blood. External factors, like "excessive living" and too much pleasure, can lead to an increase in blood, as can chocolate, coffee, and spicy foods.[18] Here, De Bienville creates a hierarchy of chocolates, writing that Spanish chocolate is the worst, the French is a little better, but the English is "the most plain and innocent."[19] Again, medical discourse relies heavily on religion, figuring the Spanish as passionate Catholics and the English as plain, innocent Protestants. Nonetheless, chocolate, like any external impurity, enters the body, circulates in the blood, produces excessive seminal fluid, and inflames the matrix.

If, De Bienville writes, the disease is not cured early, the symptoms become entirely physiological. By the third stage, the "matrix, and even the ovaria, are often infected with scirrhous, and cancerous tomours [sic] ..."[20] The excess of blood and seminal fluid produces literal excess, growths, on the uterus and ovaries, and these growths become self-propagating. Eventually, the woman becomes monstrous in all of her physiological and sexual excess. De Bienville's narratological style changes as he describes the end result of nymphomania:

> O too hideous, too alarming spectacle! Thou art, Thou always wilt be present to my sight!...What sunk, and haggard eyes! How livid is that skin! How flagging, and discolored are those cheeks! How blue, and falling are those lips! How fetid is the foam, how black and rotten are the teeth within that mouth! How shapeless is that bent, emaciated body! All, All is horrible...[21]

The horror of this "spectacle" has passed from the beautiful into the region of the sublime; it cannot be bounded by thought and will "always" be "present to [his] sight." She is reminiscent of a ghost is clearly uncontained, with foam emanating from her and her teeth putrifying in her body. At this point, her mind has been driven to an "insensible, helpless idiotism" and she is the incarnation of feminine excess.[22]

But what evokes this obsession in the first place? It is important to note that accounts of both erotomania and nymphomania emphasize not a single person, but the *idea* of that person or even of desire itself.

From the beginning, it is not the person him/herself, but the "thought" of the person that ignites this obsession: "These sufferers are continually absorbed in the same *thought*...they dwell only on the fatal object, who is the cause of their disorder; they see but him alone."[23] Later, De Bienville writes that nothing "so powerfully affects them as the obscene thoughts with which their minds are preengaged; for these, they lose hunger, thirst, and sleep, and scarcely pay the slightest attention to their natural wants."[24] We will see this pattern with Keats's Isabella and also with Dacre's Darlowitz; as De Bienville continually points out, it is the diseased imagination (the "obscene thoughts" which "pre-engage" the mind) that occasions nymphomania.

These obscene thoughts can occasion a sort of mental masturbation, as Rachel Shulkins points out in *Keats, Modesty, and Masturbation*. The repetition of a thought or idea, what Byron called the "Onanism" of Keats's poetry, leads to a feeling of (sublime) pleasure.[25] And, of course, mental masturbation, in this case, begets physical masturbation; citing the "*Onanisme* of Monsieur Tissot," De Bienville pathologizes masturbation, warning young women that the "source of such pleasure" can bring about illness and, eventually, death.[26] Since these young women will not, at this point, listen to moral injunctions, he recommends his tract as a way to frighten them into complacence with visions of their future monstrosity.

Nowhere is this monstrosity more clear than in a tract, published in the 1823 *London Medical and Physical Journal*, concerning nymphomania. The tract appears in Latin, which, the author tells us, "younger readers" should note as a superior language for medical discourse; it also, in many ways, serves to make the disturbing account less accessible. The anonymous account features an "unmarried woman about forty years old, still menstruating, and torturing herself with an unhappy passion."[27] Although she has not yet reached menopause, the woman is "unmarried" and ostensibly sexually frustrated. The account describes the woman as "obsessive" and "depressive," only speaking to her local curate, but her nymphomania manifests on

> the twenty-ninth of May, on the day of Pentecost, [when] the above-mentioned curate, to whom the woman had gone early in the morning before first light, was the first to notice symptoms of erotic delirium, manifested by inappropriate actions and shameful speech.[28]

Although the readers do not know what the woman's "inappropriate actions" and "shameful speech" might be, we do know that she approaches the curate at night, "before first light," already transgressing gendered boundaries. It is also significant that this happens on Pentecost, the day when the Holy Spirit appeared to Jesus's disciplines and inspired them to speak in tongues; it links the woman's "erotic delirium" back to the pathologiztion of "enthusiasm."

The theme of transgression against a patriarchal religious hierarchy permeates the text; the patient recites not the Bible, but the "third verse of a poem dedicated to Priapus," a rustic fertility god characterized by his permanent erection. Then, she "suddenly charged at a certain serving man, saying, 'I call you to the job, quickly follow my order, or I will kill you. I am burning with sexual desire.'" While this is a "serving man" low in the hierarchy, she nevertheless gains agency over him, "charg[ing]" at him and "order[ing]" him...not to mention that she threatens to kill him. When the curate returns to the room, she "lifted herself from the bed" and "showed herself nude to us. 'Come here, curate,' she exclaimed, in a terrifying voice, 'for I have pursued priests above all with love.'" She exposes herself, uses a loud, "terrifying" voice, and later masturbates: "she moved her hand on her vagina frequently, her clitoris swelled, whether because of the nature of her illness or because of the action of her hand." While here, the "action of her hand" is paralleled with the possible bodily causes of her nymphomania, the "nature of her illness," the patient's ability to self-pleasure, order, charge, shout out, and expose herself reveal what is truly terrifying: her agency.[29]

Medical journals attempt to diminish the anxiety associated with women's sexual agency by pathologizing it and assigning it to their bodies. While many journal articles about monomania claim that it originates in the stomach, this account mirrors the aforementioned ones in laying the blame on the errant sexual organs. After she propositions the curate, the woman "fell into a sleep, after saying these words with pleasure, 'I'm peeing,' indeed wet her private parts with a certain stinking liquid." This "stinking liquid," clearly vaginal discharge and a mark of pleasure, becomes a mark of illness, and the physicians quickly apply *twelve* leeches to "her private parts." Strangely, the leeches have no effect, and she then begins to exhibit the symptoms of monomania that we have seen with Victor Frankenstein and Emma Courtney:

> her face was wracked with convulsive twitching, her pulse was rapid and nervous, and she exhibited nearly all the symptoms described in her previous episode. Her esophagus tightened with a spasmodic strangulation, which was the source of her difficulty of breathing, involuntarily, and whenever she let forth a supply of words.[30]

The twitching, quickened pulse, and difficulty breathing are all associated, by Perfect and others, with obsession, but here, part of the symptomatology lies in her speech, as her esophagus "tightened" when she "let forth a supply of words." The woman's lack of speech also sexualizes her, resembling "involuntary" climax.

This association of nymphomania and women's speech continues as the patient recites the first two verses of the poem to Priapus and continues, *for nine hours*, to discharge a "similar" liquid from her vagina. Finally, the woman, laughing uncontrollably, dies, and the physician concludes that

> If the opportunity had been given to us by the neighbors of making an autopsy of the cadaver, perhaps the cause of this nymphomania might be found in the genitals of this woman. For the constant pain in her lower abdomen, although not terribly acute, if it does not demonstrate the truth of this assertion, goes back to a thing which is close to the truth.[31]

While the physician here cannot ascertain the cause of this woman's nymphomania, his assertion that misfunctioning genitalia must be "close to the truth" is telling. This anxiety concerning women's sexuality mirrors the anxiety about female excess, as a feminine sublime could not be anything but monstrous. Thomas Cogan, a philosopher, writes that, when the female mind becomes "depraved," it "greatly surpasses the other sex in cruelty, revenge, and every enormity."[32] Because women are associated with the small, delicate, and beautiful, the sublime woman is someone to be feared.

Both Keats and Dacre describe such monstrous women: Apollonia is driven by her "furor uterinus" to exact revenge on her love object, Weimar, and Keats's Isabella literally chops off and fawns over the head of her deceased lover. Both of these texts are taken from other texts: the former from a story in De Bienville's tract and the latter from Boccaccio. Yet both complicate this gendered dynamic. While Dacre does present Apollonia as an irrational scorned woman, she illustrates the condition of nymphomania more prominently in her *male* character, Darlowitz. And while Keats feminizes erotomania to a degree, he incorporates his medical knowledge (specifically, of herbs) to link it with contemporary-and earlier-accounts of obsession, and he attributes this obsessive thinking not only to Isabella, but also to Lorenzo and, as Shulkins points out, to the brothers. Thus these "monstrous" women are interchangeable with "monstrous" men, distorting the gender divide between the sublime and the beautiful.

Part II: The Violent Woman and the Passive Man—Dacre's Passions

In medical texts, accounts of female nymphomaniacs feature excessive appetite, both physical and sexual. William Perfect details a woman who is obsessed: "her conversation always ran upon one and the same subject."[33] She is also excessively "violent," "not the least check had been given to her unruly appetite," and she is "loud and loquacious," all qualities not conventionally connected with the feminine. Chapter 3 has already featured some accounts of women's excessive appetites (recall the woman who ate cinder walls), but this excess is most problematic when it comes to a woman's sexuality, since sexuality implies agency and desire instead of the passivity most conventionally associated with women. As Adriana Craciun observes, the greater social anxiety regarding "mad" women concerns their sexual agency.[34] Alexander Morison recounts the case of a forty-six-year-old woman (perhaps at her "critical period" in life). He describes her enormous "propensity to sexual connection," for she "seizes every person within her reach, and wantonly clings to them with her utmost strength, which is very great."[35] This notion of the woman "seizing" anyone in her proximity, and the report of her "great" strength, signify a social anxiety about women overreaching their prescribed bounds. De Bienville, describing the last stage of nymphomania, declares that women suffering from the *furor uterinus* "violently, and sometimes even without precaution, indulge their vengeance in the perpetration of the most cruel and tragical crimes."[36] The notion of violence, of "cruel... crimes," takes us from passive femininity to acts of sublime agency.

It is this portrait of nymphomania that we see in Charlotte Dacre's portrayal of Apollonia, ostensibly modeled on De Bienville's serving maid, who "educates" the simple Julia (a name that reoccurs in Dacre's book) in the "arts of Venus."[37] Apollonia is, as Craciun has observed, clearly modeled on a Wollstonecraftian "rational" woman, and she defies gendered boundaries through her violent agency. Like Dacre herself, writing and critiquing her own society (Apollonia is, after all, a female Apollo), she exists in a queer space, both masculine and feminine, both pathologized and celebrated. Perhaps this queer space stems from Dacre's own space as a Jewish writer living in England yet dealing with stereotypes of the Jewish woman as sexualized and the Jewish people, as Voltaire explains in his *Essai sur les Moeurs*, of a more primitive "religion and character." D'Holbach takes it even further in his *L'esprit de Judaïsme*, calling the Jews "frenzied imbeciles."[38] Writing about Mina Loy, a modern Jewish writer, Nadia Valman alludes to this historical trend, stating that "in the case of women, they cease to conform to a particular model of femininity once they become sexualized."[39] Thus the Jewish woman writer living in Britain is always on the outside, always queer, always in exile.

Apollonia first makes her appearance as a seemingly passive woman obsessed with the idea of Weimar. She writes to her former governess about the pain of his rejection, exclaiming:

> How inadequate the utmost stretch of imagination, how poor the extravagance of fable, in inventing degrees of torture, or of depicting them; how feeble, compared to an hour of the real unvisionary horrors which rack my soul, and convulse my reason![40]

Here, Dacre, like Mary Hays, critiques the woman affected by excessive reading of Gothic tales—these fables of the "imagination" are not "real," like her "unvisionary," psychological or maybe even immediate, horrors. She also presents us with a common symptom of obsession in that Apollonia's reason is "convulsed"; this alludes back to the idea of stretching nerves put forth by Heinroth and Bell.

If these nerves convulse, they do, at times, snap. Keats illustrates this through his use of repetition, and Dacre also showcases this formally through her use of the physical page. When Apollonia rants about Weimar's rejection, Dacre's form evinces her psychological convulsions:

> You think me mad! I believe I am; but if I am not now, I have been.—Appollonia rejected!—the love of Appollonia spurned!—Is it not enough to turn a brain, such as mine? My love, and my pride at once so outraged–for I loved the traitor–Yes! I loved, and he disdained me.———I must lay down my pen *
>
> *.[41]

Dacre uses dashes and exclamation points to illustrate Apollonia's disturbed mind. The dash after "he disdained me" is longer than the rest. Then, Apollonia communicates that she "must lay down [her] pen," and the series of asterisks indicates her mental lapse or breakdown. Dacre uses this technique consistently, not only with Apollonia, but also, later, with Darlowitz and with Julia.

In fact, Apollonia's character transitions from one who is passive and has to "lay down" her pen or her agency, to one who, in a fashion typical of Dacre's female characters, violently plots revenge. While one could argue that she herself is subsumed with thoughts of revenge, she acts on others instead of merely being acted upon. Again writing to Hauteville about her initial desire for vengeance, she claims that, "In the very heart and core of [Weimar's] security will I introduce the scorpion that shall sting him to madness!"[42] This scorpion is both internal and external: Appollonia cultivates a plan by engaging with Weimar's wife, Julia, and introducing novels, including *La Nouvelle Héloïse*, to her. Her plan is to effectively "seduce" Julia with thoughts of sexual desire, and these thoughts transfer onto the novel's chief erotomaniac, Darlowitz. Julia also becomes obsessed with Darlowitz and, when she attempts to argue herself out of it, is persuaded by Apollonia's logic: a logic gleaned straight from Wollstonecraft and contemporary notions of women as children. She persuades Julia to desire Darlowitz by asking if a child is "at fault if superior strength overpowers him? What are we but children, opposed to the power our feelings have over us?"[43] Apollonia uses conventionally gendered reasoning in order to carry out her own desires, to assume her own agency.

While Julia does assume these characteristics of a passive child, Dacre devotes significantly less space to her than to the novel's other passive character, Darlowitz. Through Julia's character, Dacre presents a counterpoint to Apollonia's, characterizing the former through images of vacancy and lack. Dacre specifically describes Julia's "madness" as "the total abstraction from and privation of all idea; that vacancy, and not confusion, was the chief characteristic of her malady."[44] Obsession with an idea, here Julia's guilt over her feelings concerning Darlowitz and her betrayal of her husband, Weimar, results in the lack of *any* idea. This lack, this "vacancy," allows Julia no violence or agency; instead, it makes her the child that Apollonia declares women to be.

Dacre not only uses Julia to heighten the reader's realization of Apollonia's sinister agency, but she also introduces a male character powerless over his own obsessive feelings: Darlowitz. When Dacre critics write about *the Passions*, they focus on Apollonia, but Dacre herself apportions more text to the character of Darlowitz. In this way, I argue, she illustrates the gender fluidity of nymphomania. When Darlowitz recounts (to his reasonable friend Rozendorf) his obsession with Julia, "effeminate" emotions dominate the text. In one of his earlier letters, he exclaims that he is "powerless to free [himself] from [his infatuation], as the madman is powerless to free himself from the delirium which shakes his brain to atoms—his soul to annihilation."[45] Not only does Dacre repeat the word "powerless" here, but she offers an image of a brain reduced to its smallest parts and a soul that becomes, again, a hole or a lack. This annihilation, or lack, is presented as both mental and physical. Using a different metaphor, Darlowitz pronounces that "Body or mind, or both, must sink under such accumulated suffering."[46] Here, the "suffering" of nymphomania is heavy enough to reduce any "self" to nothing.

As opposed to Apollonia, who maintains some agency due to her violent emotions, Darlowitz constantly exhibits not only passivity but also a sense of weakness and bodily vulnerability. "My brain," he writes, "seems to spin, and I feel as if I were on the point of death. ****************"[47] Darlowitz's pronouncement is punctuated by a group of asterisks that, again, formally visualize his mental breakdown. Yet unlike Apollonia, Darlowitz remains in this passive state, increasingly subject to the "enchantments" of Julia.[48] Death, of course, is probably the most sublime of all thoughts, but Darlowitz does not think about death or, in the mode of many Romantics, idealize suicide.[49] Instead, he is, like the pale wight in Keats's "La Belle Dame…," "in its thrall," fated to disintegrate psychologically and physically.

As with Victor Frankenstein or Emma Courtney, the suffering exhibited by the Darlowitz, unlike that of Apollonia, is physical as well as psychological. He cries that his soul will "sicken with powerful emotion" and his "sight will recede."[50] Perhaps in tandem with medical thought connecting obsession to the eyes, the eyes, already psychologically vacant, also become physiologically weakened. "I gaze till cold shudderings run through my frame, and a dimness overspreads my sight," he writes, again granting agency to the shudderings, to the dimness, but not to himself. Finally, writing to Julia, he proclaims that his "veins are parched and withered—my temples throb—I thirst—I languish to behold you…let me infold (sic) you in my arms—press you with the strength of madness to my burning breast."[51] While madness ostensibly has some "strength," the image of his parched mouth and his "withered" and "parched" veins indicate a lack of sustenance, a drying up of any vital humors.

The Passions is, in terms of gender norms, complicated. Apollonia's excess, voraciousness, and garrulousness is sublime, powerful, and threatening, especially to a patriarchal society. Darlowitz's nymphomania is somewhat passive in that his mind becomes possessed *by* the obsession, a tree waiting for his lover to water his parched veins. In this text, there is not a simple, gendered binary between erotomania and nymphomania—instead, various characters of both genders realize, question, and even subvert gendered norms.

Part III: Basil and Obsession

The very title of John Keats's *Isabella, or the Pot of Basil* evokes the obvious question of why Keats chose basil instead of, say, parsley. Scholars of Keats know that he derived his 1818 work from Boccaccio, but they have ignored the fact that Boccaccio himself wrote about a "large and beautiful pot of the sort in which marjoram or basil is planted."[52] Yet Keats, in his retelling of the story, accentuates the basil itself, placing it in the title of his poem. And, instead of "Isabella and the Pot of Basil," he chooses the "or," making Isabella interchangeable with the basil itself. If this is the case, then basil must play an important, and hitherto unstudied, role in the text.

As we think about herbs like basil, we immediately draw connections to Keats's career as a surgeon-apothecary who necessarily dealt in herbal cures for various illnesses. Critics have agreed that the 1818 poem is, in some ways, about "Illnesses of various kinds ... all of the characters are ill—psychically, physically, or spiritually—throughout the text."[53] Citing a dissertation by Charles W. Hagelman, *John Keats and the Medical Profession*, Donald Goellnicht writes that Keats's romance poem is "a study of madness."[54] Goellnicht himself goes on to say that Sir Thomas Guy's will provided for his hospital, where Keats studied and worked as a surgical dresser, "to receive lunatics, and that Keats would have had experience with 'madness'."[55] Hoeveler's perceptive essay goes further to define this "madness" as a reflection of Keats's own anxieties toward authorship, his parentage, and the genre of romance. Although Hoeveler does mention Keats's career as a surgeon-apothecary, writing that he "dabbled in herbs; he assisted in amputations; he fled into poetry," she reads his poem through the lens of psychoanalytic theory. She reads the decapitated head as material obsession, or fetish, "the voice in [Keats's] head that would not die."[56] While Hoeveler deals with the realm of obsession, she does not examine it through the medical lens of Keats's time. Instead, for her, the

> head in the pot—the central trope of the poem—stands as the essence of what Derrida has called "the trace," the residue of the father who both traps the son in the realities of the class system and proffers an escape through the metaphorically transformative power of the knife/pen.[57]

For Hoeveler, then, this is a poem about class: John Keats's own position in the class system, his vain attempts at writing his way out, and the anxiety that resulted from his constant efforts. I would like to both expand upon these readings and bring them back to Keats's medical experience and herbal knowledge—and, thus, to basil. Considering Keats's herbal education, it is not surprising that Isabella's mind is intentionally represented by a plant connected with obsession.

As early as Keats's apprenticeship with surgeon-apothecary Thomas Hammond, he learned how to compound and administer remedies, including "aconite, columbo, digitalis, jalap ... [and] opium."[58] As Hermione de Almeida has argued, Keats's apothecary training would have made him familiar with a variety of herbal and homeopathic cures, including basil.[59] Basil, *Ocimum basilicum*, was listed as one of the "medicinal and useful plants" growing at Chelsea Physic Garden in 1772, and we have no reason to suspect that the herb would not have been there during Keats's tenure. According to the Apothecaries Act of 1815, the syllabus for apothecaries required knowledge of herbals, or materia medica. By 1815, the kitchen garden at Chelsea was converted to the "purpose of instructive Horticulture."[60]

Historically, basil seems to have been associated with scorpions and poison, either drawing poison to it or breeding poison on its own. The earliest mention of its properties, in Dioscorides's *De Materia Medica* (circa 65 CE), states that "basil that has been chewed and set out in the sun breeds worms. The Libyans believe in addition that those who have consumed it and who were struck by a scorpion cannot be saved."[61] While basil paradoxically also heals inflammations and the "stroke of the ... scorpion," its healing properties quickly become overwhelming, breeding the very thing it purports to prevent. Nicholas Culpeper's 1653 *Complete Herbal* expands on Dioscorides's description, stating that

> [Basil] was an herb of Mars, and under the Scorpion, and perhaps therefore called Basilicon; and it is no marvel if it carry a kind of virulent quality with it. Being applied to the place bitten by venomous beasts, or stung by a wasp or hornet, it speedily draws the poison to it, Every like draws his like ... Hilarius, a French physician, affirms upon his own knowledge, that an acquaintance of his, by common smelling to it, had a scorpion bred in his brain...[62]

Culpepper's diction is of interest here: he describes basil as "virulent" and then connects it to a "scorpion bred in his brain." While both Dioscordes and Culpepper are, arguably, dated, Romantic-era botany combined more modern medicinal notions with classical ones; John Sibthorpe, a professor at Oxford, traveled to Greece to investigate the very medicinal plants recorded by Dioscorides, one of which may have been basil.[63]

Why a scorpion? And why in the brain? I argue that this phraseology connects scorpions, as well as basil, with the idea of obsession. In his 1819 play *The Cenci*, Percy Bysshe Shelley refers to Giacomo and his family as "scorpions ringed with fire." "What," they ask, "should we do but strike ourselves to death?"[64] This passage refers to the myth referenced in my introduction, according to which, when surrounded by a ring of fire, the scorpion will sting itself to death. Like Keats's character, an obsessive person will engage in "self-destruction," in deleterious thoughts and actions, in order to avoid "unnecessary pain," metaphorically poisoning him or herself in the process.

In addition to his botanical knowledge, Keats would have had access to medico-philosophical texts by the likes of Esquirol, Spurzheim, and Bell. Since Astley Cooper, who taught Keats at Guy's, was included on a distribution list for Bell's book, he would have read it and included information from it in his lectures. Also, Keats's friend Benjamin Haydon attended Spurzheim's lectures in 1815 and had attended Bell's 1806 anatomy lectures.[65] The likelihood of Keats's access to Bell's neurological hypotheses explains why a poem about "madness" focuses so much on Lorenzo's material head.

Aside from his medical training, Keats himself dealt with a number of "madnesses," or obsessions, most famously poetry, death, and his fiancée Fanny Brawne. An unmistakable part of his mystique and continued popularity is his ability to grasp onto one thing: to live a "life of sensation." In his letters, he often describes his need for writing poetry in physiological terms. In a May 10, 1817, letter to Leigh Hunt, he writes that he thought "so much about poetry, so long together, that I could not get to sleep at night; and, moreover, I know not how it was, I could not get wholesome food."[66] He becomes so focused on writing that he forgets to care for himself. When composing his unfinished epic, *Hyperion*, he constantly focuses on producing more, fixating on writing at least four thousand lines. For Keats, the very idea of writing becomes an obsession: "I find I cannot exist without Poetry—without eternal Poetry—half the day will not do—the whole of it—I began with a little, but habit has made me a Leviathan. I had become all in a Tremble from not having written anything of late … "[67] Of note here is his emphasis on "habit" making him unnatural, monstrous: a "Leviathan." This monstrosity evinces itself not only in his brain but also in his body, putting him "all in a Tremble."

The affective nature of Keats's constant turns to writing echoes Esquirol's notion of monomania. Keats often describes the "nervous motions" of his mind as he contemplates writing poetry or, even worse, when he cannot write due to some life occurrence. In a letter to Charles Wentworth Dilke, he describes writing as something he must do in order to prevent himself from thinking of his critically ill brother Tom:

> I am obliged to write and plunge into abstract images to ease myself of his countenance, his voice, his feebleness—so that I live now in a continual fever. It must be poisonous to life, although I feel well.[68]

Again, in a letter written the next day, September 22, Keats writes about the "feverous relief" of poetry. For Keats, here, poetry becomes a sort of illness, a "fever," that only finds relief in its compulsive repetition. It is, like obsession itself, a "cure" that eventually becomes an illness in and of itself.

Keats' letters make it clear that, as he waited for his brother and sister-in-law to leave for the United States and nursed his brother Tom, he retreated more and more inside himself. During this year, as he was working on *Isabella*, he struggled to write anything at all, writing to Benjamin Bailey that he had

> this morning such a Lethargy that I cannot write—the reason of my delaying is oftentimes from this feeling—I wait for a proper temper— … I am now so depressed that I have not an Idea to put to paper—my hand feels

> like lead—and yet it is and [sic] unpleasant numbness it does not take away the pain of existence—I don't know what to write—Monday—… even now I have but a confused idea of what I should be about my intellect must be in a degen[er]ating state—it must be for when I should be writing about god knows what I am troubling you with Moods of my own Mind or rather body.[69]

While Keats himself uses the term "depressed," he seems to mean it in a physiological way, as in "weighed down," as he continues that his "hand feels like lead." Throughout this passage, in fact, his body becomes increasingly distanced from him, "numb," and his "degenerating" intellect attempts control. Yet he realizes that the mind and body are linked, and that degeneracy in the mind does not originate, as previously thought, in humoral imbalances. Instead, for Keats, the mind is synonymous with the body.

Keats reaffirms this in a letter to George and Georgiana Keats, in which he writes that "In this state of effeminacy the fibres of the brain are relaxed in common with the rest of the body."[70] Not only is Keats numb to the world, with a "degenerating" intellect, but he genders this condition, calling it a "state of effeminacy." While critics have explored Isabella with respect to gender, neither Goellnicht nor Hagelman question why Keats would have chosen to write about "madness" or depression in a female character, Isabella. While Isabella is clearly Boccaccio's character, it bears notice that Keats himself found melancholy itself an "effeminate," passive condition.[71] Writing about an obsession, not with images of a dying brother but with a new "celebrity," Lord Byron, Ghislaine McDayter helpfully expands on the gendering of obsession. She views it as a metaphorical form of hysteria; according to medical discourse, the sufferer experiences—instead of the literal need to fill the womb—an emptiness, a Lacanian lack, that he or she still needs to fill with images, whether of Byron or, for Keats, of his brother Tom.[72] This hole is only made whole by the thoughts, the "objects," filling the brain.

This notion of thoughts as "things" that overwhelm the brain was clearly one with which Keats was familiar. Not only does his *Anatomical and Physiological Note Book* mention the danger of solitary thought for engendering melancholy, but he also wrote, in a letter to his sister Fanny, that he tried to

> think of you as little as possible and to let [brother] George dwell upon my mind but slightly. The reason being that I am affraid [sic] to ruminate on any thing which has the shade of difficulty or melancholy in it, as that sort of cogitation is so pernicious to health, and it is only by health that I can be enabled to alleviate your situation in [the] future.[73]

Although here the object of obsession is the financial situation of Keats's family, the idea of "cogitation" as "pernicious to health" is one that seeps into his writing as well.

Keats had, as remarked by scholars, read Burton's *Anatomy of Melancholy*, incorporating a story from the text into his Lamia (1819), which he was working on at the same time was working on Isabella.[74] Keats's focus on the senses—Lorenzo's sight, Isabella's hearing and touch—fits with Burton's mention of Kornmannus's *The Outline of Love*, in which he lists degrees of lust: sight, speech, "company, kissing, handling."[75] Burton also paints a scenario of lovesickness which Keats seems to adapt. While Boccaccio makes Lorenzo a "gentleman" who "as a trusty factor or servant, had the managing of the brethrens businesse and affaires," Keats writes his character as a lowly servant, much beneath Isabella in social class. Here we see echoes of Burton: " … when they come to live near one another, in the same street, village, or together in a house, Love is kindled on a sudden. Many a Serving man by reason of this opportunity and importunity inveigles his Master's daughter … "[76] While Keats paints the relationship as mutual, without any "inveigl[ing]," it is interesting to note his text's debt to Burton.

In Boccaccio's account, Isabella and Lorenzo have a respectful, mutually adoring relationship, but Keats's version is markedly different. Here, the lovers are immediately detached from the world at large, unable to see, hear, or do anything without pondering the other. Lorenzo only sees "[Isabella's] full shape" (II, 12), and as for Isabella, "Her lute-string gave an echo of his name/She spoilt her half-done broidery with the same" (II, 16).[77] Unlike in Boccaccio's tale, Isabella's actions—her ability to play the lute or embroider—are "spoilt" by her relentless thoughts of Lorenzo.[78] Isabella, overwhelmed with thoughts of Lorenzo, literally makes herself sick.

The first half of Keats's poem is a rendering of Burton's lovesickness. Writing about the lovers and their growing attraction, Keats states that they could

> ... not in the self-same mansion dwell
> Without some stir of heart, some malady;
> They could not sit at meals but feel how well
> It soothed each to be the other by;
> They could not, sure, beneath the same roof sleep,
> But to each other dream, and nightly weep. (I, 7–8)

Describing their growing attraction, Keats uses the word "malady," an interesting word choice given the slant rhyme with "by," and a choice that indicates Keats's reception of a vision of love as illness or disease. The nightly weeping transitions into literal illness as the lovers repress their feelings for one another. Isabella's "untouched cheek" falls "sick," and she herself grows "thin" (V, 33), replicating Burton's description of lovesickness as "of body, Paleness, Leanness, dryness, &c."[79] While it is true that Isabella is here compared to a young mother obsessively caring for a child, Lorenzo also exhibits these symptoms, and Isabella notices his forehead "waxing very pale and dead,/And straight all flush'd" (VII, 53–54). On one hand, lovesickness seems to be a wasting away—as Keats would have it, "degeneration"—but it also carries with it a heightened heartbeat. Burton notes this aspect when he writes about pulses, blushes, and trembling as physiological symptoms of the disease.

Throughout the poem, the mind becomes embodied; when Isabella and Lorenzo court, their "sick longing" during the month of May makes "their cheeks paler by the/break of June" (IV, 26). Isabella actually reads Lorenzo's love on his body, and it is her body that responds:

> She saw [his forehead] waxing very pale and dead,
> And straight all flush'd; so, lisped tenderly,
> "Lorenzo!" ... (VII, 53–55)

Again, Isabella "reads" Lorenzo's forehead, "pale and dead" from his obsessive love for her, and returns a bodily signal in response. The brothers also read Lorenzo's love for Isabella in his "eye / A straying from his toil" (XVIII, 139–140), a small enough clue that bears large consequences. And the brothers themselves evince their anxiety in bodily ways: "And many times they bit their lips alone" (XXII, 170). Even after the brothers come up with their dastardly plan, Keats reiterates that "... Sick and wan The brothers' faces in the ford did seem,/ Lorenzo's flush with love..." (XXVII, 213–215). Over and over again, we see mental states echoed by physical signs.

Nowhere is this clearer than in Isabella's obsession over the severed head. As time passes, Isabella "by gradual decay from beauty fell/ Because Lorenzo came not" (xxxii- xxxiii, 256–257). She talks to her brothers "with an eye all pale" (xxxiii, 258), and the dream of Lorenzo affects her bodily, making her "eyelids ache" (xli, 327). From eyes and eyelids stream Isabella's constant tears, reiterated by Keats again and again: her "thin tears" (LIV, 425), the "continual shower/from her dead eyes" (LVII, 452–453), to name a few occurrences. Isabella's relatives wonder that "seldom did she go to chapel- shrift, / And seldom felt she any hunger-pain" (LIX, 467–468). These two lines juxtapose the mind or soul with the body; not only does she seldom pray, but she also stops feeling a bodily "hunger-pain."

As Isabella moons over the basil that grows out of Lorenzo's head, she increasingly lives in her mind. And, as her obsession infiltrates her being, she falls deeper and deeper into a melancholy that not only affects her mind but, in the end, her body. As Keats himself writes, the basil drew "nurture besides, and life, from human fears" (LIV, 429). As in the beginning of the poem, Isabella obsesses; this time, though, instead of "lovesickness," Isabella gives way to obsessing over what Hoeveler calls a "fetish-object":

> And she forgot the stars, the moon, and sun,
> And she forgot the blue above the trees,
> And she forgot the dells where waters run,
> And she forgot the chilly autumn breeze;
> She had no knowledge when the day was done,
> And the new morn she saw not: but in peace
> Hung over her sweet Basil evermore,
> And moisten'd it with tears unto the core. (LIII, 417–424)

This stanza shifts between death and rebirth, emphasizing that while obsessive thoughts might help alleviate pain, they also prohibit growth. She forgets both the high, the "blue above the trees," and the low, "the dells where waters / run." Again, she might forget the "chilly autumn breeze," a phrase that, like "when the day was done," foreshadows death, but she also "saw not" the "new morn." Undisturbed, "in peace," she limply "hung" over her basil, "moisten[ing]" it with tears. Her obsession with her dead lover has indeed bred scorpions in her mind until she herself becomes one with the basil.

As with his repetition of "And she forgot…," Keats reiterates this melancholy obsession not only through his story or the use of basil, but also through his repetitive language. While Keats would have had no knowledge of psychology, specifically of Freud's *Mourning and Melancholia*, his poetry bursts with a sort of melancholy repetition. Like the repetition of "away" in his "Ode to a Nightingale" or "happy" in "Ode on a Grecian Urn," this device serves as a signifier of obsession: the words repeat until they lose their meaning, lost in all but their compulsive repetition. Irene Hsiao argues that "repetitions are a form of work: these cycles generate the characteristic heat of the lyric—emotional mania made verbal through the exercise of refrain."[80] If we consider Isabella returning again and again to her basil until it becomes, not a symbol for Lorenzo, but "her Basil sweet" (LXI, 488) or "my Basil-pot" (LXII, 496 and LXIII, 504), we begin to see how repetition lulls her—and us, the readers—into a feeling of emptiness. As Thomas Pfau has argued, the lyric itself "calls into question the symbol's redemptive power."[81] Isabella becomes a victim of her own brain, her obsessions, looking "piteous[ly]" on "dead and senseless things" (LXII, 489). Keats uses his poetic language to emphasize her growing mental illness. Throughout the poem, repetition becomes a sign of meaninglessness, a loss of control, and a spiraling into obsessive melancholy.

Yet Keats does not confine obsessive acts, or even erotomania, to his ill-fated heroine. Instead, he implicates his readers, and then the brothers, in their own acts of obsession. Keats's first use of repetition concerns his readers' obsession with the Romance genre:

> *Too many* tears for lovers have been shed
> *Too many* sighs give we to them in fee
> Too much of pity after they are dead
> *Too many* doleful stories do we see. (XII, 90–93; emphasis mine)

As Hoeveler and others have argued, Keats attempts to "deny his attraction" to the popular Romance genre, intimating that the Gothic Romance is a form of obsession.[82] Yet, as with the Grecian Urn's "happy, happy love!," the repetition belies the narrator's sincerity and s/he becomes caught up in his or her own negativity.

The poem's next instance of obsession concerns the brothers and their oft-remarked materialism:

> *Why were they proud?* Because their marble founts
> Gush'd with more pride than do a wretch's tears?—
> *Why were they proud?* Because fair orange-mounts
> Were of more soft ascent than lazar stairs?—
> *Why were they proud?* Because red-lin'd accounts
> Were richer than the songs of Grecian years?—
> *Why were they proud?* again we ask aloud,
> Why in the name of Glory were they proud? (XVI, 19–26; emphasis mine)

While this repetition bears the marks of a sermon or any popular oratorical exercise, it also reiterates the brothers' own useless obsession with wealth. After a few lines, the repetition, like the "fair orange-mounts" or "red-lined accounts," becomes a thing unto itself, a signifier that has become its own signified. This brings us to Isabella's own obsessive melancholy, with the repetition of "and she forgot."

Eventually, Keats opens his poem to his readers, inviting us to become lost in his words, in what feels like obsession:

> O Melancholy, linger here awhile!
> O Music, Music, breathe despondingly!
> O Echo, Echo, from some sombre isle,
> Unknown, Lethean, sigh to us—O sigh! (LV, 57–60)

Keats's very invocation calls us to become lost in the obsession of melancholy. His repetition of sounds, the constant O's and the m's in "melancholy and music," lull us into a sort of trance, only exacerbated by his repetition of "music," "echo" (itself a repetition), and "sigh." And to repeat the point, or lack thereof, Keats repeats almost the same refrain in stanza LXI:

> O Melancholy, turn thine eyes away!
> O music, music, breathe despondingly!
> O Echo, Echo, on some other day,
> From isles Lethean, sigh to us—O sigh! (481–484)

Here, the Lethean isles are no longer "unknown," and the narrator and reader attempt to escape the poem's obsessions. Thus Melancholy is told to "turn thine eyes away" and Echo to sigh on "some other day," but the plea is ineffective, and the damage has already been done. Due to her obsessions, "Isabel, sweet Isabel, will die" (LXI, 486).

Isabel does die, and what remains is only a signifier, a chant that has virtually no meaning, no signified. Keats initially has Isabella tell the Pilgrim "For cruel 'tis ... to steal my Basil-pot away from me" (LXII, 495–496), but this becomes a "sad ditty" that passes "from mouth to mouth through all the country" (LXIII, 501, 502). Isabella's plea, already unanchored from its original context by her empty recrimination to the Pilgrim, is further removed by the "ditty," a song "still sung": "O cruelty/To steal my Basil-pot away from me!" (LXIII, 504). Like any catchy song, from "London Bridge" to modern- day commercial jingles, the meaning evaporates, leaving only the repetition, the song itself. This is indeed a "fetish," but not merely a materialistic one. Like any obsession, the repetition becomes a thing in and of itself, overwhelming the sufferer's brain.

In their writing about nymphomania and eratomania, both Keats and Dacre point out the obvious: it is not love or sex, but, as the character in *The Breakfast Club* posited, the "state of mind" that creates an obsession. Dacre plays with the notion that it is the *idea* of Julia, the idea of Darlowitz, that so powerfully affects both Apollonia and Julia. Isabella and Lorenzo, like Romeo and Juliet, Antony and Cleopatra, or any number of ill-fated lovers, hardly know one another, but the repeated idea of love and lust ultimately assumes a sublime power. Thus, nymphomania seems less of a material fetish or an addiction than an obsession that is, again, characterized by a powerful idea (in this case, of love or lust). From excessive study to love to the subject of the next chapter, military glory, the Romantic discourse of obsession relies on ideas that assume an irrevocable agency.

Notes

1. Christopher Warley, *Reading Class Through Shakespeare, Donne, and Milton* (Cambridge: Cambridge University Press, 2014).
2. Phillis Levin, ed. *The Penguin Book of the Sonnet* (New York: Allen Lane, 2001), 3.
3. Ibid., 14.
4. Charlotte Dacre ("Rosa Matilda"), *The Passions* (New York: Arno Press, 1974), 67.
5. Ibid., 24.
6. Ibid., 92.
7. Ibid., 148.
8. Boccaccio, *Decameron*, Fourth Day, Novel V, trans. John Florio (London, 1620), http://www.brown.edu/Departments/Italian_Studies/dweb.
9. Ibid.

10. Robert Burton, *The Anatomy of Melancholy*, eds. Floyd Dell and Paul Jordan Smith (New York: Tudor, 1927), 148, 322. Galen, a Greek physician, surgeon, and philosopher, influenced many of what we would now call "medical" fields of study.
11. John Keats, *Anatomical and Physiological Note-Book*, ed. Maurice Buxton Forman (Oxford: Oxford University Press, 1934).
12. Quoted in Alan Richardson, *The Neural Sublime* (Baltimore: Johns Hopkins University Press, 2010), 31.
13. See Conan Milner, "Basil: Herb of Scorpions, Doctors, and King," August 16, 2015, http://www.theepochtimes.com/n3/1710719-basil-herb-of-scorpions-doctors-and-kings/.
14. Esquirol, *Mental Maladies*, 203–204.
15. See Ruth Formanek, ed., *The Meanings of Menopause: Historical, Medical, and Cultural Perspectives* (Routledge, 2013). Menopause or, as the Romantics would have labeled it, the "grand climacteric" for women, was (and still is) frequently pathologized and associated with mental illness. In 1820, a medical practitioner named Burns wrote that it was caused by the "violent passions of the mind, and the application of cold to the surface of the body" (quoted in Formanek, 9). Formanek hypothesizes that, with machinery doing more and more of the traditional work of women, women were consigned to the roles of domesticity and childbearing, the latter of which ended during this period of life.
16. Esquirol, *Mental Maladies*, 211 (emphasis mine).
17. T. De Bienville, *Nymphomania*, or, a Dissertation Concerning the Furor Uterinus, Clearly and Methodically Explaining the Beginning, Progress, and Different Causes of That Horrible Distemper, trans. Edward Sloane Wilmot (London, 1775), 50.
18. Ibid., 56, 58.
19. Ibid., 58.
20. Ibid., 90.
21. Ibid., 136.
22. Ibid., 91.
23. Ibid., 30 (emphasis mine).
24. Ibid., 75.
25. Quoted in Rachel Shulkins, *Keats, Modesty, and Masturbation* (Routledge, 2016), 1.
26. De Bienville, *Nymphomania*, 44. De Bienville genders the pathology of onanism, directing all of his warnings toward women.
27. I would like to thank Dr. David Frauenfelder for providing me with the English translation.
28. *London Medical and Physical Journal* (1823): 242.
29. Ibid.

30. Ibid., 243.
31. Ibid.
32. Cogan, *Philosophical Treatise*, 225.
33. William Perfect, *Select Cases in the Different Species of Insanity, Lunacy, or Madness* (Rochester, 1787), 267.
34. See Adriana Craciun and Kari Lokke, eds., *Rebellious Hearts: British Women Writers and the French Revolution* (Albany: SUNY Press, 2001).
35. Morison, *Lectures on Insanity*, 94.
36. De Bienville, *Nymphomania*, 37.
37. Ibid., 167.
38. Quoted in George Rousseau, *The Languages of Psyche: Mind and Body in Enlightenment Thought: Clark Library Lectures, 1985–1986* (Berkeley: University of California Press, 1990), eBook Collection, 436.
39. Nadia Valman, *Jewish Women Writers in Britain* (Detroit, MI: Wayne State University Press, 2014), 78.
40. Dacre, *Passions*, 41.
41. Ibid., 42.
42. Ibid., 155.
43. Ibid., 76.
44. Ibid., 270.
45. Ibid., 106.
46. Ibid., 109.
47. Ibid., 273.
48. Dacre, vol. 3, 3.
49. For more on Romanticism and suicide, see Koretsky, "'Unhallowed Arts' and Gabriele Dillmann, 'Wertherwirkung': Goethe's Suicidal Fantasies and Their Literary Manifestation," *Prism(s): Essays in Romanticism* 11 (2003): 87–99.
50. Dacre, vol. 3, 7.
51. Ibid., 190.
52. Boccaccio, *Decameron*.
53. Diane Hoeveler, "Decapitating Romance: Class, Fetish, and Ideology in Keats's *Isabella*," *Nineteenth-Century Literature* 49 (1994): 326.
54. Donald Goellnicht, *The Poet-Physician: Keats and Medical Science* (Pittsburgh: University of Pittsburgh Press, 1984), 191.
55. Ibid., 191.
56. Hoeveler, "Decapitating," 324.
57. Ibid., 323.
58. Goellnicht, *Poet-Physician*, 20.
59. Hermione de Almeida, *Romantic Medicine and John Keats* (New York: Oxford University Press, 1990), 127.

60. Sue Minter, *The Apothecaries' Garden: A New History of the Chelsea Physic Garden* (Phoenix Mill, UK: Sutton Publishing, 2000), 63.
61. Lily Y. Beck, trans., *Pedanius Dioscorides of Anazarbus: De Materia Medica* (New York: Olms-Weidmann, 2005), 152.
62. Nicholas Culpeper, *Culpeper's Complete Herbal, Consisting of a Comprehensive Description of Nearly All Herbs* (London: W. Foulsham and Co., 1954), 39.
63. Gareth Evans, "Poison Wine—John Keats and the Botanic Pharmacy," *Keats-Shelley Review* 16 (2002): 46.
64. Percy Bysshe Shelley, *The Cenci*, The Portable Library, Kindle Edition. See also note number 2. While Shelley did publish his work a year after Keats wrote *Isabella*, the myth was, and still is, a popular one.
65. Richardson, *British Romanticism*, 118.
66. John Keats, *Letters of John Keats to His Family and Friends*, ed. Sidney Colvin (London, 1925), Kindle Edition.
67. Keats, *Letters*, April 18, 1817.
68. Keats, *Letters*, September 21, 1818.
69. Keats, *Letters*, May 21 and 25, 1818.
70. Ibid.
71. This very notion of melancholy as gendered has been explored in interesting and productive ways. See Elizabeth Dolan, "British Romantic Melancholia."
72. Ghislaine McDayter, *Byromania and the Birth of Celebrity Culture* (Albany: SUNY Press, 2009), eBook Collection, 47.
73. Keats, *Letters*, May 4, 1820.
74. For more on this, see Jane Chambers, "'For Love's Sake': Lamia and Burton's Love Melancholy," *Studies in English Literature, 1500–1900* 22, no. 4 (1982): 583–600.
75. Burton, *Anatomy of Melancholy*, 664.
76. Ibid., 695.
77. All quotations from *Isabella* are taken from Susan Wolfson, ed., *John Keats*: A Longman Cultural Edition (New York: Pearson Education, Inc., 2007).
78. Here, playing the lute could easily be a metaphor for composing poetry; Apollo, the god of poetry (and medicine), supposedly invented the lute. Keats was also familiar with the myth of Orpheus and his lute, in which Orpheus leads Eurydice from the underworld with his music, the form from which poetry originally derived. Keats would also have been familiar with the idea of the muses as associated with lutes, as evidenced by Sir Thomas Wyatt's poem of 1557, "My Lute Awake." In this version, Isabella becomes the artist unable to create due to repetitive thoughts.
79. Burton, 695.

80. Irene Hsiao, "Blackberry, Blackberry, Blackberry: Melancholic Repetition and the Romantic Lyric" (PhD diss., University of Chicago, 2008), 10.
81. Thomas Pfau, "'The Purest English': Serialization, Eros, and Melancholy in the Early Keats," in *Romantic Moods: Paranoia, Trauma, and Melancholy, 1790–1840* (Baltimore: The Johns Hopkins University Press, 2005), 314.
82. Hoeveler, "Decapitating," 324.

Bibliography

Boccaccio. *Decameron*. Fourth Day, Novel V. Translated by John Florio. London, 1620. http://www.brown.edu/Departments/Italian_Studies/dweb.

Burton, Robert. *The Anatomy of Melancholy*. Edited by Floyd Dell and Paul Jordan Smith. New York: Tudor, 1927.

Cogan, Thomas. *A Philosophical Treatise on the Passions*. London, 1800.

Craciun, Adriana, and Kari Lokke, eds. *Rebellious Hearts: British Women Writers and the French Revolution*. Albany: SUNY Press, 2001.

Dacre, Charlotte ("Rosa Matilda"). *The Passions*. New York: Arno Press, 1974.

de Almeida, Hermione. *Romantic Medicine and John Keats*. New York: Oxford University Press, 1990.

De Bienville, T. *Nymphomania, or, a Dissertation Concerning the Furor Uterinus, Clearly and Methodically Explaining the Beginning, Progress, and Different Causes of That Horrible Distemper*. Translated by Edward Sloane Wilmot. London, 1775.

Esquirol, Etienne. *Mental Maladies: A Treatise on Insanity*. Philadelphia: Lea and Blanchard, 1845.

Evans, Gareth. "Poison Wine—John Keats and the Botanic Pharmacy." *Keats-Shelley Review* 16 (2002): 31–55.

Formanek, Ruth, ed. *The Meanings of Menopause: Historical, Medical, and Cultural Perspectives*. New York: Routledge, 2013.

Goellnicht, Donald. *The Poet-Physician: Keats and Medical Science*. Pittsburgh: University of Pittsburgh Press, 1984.

Hoeveler, Diane. "Decapitating Romance: Class, Fetish, and Ideology in Keats's *Isabella*." *Nineteenth-Century Literature* 49 (1994): 321–338.

Hsiao, Irene. "Blackberry, Blackberry, Blackberry: Melancholic Repetition and the Romantic Lyric." PhD diss., University of Chicago, 2008.

Keats, John. *Letters of John Keats to His Family and Friends*. Edited by Sidney Colvin. London, 1925. Kindle Edition.

———. *Anatomical and Physiological Note-Book*. Edited by Maurice Buxton Forman. Oxford: Oxford University Press, 1934.

Levin, Phillis, ed. *The Penguin Book of the Sonnet*. New York: Penguin, 2001.

London Medical and Physical Journal, vol. 47. London: J. Souter, 1823.
McDayter, Ghislaine. *Byromania and the Birth of Celebrity Culture*. Albany: SUNY Press, 2009. eBook Collection.
Milner, Conan. "Basil: Herb of Scorpions, Doctors, and King." Last updated August 16, 2015. http://www.theepochtimes.com/n3/1710719-basil-herb-of-scorpions-doctors-and-kings/.
Morison, Alexander. *Lectures on Insanity, for the Use of Students*. Edinburgh, 1841.
Perfect, William. *Select Cases in the Different Species of Insanity, Lunacy, or Madness*. Rochester, 1787.
Pfau, Thomas. "'The Purest English': Serialization, Eros, and Melancholy in the Early Keats." In *Romantic Moods: Paranoia, Trauma, and Melancholy, 1790–1840*. Baltimore: The Johns Hopkins University Press, 2005.
Richardson, Alan. *British Romanticism and the Science of the Mind*. Cambridge: Cambridge University Press, 2001.
———. *The Neural Sublime*. Baltimore: Johns Hopkins University Press, 2010.
Rousseau, George. *The Languages of Psyche: Mind and Body in Enlightenment Thought: Clark Library Lectures, 1985–1986*. Berkeley: University of California Press, 1990. eBook Collection.
Shelley, Percy Bysshe. *The Cenci*. The Portable Library. Kindle Edition.
Shulkins, Rachel. *Keats, Modesty, and Masturbation*. Routledge, 2016.
Valman, Nadia. *Jewish Women Writers in Britain*. Detroit, MI: Wayne State University Press, 2014.
Warley, Christopher. *Reading Class through Shakespeare, Donne, and Milton*. Cambridge: Cambridge University Press, 2014.

CHAPTER 5

Revolutiana and the Sublime in George Gleig's *Subaltern*, Lord Byron's *Siege of Corinth*, and Joanna Baillie's *Count Basil*

As our current post-9/11 era makes clear, war can engender a number of obsessions ranging from an obsession with the experience of warfare to an obsession with wartime memories, both glorious and traumatic. American physician Benjamin Rush, writing in the aftermath of the American Revolution, named this "Revolutiana," declaring that

> enthusiasm at the beginning of a battle excited, both in officers and men, great thirst, though no exertion had been used; and at the first onset, even in the severest cold, a glow of heat was perceptible in both ears. Soldiers were found dead on the field at the battle of Monmouth, without any sign of wound, injury, or exhaustion: he therefore supposes they died from emotions of the mind.[1]

This snippet, extracted from Dr. George Man Burrows's tract concerning the treatment and causes of "insanity," again explains how emotions, in this case "enthusiasm," can produce remarkably physiological symptoms, including death. Thirst, cold, and heat are all occasioned by "emotions of the mind," but which emotions are these? The trauma of war can, and does, cause significant emotional and physiological damage, what we now pathologize as PTSD. This chapter will superficially explore the ways in which repeated memories of violence become destructive obsessions. Yet Burrows and Rush point to a different type of emotional reaction: an aesthetic reaction to the sublimity of war that the soldier begins to crave.

K. Béres Rogers, *Creating Romantic Obsession*,
Palgrave Studies in Literature, Science and Medicine,
https://doi.org/10.1007/978-3-030-13988-9_5

Because the full-scale violence of war evokes both awe and fear, the obsession with war relates closely to the discourse of the sublime, one that, in itself, obsessed Romantic-era thinkers. Burke, whose ideas of the sublime are most evident in wartime memoirs and literature, posits the sublime as bodily—physiological—and later connects it to the events of the French Revolution. In his *Philosophical Enquiry*, Burke analyzes the sublime in terms of its effects, namely, the "astonishment" of the brain: "all [of the mind's] motions are suspended, with some degree of horror … the mind is so entirely filled with its object that it cannot entertain any other."[2] Burke's sublime, as Vanessa Ryan has convincingly argued, is physiological, with the physiological reaction preceding a psychological one.[3] In Rush's account, the mind's physiological motions produce a degree of horror. Horror, for Burke, leads to a loss of reason: "the mind," he writes, "by a sort of mechanism repeats [a sublime thought] long after the first cause has ceased to operate," driving the thinker to become a "madman."[4] Here, astonishment, the paralysis of the brain upon experiencing the sublime idea, can, through association, lead to obsession. It is not surprising that Burke, whose *Enquiry* posits the sublime in such a physiological way, returns to the concept in his 1790 *Reflections on the Revolution in France*.

Astonishment is also central to Burke's description of the French revolution, which he posits as "the most astonishing thing that has hitherto happened in the world. The most wonderful things are brought about in many instances by means the most absurd and ridiculous."[5] Although the event itself is posited as somewhat carnivalesque, "absurd" and "ridiculous," the emotions evinced are the "astonishment" and "awe" (here expressed as "wonder") that he earlier linked with the sublime.

Elevated feelings, a fear of and curiosity about death, and a sense of continuous novelty also form part of Burke's sublime. "Whatever," he writes,

> is fitted in any sort to excite the ideas of pain, and danger, that is to say, whatever is in any sort terrible, or is conversant about terrible objects, … is a source of the sublime; that is, it is productive of the strongest emotion which the mind is capable of feeling.[6]

War, as indicated by firsthand accounts, is clearly "terrible"; the literature about war, including De Quincey's essays, Lord Byron's *The Siege of Corinth*, and Joanna Baillie's *Count Basil*, one of her plays on the passions, is "conversant about terrible objects." In all of these depictions of both negative and positive sublimity, "strength, violence, pain and terror, are ideas that rush in upon the mind together."[7] Again, it is the ideas of strength and violence that are sublime, not necessarily the scenes themselves.[8]

These elevated feelings are often connected to patriotism or national identity. For Georg Hegel, in his *Grundliniender Philosophiedes Rechts* (1821), war was necessary to elevate a nation above its mundane concerns. In his account, the common idiom that war creates an elevated, more serious character is a valid one. He describes war as moving, like a breeze over the ocean, over the stagnating "moral health" of the people, shifting and elevating it.[9] War, argued Kant and Hegel, might be barbarous, but they had difficulty imagining an alternative route to an elevated sense of national character. Similarly, in "On the Sublime," Thomas De Quincey writes that "the risk-taking impulse of the sublime preserves a social function insofar as it exists to prevent men from becoming 'slaves to [luxury].'"[10] One of the most important effects of this collective "risk taking" is that slaves to luxury were grouped with the poor, the disenfranchised; they were all, as Linda Colley argues in *Britons*, united in the defense of their nation. The rich, the poor, voters and the disenfranchised, were all drawn into the military by "the excitement of it all, by a pleasureable sense of risk and imminent drama."[11] In this sense, the "risk-taking" inherent in war allows for a developing personal—and national—narrative.

Of course, personal growth and national development does not happen in the thick of war; one cannot, for instance, experience individual or collective elevation, what Kant refers to as sublime, during a bone-shattering explosion. Burke writes about the distance necessary for the sublime to create both awe and fear. Perhaps this is why "there is no spectacle we so eagerly pursue, as that of some uncommon and grievous calamity; so that whether the misfortune is before our eyes, or whether they are turned back to it in history, it always touches with delight."[12] This distancing might explain the uncomfortable aesthetic response noted by some film critics to the events of September 11, 2001. None would argue that the calamity was "uncommon" and definitely "grievous," but there is a morbid "delight" we gain by watching what fills the screen, and our minds, with the excess of spectacle. Joanna Baillie, famously detailing the curious excitement surrounding executions, also places part of this delight in the fact that we can safely sympathize: "With limbs untorn, with head unsmitten, with senses unimpaired by despair, we know what we ourselves might have been on the rack, on the scaffold, and in the most afflicting circumstances of distress."[13] Distance is indeed part of what makes war sublime, as is novelty, but the most sublime element of war, the one that spurs Romantic accounts of obsession, is its inexpressibility.

Dennis, a philosopher featured in Chapter 3, ties this notion of terror and distance to the concept of enthusiasm. Even though, according to Dennis, terror is the

> violent'st of all the Passions, it consequently makes an impression which we cannot resist, and which is hardly to be defac'd, and no Passion is attended with greater Joy than Enthusiastick Terrour, which proceeds from our reflecting that we are out of Danger at the very time that we see it before us.[14]

For Dennis, both joy and terror (like awe and fear) exist simultaneously, and his version of "enthusiasm" shares much with Burke's sense of the sublime. As opposed to the religious connotations of the term, which imply a lack of distance from an emotional stimulus, Dennis posits that it is the very knowledge *of* the danger- a knowledge that requires distance—that makes terror "enthusiastic." Kant also examines the rhetoric of "enthusiasm," mentioning that the "spectators" who are "not engaged in the game themselves" feel "a wishful participation that borders closely on enthusiasm, the very expression of which is fraught with danger."[15] Here, we have the expression of what Mary Favret terms "war at a distance," the almost "wishful" spectatorial quality associated with looking, from a distance, at sublime events.[16]

This distancing might account for Rush's categorization of "revolutiana," as the term implies an emotion experienced during revolution which, of course, can only be labeled as such retroactively. In other words, the revolutionary can classify his emotions *as* revolutionary only after the event has been classified as a revolution. This after-the-fact-ness occurs not only in memoirs, which are published after a military event, but also in letters that reach home months after something has taken place. It also accounts for the traumatic remembrance of war, as detailed by Rush when he describes "fevers," "convulsions," and other "affections of the body" produced

> by the sudden abstraction of that tone in the system which was excited by a sense of danger, and the other invigorating objects of a military life.[17]

Here, the objects excite a "tone," a "sense of danger" which, then, translates, over and over again, into physiological symptoms.

This sense of sublimity, and the obsession with these wartime experiences, fill Romantic-era memoirs and literature by soldiers and civilians alike. While military glory and violence have always been common in literature, the sheer number of soldiers reflecting on their military experiences in venues ranging from the *London Times* to the increasingly popular military memoir supports Neil Ramsey's thesis that the Romantics pioneered the "modern culture of war" in which the experience is mediated, in part, through the experience of the soldier. Due to the proliferation of media and increasing literacy rates, people could now write and read about soldiers' experiences. No longer was the soldier merely a tool for the state, an "arm" of the greater social body, but an autonomous individual with "personal motivations."[18] In his 1809 *Convention of Cintra*, William Wordsworth insisted that every soldier who traveled to fight the French in Spain had taken with him "not only the virtues which might be expected from him as a soldier, but the antipathies and sympathies, the loves and hatreds of a citizen—of a human being—acting, in a manner hitherto unprecedented under the obligation of his human and social nature."[19] The Romantics were interested in sympathy toward human suffering, the "universal human sympathy" that enabled Wordsworth's narrator to provide shelter to his discharged soldier, and also in the sublime landscape of war: a landscape simultaneously far removed from yet, as Favret argues, all too close to home. In fact, many military memoirs, some of which I will explore in this chapter, served as travel memoirs, enabling readers of newspapers and books at home to travel to places like France and Russia, experience large-scale explosions, and feel, from afar, the "enthusiasm" of the soldier.

This feeling, termed as "enthusiasm" by Rush, was also associated, in both medical and philosophical writing, with the sublime. Not only does Rush write about Revolutiana, but Pinel argued that violent political events often caused "insanity."[20] One can even observe what we now call PTSD in descriptions of asylum patients. According to the 1823 *Sketches in Bedlam*, Charles P. Traille, one such inhabitant, had been a lieutenant in the 95th, serving in Spain and other parts of the continent. He, the author writes, "was affected by a bitter sense of remorse for ideal crimes, a horror of death, and a perpetual suspicion that every person about him intended to assassinate or poison him." He was "found dead, hung by his neck-kerchief to the wire-guard over his door."[21] It is a story we still hear all too often: a story of repeated, obsessive memories that culminate in self-destruction.

This sense of traumatic, repeated memories falls in line with recent theorists of trauma, such as Richard J. McNally's argument in his 2003 *Remembering Trauma*. Whereas Cathy Caruth's 1996 *Unclaimed Experience: Trauma, Narrative, and History* argued that the traumatic experience is one that cannot be put into words by the sufferer and requires narrativization through imaginative, figural literature, McNally argues the opposite, positing that traumatic experiences do remain in our memories. In fact, it is consistent flashbacks, associations, and nightmares that result from trauma. The question is not in *whether* people remember their experiences, but *how* those experiences are remembered and told. "[P]eople who have experienced harrowingly close brushes with death (such as falling off a mountain) often report extreme dissociative alterations of consciousness (time slowing down, everything seeming unreal), yet they remain fully capable of providing detailed accounts of their experiences."[22] Seen in this way, the aforementioned Bedlam resident remembers his "crimes" but views them as "ideal," perhaps infiltrated by associations. He clearly remembers death but has endowed it with an additional "horror," and these emotions then precipitate an extreme, (mostly) unwarranted fear of assassination. A memory, repeated and revised, becomes so disturbing that it culminates in suicide. This exemplifies what Thomas Weiskel refers to as the "negative sublime": the sublime that, unresolved, results in trauma.

Although De Quincey's later writings lament the barbarity of war, "The English Mail Coach" and "On War" both exemplify the tensions between the negative sublime occasioned by human suffering and the positive occasioned by novelty, anticipation, and spectacle. One passage in "The English Mail Coach" expresses, much like Benjamin Rush's medical work, the excitement inherent in the anticipation of war:

> The sensibility of the horse, uttering itself in the maniac light of his eye, might be the last vibration of such a movement; the glory of Salamanca might be the first. But the intervening links that connected them, that spread the earthquake of battle into the eyeballs of the horse, were the heart of man and its electric thrillings–kindling in the rapture of the fiery strife, and then propagating its own tumults by contagious shouts and gestures to the heart of his servant the horse.[23]

De Quincey's passage recalls Hartley's doctrine of associationism, with the Peninsular War battle in Salamanca igniting the emotional equivalent of the "earthquake of battle." He details the links that connect the sublime emotions of military glory, through "vibrations," into the heart of man, then to more men, and then, finally, to the "eyeballs" of the horse. These eyeballs reveal madness through a "maniac light." Thus, in a passage about a stagecoach, De Quincey nonetheless manages to incorporate distance, the sublimity of war, and the possibility of madness.

In fact, the notion of the mail invokes the Burkean idea of repetition bringing the sublime to a state of madness. With multiple readers reading accounts multiple times, and then recalling their ideas in their imaginations, the incidents become repetitive, almost infinite. Here De Quincey uses the metaphor of a "train of gunpowder" that not only allows for continued fire but also multiplies its intensity. The mail, he writes, "has an obscure effect of multiplying the victory itself, by multiplying to the imagination into infinity the stages of its progressive diffusion."[24] The idea of war, repeated both in writing and in the readers' imaginations, begins as a spark but kindles into a raging fire.

For De Quincey, it is significant that this fire is flamed by technologies, the stagecoach being a new technology that delivered news to more people more quickly, allowing for an entire nation to virtually participate in war. However, the stagecoach is not the only technology that De Quincey lauds; in "On War," he writes about strategies, tactics, "castrametation" (the laying out of a military camp), "poliorcetics" (the art of siege warfare), and "all the processes through which the first rude efforts of martial cunning finally connect themselves with the exquisite resources of science."[25] Science, or knowledge, allows for "rude" or primitive efforts to become more civilized, more elevated, and more sublime through, as discussed in Chapter 3, an investment in knowledge.

Part I: The Subaltern

Civilization and nationalism have, in these accounts, a tension-filled relationship with the sublime. While military glory clearly, as per De Quincey, Kant, and Hegel, elevates the idea of the nation into a higher sphere, the terror and awe associated with the sublime often finds itself in what Edward Said calls the subaltern (perhaps significantly, this term was the term used to refer to subordinate soldiers). One of Byron's Turkish Tales, *The Siege of Corinth*, connects sublimity not only with the experience of battle but with Muslim culture, and with the idea of existing as a renegade, outside of cultural (and, perhaps for Byron, other) borders.

Importantly, it is not national identity or affiliation that motivates Byron's protagonist Alp, but rather the notion of revenge and, perhaps more, the exhilaration of violence itself. Simon Bainbridge, writing about the popularity of the siege, writes that "Byron exploits (and increasingly scrutinizes) the exhilaration of this form of combat…"[26] The very ideology of a "siege," a fast, unexpected, loud, often blood-soaked invasion of a town, resonates with the terror and awe of the sublime, leaving the participant no mental space in which to examine his thoughts. The synaesthesia of Byron's passages attests to the overwhelming nature of the sounds, smells, and sights of war:

> …Here and there some crackling dome
> Was fired before the exploding bomb;
> And as the fabric sank beneath
> The shattering shell's volcanic breath,
> In red and wreathing columns flashed
> The flame, as loud the ruin crashed,
> Or into countless meteors driven,
> Its earth-stars melted into heaven…. (6, 120–127)[27]

Sounds infiltrate the passage: the dome "crackl[es]," the ruin crashes loudly, and the bomb explodes. The shell, personified, breathes fire which, then, ascends as a meteor to the sky. As the "fabric" of the earth "sinks," the image of fire becomes that of stars and then meteors, elevated into the skies as it becomes more and more sublime. In this same passage, Byron takes care to magnify the effect of the exploding bomb ascending into the skies by stressing the obscurity of everything else:

> Whose clouds that day grew doubly dun,
> Impervious to the hidden sun,
> With volumed smoke that slowly grew
> To one wide sky of sulfurous hue. (6, 128–131)[28]

The clouds are "doubly dun," an effect achieved not only through word choice but also alliteration, and the "sulfurous" hue evokes not only a bland yellow color, but also the smells associated with many explosives that contain the compound. The explosives shooting up into the sky, the yellowish smoke, and the unusual smells all make this scene somewhat other-worldly. It is the removal from, as Byron would have it, the "fabric" of everyday life, which renders this scene sublime.

Not only is the novelty of the scene here attributed to the sounds and sights of war, but this is, as Favret would have it, war "at a distance," in a foreign land dominated by different religious customs. Here, the sounds of gunfire merge with the sounds of prayer to form an even more surreal landscape. For instance, Byron's narrator writes about the Muezzin's voice as he calls people to prayer, claiming that

> It struck even the besieger's ear
> With something ominous and drear,
> An undefined and sudden thrill,
> Which makes the heart a moment still,
> Then beat with quicker pulse, ashamed
> Of that strange sense its silence framed. (11, 231–236)[29]

Again, the narrative begins by focusing on the sound of the call, which strikes the "ear" of "even the besieger"—and one would do well to ask who else—as something "ominous." The language here mirrors both the discourse of obsession and of the sublime: the "sudden thrill" that, in a Burkean moment of astonishment, makes the "heart a moment still," is followed by the quickening pulse mentioned in medical journals. The reader is left to think about the "strange sense" evoked by this distinctive sound in an "oriental" land.

As Bainbridge and others argue, Byron both focuses on the exhilaration, the "strange sense," of a foreign war, and on the inevitable trauma that war will produce:

> ...when all is past, it is humbling to tread
> O'er the weltering field of the tombless dead,
> And see worms of the earth, and fowls of the air,
> Beasts of the forest, all gathering there;
> All regarding man as their prey,
> All rejoicing in his decay. (17. 442–449)[30]

The language turns purely visual as the narrator asks us to see the weltering (steeped in blood) field of innumerable casualties. As opposed to turning upward and outward, like the firing of explosives or the echoing call of the Muezzin, everything here turns inward as the worms on the ground, the birds in the air, and the beasts coming from the forests all "gather" there. They all prey on the dead, and the reader cannot help but think that this image would, similarly, prey on the narrator's (and readers') minds.

This juxtaposition between war as exalted and localized, exhilarating and traumatic, also appears in popular military memoirs of the time. George Gleig's *Subaltern*: Chronicle of the Peninsular War, published initially as anonymous contributions to *Blackwood's Magazine* and then released as a book in 1825, recounts Gleig's experience as a new, young soldier, stressing both the excitement and trauma of warfare. Here, for instance, is a passage reminiscent of Byron's poem:

> It was a spectacle as appalling and grand as the imagination can conceive, the sight of that explosion. The noise was more awful than any which I have ever heard before or since; whilst a brief flash, instantly succeeded by a smoke so dense, as to obscure all vision, produced an effect upon those who witnessed it, such as no powers of language are adequate to describe.[31]

The flash, the smoke, and the awful noise recall the siege of Corinth, as does the juxtaposition of "appalling" and "grand." We have here the same synaesthesia, the same tension between the positive and negative sublime.

The "effect," like Byron's "strange sense" and Burke's sublime, is prelinguistic, unable to be adequately signified, a trope that recurs often in military literature of the time. Gleig himself mentions the inability of language to express the sublime, writing that a scene was one "to which the pencil might perhaps do justice, but which defies all the powers of language adequately to describe."[32] Interestingly, Gleig sees art, the "pencil," as better able to convey the overwhelmingly strange feeling he feels. Later, he states that the "roar" of a waterfall accompanied by the voice of a military sentinel "produced an effect altogether too powerful for me to pourtray, at this distance of time, even to myself."[33] Not only can he not convey the effect in words to his audience, but the power of his feelings leaves them inexpressible, even to his own self-understanding.

What might this feeling be: the feeling that evades words altogether? In *The Body in Pain*, Elaine Scarry posits that extreme pain and extreme pleasure both exist outside of the linguistic realm.[34] One is tempted to only think of the former in terms of war, but Gleig, Robert Ker Porter, and Moyle Sherer definitely posit pleasure as one element of the martial sublime. Gleig writes that the "species of feelings" accompanying his military experience "was not terror, it can hardly be called alarm—for we followed our occupations unceasingly, and even our mirth was uninterrupted; but it kept the mind wound up to a pitch of excitation, from which it was by no means an unpleasant matter to relieve it."[35] Gleig specifically deflects the reader's assumption that the strange feeling of wartime is "terror" or "alarm." Instead, he uses the word "mirth" and, echoing the physiological language of proto-psychologists Tissot and Brown (mentioned in Chapter 3), writes about the strings of the mind "wound up" to a "pitch of excitation." Later, he uses the term "feverish excitement." In Brunonian medicine, a person with too much excitability would indeed possess nerves wound up in excess: an excess that results in nervous disorders. In his later (1827) *Recollections of the Peninsula*, Moyle Sherer makes it clear that this excitation is not only due to novelty or military glory, but to the violence itself. As the passage is pivotal to understanding military obsession, I quote it at length:

> we talked long, and with an undefined pleasure, about the carnage. Yes, strange as it may appear, soldiers, and not they alone, talk of the slaughter of battle-fields with a sensation, which, though it suspends the lively throb of the gay and careless heart, partakes, nevertheless, of pleasure. Nay, I will go farther : in the very exposure of the person to the peril of sudden and violent death, cureless wounds, and ghastly laceration, excitement, strong, high, and pleasurable, fills and animates the bosom : hope, pride, patriotism, and awe, make up this mighty feeling, and lift a man, for such moments, almost above the dignity of his nature.[36]

Like Gleig, he posits the feeling as inexpressible, "undefined" pleasure, but he goes on to attempt a definition. He links the pleasure, not only to patriotism and awe, but also to the "slaughter of battle-fields...violent death, cureless wounds, and ghastly laceration." Paradoxically, it is the violence itself which awakens the "mighty feeling" of sublimity and "lifts" a man to an elevated, almost God-like sphere.

Part II: War as Spectacle

It bears repeating that the soldiers here discuss the carnage of the battlefield after the battle, at a remove, giving them the distance necessary to aestheticize their experience. Gleig describes war from afar as a "spectacle," another term used often in conjunction with warfare and its literary, theatrical, and artistic representations. Early in his narrative, he calls the military "spectacle in the highest degree interesting and grand, especially to my eyes, to whom such spectacles were new." For Gleig, this spectacle is connected to the sublimity of the foreign landscape in which he fights, a landscape whose sublime and picturesque conventions are compared by Ramsey to the staples of the travel narrative. He even refers to the landscape as a "picture" and writes that,

> To complete the picture, the back-ground behind Passages is on all hands beautifully romantic. Hills rise, one above another, to a very considerable height, all of them covered with rich herbage, and the most ample foliage; whilst far away in the distance are seen the tops of those stupendous mountains, which form a barrier, and no imaginary barrier, between France and Spain.[37]

Here, the high hills and "stupendous" mountains, much like Byron's explosive meteors/stars, literally elevate the scene, raising it above the everyday. Later in the narrative, Gleig refers to an "amphitheater" of mountains, a word choice that both elevates and lends distance to the unfolding events of war.

As Sherer makes clear, the "spectacle" of war, an element of the experience that connects it to both visual art and theater, can be both glorious and traumatic. Gleig writes about entering a field from the street and encountering a "dreadful spectacle...We found it covered – literally covered – with fragments of dead carcases, to bury which it was evident that no effectual attempt had been made."[38] The many "fragments" of human bodies that literally cover the ground lend the scene a sense of infinite horror, a horror that, repeated in the viewer's mind, converts the awe and fear of the sublime into a form of obsession. Robert Ker Porter, in his 1812 *Narrative of the Campaign in Russia*, hints at the repeated memories of military spectacle:

> But I will not attempt a further enumeration of the varieties of human miseries I have seen. Only those who have witnessed such extremes of distress, can form any idea of the horrors I have left yet untold of the hideous spectacle exhibited between the Berezina and the Neimen, and whose parallel for miseries is not to be found in the annals of the world.[39]

The reader is left to wonder at the untold horrors, but Ker Porter does describe the scene as a "hideous spectacle," one that, again, cannot be found in written or recorded form. It is this strange amalgam of pleasure, horror, excitement, and distress that characterizes war and begins to explain soldiers'—and the public's—obsession with it.

It is this "strange" interest in war that explains the national obsession with the military panorama. Robert Barker, who mastered the difficulty of presenting straight lines on a curved canvas, patented his panorama at Leicester Square in 1787. The idea was to literally surround the viewers with the scene at hand, making it as authentic as possible. To this end, Barker's patent explicitly mentioned the circular framing, top-lighting, "inclosure" to keep the viewers from coming too close, and "interceptions" to block the top and bottom of the painting, so that the viewer would "feel as if really on the very spot."[40] In his 1804 *Prelude*, Wordsworth alludes to the sheer magnitude and power inherent in these panoramas:

> ...The Painter, fashioning a work
> To Nature's circumambient scenery,
> And with his greedy pencil taking in
> A whole horizon on all sides, with power,
> Like that of angels or commissioned spirits,
> Plant[s] us upon some lofty pinnacle,
> Or in a ship on waters, with a world
> Of life, and life-like mockery, to east,
> To west, beneath us, behind us, and before... (VII, 240–247)[41]

The painter is characterized here with "power," significantly compared to the exalted and divine, the "angels" or "spirits" commissioned by God. The painter, in turn, grants the viewer power by planting him or her upon a "lofty pinnacle," perched above a city, landscape, or military scene, looking down at the spectacle below. Everywhere the viewer looks, east, west, behind, and before, his or her view is overwhelmed by the large, circular painting. As Richard Altick argues in *The Shows of London*, "Sheer magnitude, combined with the powerful feeling inherent in the subject and amplified by the artist, was intended to overwhelm the spectator."[42] Magnitude, power, and an ability to overwhelm again connect these "realistic" scenes with the sublime.

Probably the most commented-upon panorama at Leicester Square was Robert Ker Porter's *Conquest at Seringapatam*, a spectacle that, like Byron's poem or the military memoirs, placed the viewer in a foreign land to view an already sublime battle scene. The painting, replete with temples, a huge quantity of smoke, people falling from turrets, and shooting, visually replicates the scenes described by Byron, Gleig, and Sherer (and perhaps posits visually some of the horrific violence Ker Porter could not share on paper). The viewer sees soldiers wading through water, one seriously wounded soldier being carried by his comrades. Others lie dead on the side of the road, while the background is obscured by smoke that seems to blend with the clouds, creating an air of mystery. While, as William Galperin argues, Ker Porter preferred the title of "historical picture," privileging accuracy over the sensationalism of the panorama, the prospect was nonetheless "overwhelming."[43] In keeping with the sublime, the panorama both depended on and negated the viewers' subjectivity.

While some panoramas experienced relatively short runs, military topics always garnered public interest. According to Thomas Frognall Dibdin, "such a sight was as marvelous as it was novel. You carried it home, and did nothing but think of it, talk of it, and dream of it."[44] Here, Dibdin praises the novelty of the panorama; not only does it overwhelm the viewer, but the image remains lodged in the viewer's mind, causing him or her to insistently, repeatedly "think of it, talk of it, and dream of it." In other words, the sublimity of the panorama, by capturing the viewer's imagination, allowed it to become an obsession.

Part III: Make Love, Not War

It is perhaps not accidental that the panorama shared much in common with the developing—and increasingly complex—theater set. Both allow for the viewer to view a scene from afar, identify with characters, and experience the martial sublime. The theater is an experience that became more and more spectacular as technologies became more and more complex. Yet Joanna Baillie was not as interested in the sublimity of explosions and gruesome war scenes as the sublimity of human emotion. Her play *Basil: A Tragedy* delineates the title character's twin obsessions with war and with love. In fact, I argue that Basil's obsession with Victoria, herself named after the notion of "victory," serves here as what David Mitchell and Sharon Snyder call a "narrative prosthesis," the use of one narrative device to stand in for another.[45]

This conflation of war and love is by no means a new one, and I do not presume, here, to trace its history. Conquest, whether of a city or a woman, has long been associated with masculinity; as Tim Fulford argues in *Romanticism and Masculinity*, it is this ability to "command himself and others" that qualified Horatio Nelson's "body, mutilated by many battles in which he had exposed himself to fire," as "proof of... manliness."[46] This "command" can be either military or romantic; Byron mocks the convention in *Don Juan*, ironically invoking "fierce loves and faithless wars," comically switching the adjectives to illustrate the convention.[47] Byron's title character is "trained to scale a fortress/ or a nunnery" (I, 38), both means of attaining a desired end.[48] Yet I argue that the passion delineated here, supposedly the passion of love, only stands in for Basil's real obsession with war, spectacle, and the martial sublime.

Baillie's preface, intended to explain why she would trace one chief passion per play, already hints at the intersectionality between many of the passions (love, hatred, jealousy) and a desire for violence. "Great and bloody battles," she writes, "are to us battles fought in the moon, if it is not impressed upon our minds, by some circumstances attending them, that men subject to like weaknesses and passions with ourselves, were the combatants."[49] In her footnote, Baillie details two battles, one described as a "compleat and glorious victory" and the other as a more complex battle in which the soldiers, fleeing due to the trauma of seeing so many of their compatriots die, are reinvigorated by their leader to reflect on "everything that kindles in the bosom of man the high and generous passions."[50] With this in mind, they now return to battle "with the fury of wild beasts."[51] This analogy to beasts is referenced again when Baillie describes the soldiers as "rude" and "uncultivated"; in the trenches, war and violence are bestial, but viewed as a spectacle, they are unquestionably sublime.[52]

As spectators, we—and also the spectators of the play within Baillie's play—are expected to approach characters as proto-psychoanalysts, tracing their "passions" through their voice inflections and facial characteristics. Viewing them from a distance, we "partake[ ], in some degree, of the entertainment of the Gods, who were supposed to look down upon this world and the inhabitants of it, *as we do upon a theatrical exhibition*" (emphasis mine).[53] As spectators, we therefore possess a sublime power, looking down from an elevated position (much like Gleig's position looking down at a battlefield). From this distanced vantage point, we can "read" expressions, people, and passions, viewing battles, and characters themselves, as spectacles.

Yet the problem with theater, as Alan Richardson points out in "A Neural Theater: Joanna Baillie's Plays on the Passions," is that theaters during Baillie's time were generally large. Peter Duthie, in his introduction to Baillie's plays, writes that intimate Augustan theaters were replaced by "industrial monoliths that would seat as many as three thousand spectators."[54] In such a depersonalized setting, viewers would be distanced but hard-pressed to really see the actors' faces. How, then, would one express emotion, especially the finer expressions and tics necessary for psychic dissection? Richardson convincingly argues that, to deal with this problem, Baillie uses meta-theater—"pageants, processions, and masks within the play, on-stage spectators…"—so that observers could "report" on what the audience could not see. In other words, we might see a military procession, and a minor character might then report on Basil's reaction to it.[55] In this way, Baillie could psychologically dissect Basil's obsession with love and, even moreso, with war. In fact, Baillie performs this move often, placing Geoffrey, the visibly wounded soldier, as a spectator of Basil's unrequited love. And she takes it even further, including numerous spectacles and processions in her play for her viewers to observe.

Thus viewers might not see the facial expressions of Baillie's characters, but they can still, through others' comments, dissect an individual passion of the mind, tracing its various stages of growth, and clinically examining what she calls its "thousand delicate traits" and its "bold and prominent features."[56] As Dwyer argues, Baillie treats the mind from a medical vantage point as "a pathological entity, rooted in the vital organs, circulating through the body, expressing itself upon the countenance, exhibiting itself in symptomatic behavior."[57] When characters like Geoffrey remark upon others' facial expressions, they give the audience a clue as to the passions and their physiological effects, "reading" the characters for us.

This proto-psychological view of the emotions is not surprising, considering that her brother, Matthew Baillie, not only worked as a doctor and attended King George III, but also wrote quite extensively about the brain in his 1825 *Lectures and Observations on Medicine*. Here, Matthew, like Joanna, espouses a materialist notion of mental illness: "we know that the brain is frequently changed from its healthy structure, so as to receive false impressions, as in many instances of mania…"[58] Also, these patterns do not remain in the brain but are exhibited throughout the body, lending themselves to observance: "the different emotions of the mind are also conveyed along nerves to different muscles of the body, exciting them to contraction…the expressions of the countenance and attitude in anger, revenge, fear, &c., when strongly excited, are the same in every country, and are universally understood."[59] This statement by Matthew Baillie might as well have been part of his sister Joanna's Preface.

Dwyer argues that "compilation and classification lend Baillie's passion project a systematic, scientific appearance but also ties it, like Hunter's cabinet, to collecting, one of the most popular pastimes of eighteenth-century England."[60] Here, she references Dr. William Hunter, Baillie's uncle and a prominent influence in her life. In the *Universal Magazine* in 1784, Hunter writes that "To form a solid judgment about the birth of a new-born child, from the examination of its body, a professional man should have seen many new-born children, both still-born, and such as had outlived their birth a short time only; and he should have dissected, or attended the dissections of a number of bodies in the different stages of advancing putrefaction."[61] From this description, it becomes clear that Joanna Baillie also wished to examine "many" people in "many" mental states, and metaphorically "dissected" their thoughts and actions.

Given this emphasis on spectacle, the sublime, and psychology, it is not surprising that war should be central to this play. In 1798, when Baillie's play was first published, England was still embroiled in the French revolutionary wars. Not only does Baillie set this drama in the time of the Battle of Pavia (significantly fought by the Spanish against the French), but her play also focuses on Basil's military experience. In "Joanna Baillie's Theatre of Cruelty," Victoria Myers argues that cruelty, and the passions that lead to it, are very much present in Baillie's theatrical works. "If," she writes, "Baillie recognizes the presence of cruelty in her society, it is not in order to reject the savage component in contemporary life, but to identify and release it in art."[62] Basil's cruelty lies in his "obsession with military reputation," an obsession so damaging that it costs him relationships with his soldiers and, eventually, his own life.[63] Reputation is another form of spectacle—it involves others reading and judging a person. Thus, the issues of seeing and how we are seen become central to this play.

It is therefore not surprising that Baillie immediately introduces the element of spectacle. The very first stage direction she gives is "an Open Street, crowded with people, who seem to be waiting in expectation of some show."[64] Already, Baillie gives us an atmosphere of expectation and anticipation—we, the audience, are those people, and, like Gleig before a battle, we feel sublime anticipation for what is to come. Initially, we only hear about a "grand procession" and await Victoria, the "fairest lady of the train/ And all the fairest beauties of the court/ Are in her train."[65] This train will later be paralleled with Basil's military procession, as masculine and feminine spectacles merge, the feminine highlighted by "soft musick" and the masculine by "martial musick."[66] Baillie's reference to music is not irrelevant, as martial music exerted a powerful "seduction" on the people.[67] Many of the poor who volunteered for military service had never had access to any sort of instrumental music, so the combination of loud, glorious tones mixed with brightly colored military uniforms acted as a glorious spectacle.

Nor is it coincidental that Geoffrey, "an old soldier very much maimed in the wars," is one of the first named characters to witness this spectacle.[68] Geoffrey is missing an arm; according to the OED, the word "arm" would have been used as a military verb as early as 1250, so he is missing an "arm" both literally and figuratively. He describes this period of his life nostalgically, citing his "gay attire" and the "grand accouterments of war."[69] Geoffrey's descriptions of wartime reiterate the element of spectacular sublimity:

> I left my peaceful home: Then my first battles
> When clashing arms, and sights of blood were
> New:
> Then all the after chances of the war:
> Ay, and that field, a well-fought field it was,
> When with an arm (I speak not of it oft)
> Which now (pointing to his empty sleeve) thou
> Seest in no arm of mine,
> In a straight pass I stopp'd a thousand foes…[70]

Although he substitutes his "peaceful" (read beautiful) home for the sublimity of war, the latter holds an attraction for him (and, when reading the play, for us). Baillie's enjambment here of "new" highlights it in our minds, allowing us, her readers, to also experience a "new" event. In addition, the language and alliteration of the "well-fought field" adds to the pace of the passage, as does the assonance in "stopped a thousand foes."

While Geoffrey is maimed and cannot return to battle, his dedication serves as a counterpart to Basil's. During the military procession, Geoffrey hears music and "walks up and down with a military triumphant step," causing someone to ask why he moves that way. He responds that "I've marched to this same tune in glorious days./ My very limbs catch motion from the sound."[71] Music has become so conflated with "glorious days" that his body unconsciously repeats military routine.

In addition to Geoffrey, Baillie introduces Frederick, who attempts to incite revolt among Basil's soldiers. Although a minor character, he also reveals much about the psychology of power when he says that

> My soul for war and danger pants,
> As doth the noble lion for his prey.
> My soul delights in battle.[72]

Interestingly, war is here aligned with "danger"; like a lion hunting his prey, he can only, selectively, focus on opportunities for danger and fame.

These musings parallel with the first descriptions we have of Count Basil—again, because a large theater cannot allow for close facial recognition, we are to use these descriptions to read his character. Rosinberg, his kinsman, calls Basil his "pride," to which Frederick responds that it is his "foolish admiration/ which raises [Basil] to such superiour height."[73] Closely following this metaphor of Basil as exalted or "raised" up, Frederick adds that he has "felt at times an awe before him,/ I know not why."[74] Early on, we are told that Basil himself is in awe of military "fame," "Destroys his thoughts, and makes him oft appear/ Unsocial and severe."[75] Baillie gives her audience the first hint that the sublimity of military life comes at a great cost; Geoffrey might have lost a physical body part, but Basil loses "his thoughts" to one overwhelming idea.

Because war occupies all of his thought, Basil has trouble forming relationships and functioning in the world. He draws a parallel between war and love, stating that

> From early youth, war has my mistress been,
> And though a rugged one, I'll constant prove
> And not forsake her now.[76]

In a play purportedly about love, the choice of the word "mistress" is not accidental. Arguing with Rosinberg that Victoria has not "conquered" him, he contends that the "hasty flashes of contending steel/ Must serve instead of glances from my love,/ And for soft breathing sighs the cannon's roar."[77] Masculine and feminine are, much as in the beginning of the play, juxtaposed with both sight (the flashes of steel and the glances from his love) and sound (soft breathing sights and the cannon's roar). Yet love is, for him, also a form of conquest, and Baillie troubles the distinction with her mixed use of military and romantic diction.

Throughout the play, Baillie plays with the languages of sexual and military tyranny. In one of his soliloquies about Victoria, Basil muses that her dark blue eyes "command the inmost soul."[78] Later, this notion becomes more pronounced when, in the Mask, Rosinberg dresses "fantastically," with a "willow upon his head, and scraps of sonnets, and torn letters fluttering around his neck."[79] He plays his part with a masked woman, later discovered to be the countess of Albini, Victoria's (older) governess. Not knowing her identity, he courts her by stating that he is ready to "engage" with any "mistress," recalling Basil's earlier statement about war being his "mistress." When a masker asks him what dangers he will "brave," he mentions that he is "something loth/ To storm a convent's walls for one dear glance."[80] Again, the notion of "storming" the convent walls, one repeated by Byron in *Don Juan*, parallels storming a fortress to defeat the enemy and gain the prize (here, virginity).

Images of "conquest" and "storming" give way quickly in this play to those of body parts and blood, the images of battle. The fifth mask, who turns out to be Albini, turns the language of conquest on Rosinberg:

> …I'll careful be
> In feigned admiration of thy parts…
> To bind thy giddy soul with flatt'ry's charm:
> For well thou knowst that flatt'ry ever is
> The tickling spice, the pungent seas'ning,
> Which makes this motley dish of monstrous scraps
> So pleasing to the dainty lover's taste…[81]

The "feigned admiration of thy parts," a reference to the sonnet *blazon* (recall that Rosinberg wears sonnet scraps), quickly becomes something more gruesome, a dish of "monstrous scraps" that dehumanizes its victim, making her a collection of her body parts (here, Albini mentions a "pretty leg"), much like Geoffrey is characterized by his missing arm. Love, like war, reduces its players to their reproductive or military functions.

Subverting his own military function, Basil decides to dress as the second; he attends the mask as a "wounded soldier," a bandage on his arm, aligning himself with Geoffrey.[82] Baillie has Victoria dress as a "female conjurer" who examines Basil using medical diction. Much like Baillie's viewers, she can see Basil (he has taken off his mask), but he cannot "see" her. She offers him healing—"I have some potent drugs may ease thy smart," she says—but he cannot be healed from his pain, only "examin'd."[83] Since he has been "wounded" by Victoria herself, she is both examiner, audience/physician, and conqueror. Knowing this, she plays with his disguise as a wounded soldier:

> Mask: Art thou a soldier, and no weapon
> Bear'st
> To send her wound for wound?

To this, Basil replies:

> Alas! She shoots from such a hopeless
> Height
> No dart of mine hath plume to mount so far...[84]

Baillie's image is a spatial one; Victoria shoots her weapon from on high while Basil remains on the ground. His heart, he says, would have "bled for her."[85] Like cupid's dart, it finds its mark and devastates his psyche. This metaphor gains strength when Baillie inserts Mirando, Victoria's young, doting charge, as cupid in the mask. When Basil finds out that Victoria dotes on the young boy, he "takes him eagerly up in his arms, and kisses him" to which Mirando/Cupid complains: "No, let me down, thy kisses are so rough/ So furious rough–she doth not kiss me so."[86] Only a few lines later, Baillie turns Basil's roughness around when she has a group of maskers sing a "glee" about Cupid, calling him "The tyrant of the human race."[87]

The mask itself, including the rituals and carnivalesque twists and turns, is a sublimation of the violence that dominates both military and romantic connections. "Ritual," whether it be the procession, the mask, or an organized battle, "is the imitation and reenactment of spontaneous, unanimous, violence."[88] René Girard argues that the sublimity of our violent impulses, like the ones voiced in the subaltern memoirs, is reenacted and cultivated through ritual. Discussing Dionysus and *The Bacchae*, Girard refers to celebrations in which promiscuity, incest, and other social taboos are "celebrated": "Family and social hierarchies are temporarily suppressed or inverted; children no longer respect their parents, servants their masters, vassals their lords."[89] In this way, the festival celebrates a temporary elimination of sexual and gender differences. Both Victoria and Basil enact their own forms of tyranny upon one another (Basil's love is unrequited and therefore nonconsensual), and Basil's soldiers even plan an insurrection against him. Social roles are subverted until, in the end, Cupid and his votaries are chased away by a group of satyrs. This plot point aligns Baillie's play with the classical drama, namely with the satyr play at the end which, in and of itself, served a subversive function.

A small plot point, the figure of the satyr nonetheless points to the violent nature of Basil's obsessions, not only with the military but also with Victoria herself. As Hatab writes, Satyrs were "wanton drunkards, thieves, and gluttons, beings who could not control or still their desires."[90] In a play about the passions, this aspect could not have been lost on Baillie; in addition, the satyrs appear after Basil is "too rough" with Cupid, and they literally chase love away. Basil's "rough" ness reminds us of Baillie's footnote comparing soldiers to "wild beasts," and again, it is no accident that Satyrs were, in fact, half-goat, half-man. To quote Hatab again, "the satyr embodies [an] ambiguous animal-human hybrid who lives on the fringes of the human world, and who exhibits astonishment at the unfolding of that world, and whose transgressions and crossings are experienced as comical—which is not to say repulsive but pleasurable, interesting, revelatory, and rejuvenating."[91] I equate this form of "pleasure" with the pleasure experienced upon witnessing an execution or transgressing sexual norms; as Girard argues, it is this "off-letting" of violent instincts that allows for, and even calls for, ritualistic behavior.

Another important, and heretofore undiscussed, element of ritual is sound; sound, which does not need verbal signification, also recalls the sublime. Even though western society privileges sight as a primary sensation, philosopher and Gothic author Carl Grosse argues that the ear is "most suited to an indefinite Schwärmerei of imagination…," elaborating that "the ear is more suitable than the eye to create images and agitate the passions."[92] In his 1735 treatise, Hildebrand Jacob states that hearing works "on our imaginations much after the same way…" as sight. Specifically, he mentions water in cataracts, thunder, "the clash of arms, and voice of war."[93] While Kant's—and to some degree, Burke's—sublime begs to be resolved, Kiene Wurth argues that in musical "interactions the sublime feeling often turns out unfinished or unaccomplished: it hangs suspended in between pain and pleasure, caught in a repetitive strain that obstructs a set thoroughfare."[94] The "repetitive strain" and the obstruction of the "thoroughfare," a word that resembles the chain of association or the strain of thought, recalls the discourse of obsession.

Distance combined with sound only increases the element of sublimity: the astonishment of the brain. According to Grosse, "A soft music heard from afar is much more stirring than if heard in the concert hall; and the wavering tones of the distant [entfernung] set off the power of imagination into the realm of scattering images."[95] These "wavering tones" of distant sound are replicated by Baillie in the procession of the ladies and the military procession, both of which would have sounded even more distant and "wavering" to theater audiences. Basil himself claims that

> A sound, a simple song without design,
> In revolutions, tumults, wars, rebellions,
> All grand events, have oft effected more
> Than deepest cunning of their paltry art.[96]

Baillie here plays with our sense of hearing, both by evoking simple songs and by using alliterative "s" words to mimic musicality.

Twentieth-century psychological theories of attention argue that we all maintain a bottleneck for sensory input; we either do not hear what we cannot attend, or we hear it at a reduced "volume." This metaphor of hearing–and of sound–becomes important to Baillie's play and to Basil's obsession with Victoria. Dorothy McMillan argues, "The passions must be fully embodied to be understood…even unperformed drama embodies its characters more fully than narrative verse or dramatic monologue, where voice is always more important than presence."[97] Again, since Baillie wished this play to be performed, the audience would also have heard Victoria's words. Basil himself claims that he can hear nothing else. When he repeats everything she says, word for word, she exclaims: "my lord, it is uncivil in you thus/ My very words with mock'ry to repeat."[98] Instead of being "uncivil" and "mocking" her, he replies that "when I hear thee speak,/So sweetly dwells thy voice upon mine ear,/ My tongue e'en unaware assumes the tone."[99] If Basil's previous bottleneck was the thought of war, he can now only hear Victoria's voice, see her face, and even repeat her words.

This notion of an auditory bottleneck and its connection to obsessive thinking becomes even more pronounced when the element that brings Basil's attention back to the idea of war is connected to hearing. Ringing in the ears was initially connected with Victoria; the second time he sees her, Basil reports that "A dizzy mist…swims before my sight—/ A ringing in my ears—'tis strange enough."[100] Now, when he realizes that he has, due to his obsession with Victoria, missed the war's defining battle, he says

> Thou said'st, the words do ring so in
> mine ears,
> I cannot catch their sense—the battle's o'er?[101]

Here, the words "ring in" Basil's ears, but he cannot process or understand them. Literally, he cannot "catch their sense." When he does understand, he becomes overwhelmed (again) by one passion: the idea of shame.

This passion, as per Baillie's preface, manifests on Basil's body when he enters, "with his hat off, his hair and his dress in disorder, stepping slowly, and stopping several times to listen, as if he was afraid of meeting any one."[102] His military hat is off, he cannot attend to grooming or dressing himself, and, again, Baillie emphasizes his auditory response when she writes that he stopped "several times to listen." It is also, significantly, a sublime night, a "dark night" with "no moon," and Basil finds himself in a graveyard. When he speaks of his sense of shame, it overwhelms any other sensory response:

> I can bear scorpions' stings, tread fields of fire
> In frozen gulfs of cold eternal lie
> Be toss'd aloft through tracts of endless void
> But cannot live in shame…[103]

The titular image of the scorpion returns here, and the use of "fields of fire" hearkens back to the myth about scorpions ringed with fire who sting themselves to death. Surrounded by this field of fire, unable to live with this passion—significantly not the passion of love, but of shame—Basil kills himself.

How can one make sense of the "passion" in this particular play? If, as I argue, Basil is a play about obsessions (with war, love, or shame), these obsessions play out through the senses. When Geoffrey mentions the "sights of blood," Basil views Victoria in the procession, or we think about our own distanced images of war, we privilege sight. Yet, as I have argued, this particular play foregrounds the auditory nature of obsession, whether with the sounds of a woman's voice, or the sounds of battle. Significantly, both of these sensory responses become sublime when we, the theater viewers, see and hear them at a distance.

One can add that this passion is, like the others I have examined in this book, a "delusion," an obsession not with war per se, but with the *idea* of war. The last scene of Baillie's play takes place in a cave placed in a "wood, wild and savage."[104] She takes care to tell us that the time is the "dawn of morning," and all of these images project a sense of primitivity, infancy, or, as Baillie herself put it, "uncultivated" thought. The cave itself is a platonic image, and, when Basil kills himself and says to Rosinberg that his superiority was "delusion, all delusion" we remember that, philosophically speaking, most ideas are delusions, signifiers for the thing we might never understand. When we cling to these ideas, becoming unaccountably attracted to "one thing," we run the risk of being perceived as "mad." As Baillie herself puts it, "such singularities (like unaccountable aversion or attraction to/for one thing) can no where be sought for, with such probability of success, as in Bedlam."[105] Yet it is these ideas, these delusions, which elevate us from the din of common life. The next chapter will examine "ideality," an obsession with "irrational" ideas that, unlike the idea of reading, love, or the military, cannot be so easily categorized.

Notes

1. Quoted in George Man Burrows, *Commentaries on the Causes, Forms, Symptoms, and Treatment, Moral and Medical, of Insanity* (London, 1828), 20.
2. Edmund Burke, *A Philosophical Enquiry into the Origin of Our Ideas of the Sublime and Beautiful* (Oxford: Oxford World's Classics, 2013), 53.
3. Vanessa L. Ryan, "The Physiological Sublime: Burke's Critique of Reason," *Journal of the History of Ideas* 62, no. 2 (April 2001) 267.
4. Ibid., 67–68.
5. Edmund Burke, *Reflections on the Revolution in France* (Oxford: Oxford World's Classics, Oxford University Press, 1993), 10.
6. Burke, *Enquiry*, 39.
7. Ibid., 65.
8. Women are also affected by violent events but, as with intellectual monomania, the effects are often bodily. Burrows details that women during the American Revolution experienced "hysterical and different" complaints, and that the 1814 siege of Paris by the Allies "occasioned in the female inhabitants much irregularity in the menstrual flux" (*Commentaries*, 20–21).
9. Der Krieg, als der Zustand, in welchem mit der Eitelkeit der zeitlichen Gűter und Dinge, die sonst eine erbauliche Redensart zu sein pflegt, Ernst gemacht wird, ist hiermit das Moment, worin die Idealität des

Besonderen ihr Recht erhält und Wirklichkeit wird; -er hat die hőhere Bedeutung, dass durch ihn, wie ich es anderwärts ausgedrückt habe, die sittliche Gesundheit der Völker in ihrer Indif- ferenz gegen das Festwerden der endlichen Bestimmtheiten erhalten wird, wie die Bewegung der Winde die See vor der Fäulnis bewahrt, in welche sie eine dauernde Ruhe, wie die Völker ein dauernder oder gar ein ewiger Friede, versetzen wiirde (My translation). Georg Hegel, *Grundlinien der Philosophie des Rechts* (Leiden: A.H. Adriani, 1902), 492–493, accessed via Google Books.

10. Quoted in Philip Shaw, *The Sublime (The New Critical Idiom)* (Taylor and Francis, 2007), Kindle Edition, 26.
11. Linda Colley, *Britons* (New Haven, CT and London: Yale University Press, 1992), 306.
12. Burke, *Enquiry,* 56.
13. Joanna Baillie, *Plays on the Passions*, ed. Peter Duthie (Peterborough, ON: Broadview, 2001), 74.
14. John Dennis, *The Grounds of Criticism in Poetry* (London, 1704), 86. Google Books.
15. Immanuel Kant, *Religion and Rational Theology,* ed. Alan W. Wood (Cambridge: Cambridge University Press, 2001), 302.
16. See Mary Favret, *War at a Distance: Romanticism and the Making of Modern Wartime* (Princeton and Oxford: Princeton University Press, 2009).
17. Benjamin Rush, *Medical Inquiries*, 285.
18. Neil Ramsey, *The Military Memoir and Romantic Literary Culture, 1780–1835* (New York: Ashgate, 2011), 12.
19. W. J. B. Owen and Jane Worthington Smyser, eds., *The Prose Works of William Wordsworth,* vol. 1. (Oxford: Oxford University Press, 1974), 225.
20. Helen Small, *Love's Madness: Medicine, the Novel, and Female Insanity* (Oxford: Clarendon, 1996), 107.
21. "Constant Observer," *Sketches in Bedlam* (London, 1823), 39.
22. Richard J. McNally, *Remembering Trauma* (Cambridge: Harvard University Press, 2003), 182.
23. Thomas De Quincey, *The Complete Works of Thomas De Quincey (20 Complete Works of Thomas De Quincey Including The Caesars, The Confessions of an English Opium-Eater, The English Mail-Coach & Joan of Arc, and More)*, Kindle Edition, location 38222.
24. Ibid., location 38358–38360.
25. Ibid., location 32668–32671.
26. Simon Bainbridge, *British Poetry and the Revolutionary and Napoleonic Wars* (Oxford and New York: Oxford University Press, 2003), 193.

27. George Gordon Byron, *The Siege of Corinth*, ed. Peter Cochran (https://petercochran.files.wordpress.com/2009/03/the-siege-of-corinth.pdf), 6.
28. Ibid.
29. Byron, 8.
30. Byron, 13.
31. George Gleig, *Subaltern: Chronicle of the Peninsular War* (London: Leo Cooper), Kindle Edition, location 778–780.
32. Ibid., location 604–604.
33. Ibid., location 1142–1144.
34. Elaine Scarry, *The Body in Pain: The Making and Unmaking of the World* (New York and Oxford: Oxford University Press, 1987).
35. Gleig, *Subaltern*, location 3556–3559.
36. Moyle Sherer, *Recollections of the Peninsula* (London, 1827), 56.
37. Gleig, *Subaltern*, location 551–554.
38. Ibid., location 1091–1093.
39. Robert Ker Porter, *A Narrative of the Campaign in Russia* (London, 1812), 246.
40. Ralph Hyde, *Panoramania! The Art and Entertainment of the 'All-Embracing' View* (London: Barbicon Art Gallery, 1988), 17.
41. William Wordsworth, *The Prelude: 1799, 1805, 1850*, eds. Jonathan Wordsworth, M. H. Abrams, and Stephen Gill (New York: W. W. Norton, 1979), 239–240.
42. Richard D. Altick, *The Shows of London* (Cambridge, MA: Harvard University Press, 1978), 187.
43. William H. Galperin, *The Return of the Visible in British Romanticism* (Baltimore: Johns Hopkins University Press, 1993), 50–51.
44. Quoted in Altick, 135.
45. See David T. Mitchell and Sharon L. Snyder, *Narrative Prosthesis: Disability and the Dependencies of Discourse* (Ann Arbor: University of Michigan Press, 2000).
46. Tim Fulford, *Romanticism and Masculinity: Gender, Politics, and Poetics in the Writings of Burke, Coleridge, Cobbett, Wordsworth, De Quincey, and Hazlitt* (London: Macmillan, 1999), 6.
47. George Gordon Byron, *Don Juan*, eds. T. G. Steffan, E. Steffan, and W. W. Pratt (London: Penguin, 2004), 297.
48. Byron, *Don Juan*, 55.
49. Joanna Baillie, *Plays on the Passions,* ed. Peter Duthie (Peterborough, ON: Broadview, 2001), 77.
50. Ibid., 77.
51. Ibid.
52. Ibid., 107.

53. Ibid., 75.
54. Ibid., 37.
55. Alan Richardson, "A Neural Theatre: Joanna Baillie's Plays on the Passions," in *Joanna Baillie, Romantic Dramatist, Critical Essays,* ed. Thomas C. Crochunis (London and New York: Routledge, 2004), 136.
56. Karen Dwyer, "Joanna Baillie's Plays on the Passions and the Spectacle of Medical Science," *Studies in Eighteenth-Century Culture* 29 (2000): 31, 36.
57. Ibid., 34.
58. Matthew Baillie, *Lectures and Observations on Medicine* (London, 1825), 13.
59. Ibid., 146.
60. Dwyer, "Joanna Baillie's Plays," 29.
61. Quoted in Nathan Elliott, "'Unball'd Sockets' and 'The Mockery of Speech': Diagnostic Anxiety and the Theater of Joanna Baillie," *European Romantic Review* 18, no. 1 (2007): 90.
62. Victoria Myers, "Joanna Baillie's Theater of Cruelty," in *Joanna Baillie, Romantic Dramatist: Critical Essays,* ed. Thomas C. Crochunis (New York: Routledge, 2004), 104.
63. Richardson, "Neural Theater," 143.
64. Baillie, *Passions,* 119.
65. Ibid., 119.
66. Ibid., 122.
67. Colley, *Britons,* 307.
68. Baillie, *Passions,* 117.
69. Ibid., 120.
70. Ibid.
71. Ibid., 122.
72. Ibid., 157.
73. Ibid., 123.
74. Ibid.
75. Ibid., 124.
76. Ibid., 127.
77. Ibid., 168–170.
78. Ibid., 137.
79. Ibid., 162.
80. Ibid., 63–64.
81. Ibid., 164, 98–105.
82. Ibid., 161, 167.
83. Ibid., 167, 174.
84. Ibid., 167, 188–191.
85. Ibid., 167, 201.
86. Ibid., 171, 281.

87. Ibid., 306.
88. René Girard, *Violence and the Sacred* (Baltimore: Johns Hopkins University Press, 1979), 99.
89. Ibid., 119.
90. Lawrence J. Hatab, "Human-Animality in Nietzsche," in *A Nietzschean Bestiary: Becoming Animal Beyond Docile and Brutal*, eds. Christa Davis Acampora and Ralph R. Acampora (Lanham, MD: Rowman and Littlefield, 2004), 214.
91. Ibid., 217.
92. Quoted in Kiene Wurth, *Muscially Sublime: Indeterminacy, Infinity, Irresolvability* (New York, NY: Fordham University Press, 2009), 58.
93. Andrew Ashfield and Peter De Bolla, eds., *The Sublime: A Reader in Eighteenth Century Aesthetic Theory* (Cambridge: Cambridge University Press, 1996), 41.
94. Wurth, *Musically Sublime*, 2.
95. Quoted in Wurth, 58.
96. Baillie, *Passions*, 184, 17–20.
97. Quoted in Barbara Judson, "'Sympathetic Curiosity': The Theater of Joanna Baillie," *Tulsa Studies in Women's Literature* 25, no. 1 (2006): 51.
98. Baillie, *Passions*, 195.
99. Ibid., 195.
100. Ibid., 132.
101. Ibid., 199, 143–144.
102. Ibid., 201.
103. Ibid., 204, 9–12.
104. Ibid., 204.
105. Ibid., 100.

Bibliography

Ashfield, Andrew, and Peter De Bolla, eds. *The Sublime: A Reader in Eighteenth Century Aesthetic Theory*. Cambridge: Cambridge University Press, 1996.

Baillie, Joanna. *Plays on the Passions*. Edited by Peter Duthie. Peterborough, ON: Broadview, 2001.

Baillie, Matthew. *Lectures and Observations on Medicine*. London, 1825.

Burke, Edmund. *A Philosophical Enquiry into the Origin of Our Ideas of the Sublime and Beautiful*. Oxford: Oxford World's Classics, 2013.

———. *Reflections on the Revolution in France*. Oxford: Oxford World's Classics, Oxford University Press, 1993.

Burrows, George Man. *Commentaries on the Causes, Forms, Symptoms, and Treatment, Moral and Medical, of Insanity*. London, 1828.

Byron, George Gordon. *Don Juan*. Edited by T. G. Steffan, E. Steffan, and W. W. Pratt. London: Penguin, 2004.

Colley, Linda. *Britons*. New Haven, CT and London: Yale University Press, 1992.

Fulford, Tim. *Romanticism and Masculinity: Gender, Politics, and Poetics in the Writings of Burke, Coleridge, Cobbett, Wordsworth, De Quincey, and Hazlitt*. London: MacMillan, 1999.

Galperin, William H. *The Return of the Visible in British Romanticism*. Baltimore: Johns Hopkins University Press, 1993.

Girard, René. *Violence and the Sacred*. Baltimore: Johns Hopkins University Press, 1979.

Hatab, Lawrence J. "Human-Animality in Nietzsche." In *A Nietzschean Bestiary: Becoming Animal Beyond Docile and Brutal*, edited by Christa Davis Acampora and Ralph R. Acampora, 211–219. Lanham, MD: Rowman and Littlefield, 2004.

Hegel, Georg. *Grundlinien der Philosophie des Rechts*. Leiden: A.H. Adriani, 1902. Google Books.

Judson, Barbara. "'Sympathetic Curiosity': The Theater of Joanna Baillie." *Tulsa Studies in Women's Literature* 25, no. 1 (2006): 49–70.

Mitchell, David T., and Sharon L. Snyder. *Narrative Prosthesis: Disability and the Dependencies of Discourse*. Ann Arbor: University of Michigan Press, 2000.

Richardson, Alan. "A Neural Theatre: Joanna Baillie's Plays on the Passions." In *Joanna Baillie, Romantic Dramatist, Critical Essays*, edited by Thomas C. Crochunis, 136. London and New York: Routledge, 2004.

Ryan, Vanessa L. "The Physiological Sublime: Burke's Critique of Reason." *Journal of the History of Ideas* 62, no. 2 (April 2001): 265–279.

Shaw, Philip. *The Sublime (The New Critical Idiom)*. Taylor and Francis, 2007. Kindle Edition.

Wurth, Kiene Brillenburg. *Musically Sublime*. New York: Fordham University Press, 2009.

CHAPTER 6

Ideality and Art in Samuel Taylor Coleridge's "Rime of the Ancient Mariner" and Edgar Allan Poe's "Berenice" and "The Tell-Tale Heart"

Anna Louisa Karsch, a German "peasant poet," was often linked, by readers including Goethe, to notions of inspiration and "original genius."[1] While the figure of the unlettered poet was clearly of interest to the Romantics (one need only recall peasant-poets Anne Yearsley or John Clare), what made Karsch different was her appearance.

Quite bluntly, she was considered "ugly." Yet, unlike Frankenstein's creature, Karsch was not a study in asymmetry or the "monstrous." Instead, according to her daughter Caroline von Klencke, her ugliness lay in her eyes, in her gaze. "If," she wrote in her biography, "she had had any control over her body and her facial expression, she could almost have been considered beautiful." Instead,

> When she displayed that searching gaze that predominated in her face most of the time, she was difficult to tolerate, and one could not have borne to be in her company…her eyelids contracted in this gaze, her eye became smaller, and like the sun concentrated through a burning glass its rays shot towards the object of its contemplation. It was an all-consuming gaze.[2]

In fact, Klencke continues, this gaze is due to the "poetic fire burning with her," and she would gladly have exchanged her poetic gifts for an acceptable appearance. Aside from the poor marketing involved in

K. Béres Rogers, *Creating Romantic Obsession*,
Palgrave Studies in Literature, Science and Medicine,
https://doi.org/10.1007/978-3-030-13988-9_6

Klencke's placing this description before a series of her mother's poetry, this passage is remarkable in that Karsch's "poetic fire," her ideas, cannot be contained. Instead, they appear on her face, her physiognomy, and even travel, like the rays of the sun, toward their objects.

The idea of ideas traveling, of ideas as things-in-themselves, recalls Anton Mesmer's theory of animal magnetism (the term "mesmerism" would be coined later), in which the idea, here viewed as a force that flowed from one person to another, could be communicated between individuals. Samuel Taylor Coleridge also connected this to poetry, specifically the recitation of a poem. For Coleridge, the recitation of a poem is

> a species of animal magnetism, in which the enkindling reciter, by perpetual comment of looks and tones, lends his own will and apprehensive faculty to his auditors. They live for a time in the dilated sphere of his own being.[3]

Again, we see the image of poetic fire in the "enkindling reciter." It is through the reciter's "looks and tones," his or her eyes and voice, that the listeners receive his "own will and apprehensive faculty." In other words, this transmission of ideas not only allows the mesmerist/poet to control listeners, but it also gives listeners access to the poet's intelligence or method of understanding the world at large. Like the glance of the mesmerist, words, too, could lead to healing.[4] The idea, like a mesmerist's glance or a physical medicine, could travel to the reader, possessing and possibly healing him or her.

In order for this linguistic transfer to take place, the reader/listener had to maintain a focus on a single idea. By focusing on and *repeating* this idea, the transfer would become most effective. George Winter, in his *Animal Magnetism*, speaks of the need to "abstract the thoughts from every other idea whatever."[5] Joseph Deleuze, in *Practical Instruction in Animal Magnetism* (trans. 1837), also privileges the singular idea, claiming that the more the patients' "attention is distracted by various objects, the less of it will they give to the essential object."[6] Thus we see repetition as an important element not only in mesmeric tracts, but also in poems like *Rime of the Ancient Mariner*, Poe's "The Bells" and "The Raven," and in later prose works like "Berenice" and "The Tell-Tale Heart."

How was an onlooker to know that the subject had been successfully magnetized? The answer lay in the person's physiognomy: in his or her external appearance. Johann Caspar Lavater claimed that enthusiasts (a complex word that I have examined at length in Chapter 3) were likely to have "flat" foreheads, probably due to the one-dimensional nature of their obsessions. In many long treatises detailing how to "read" eyes, ears, foreheads, and noses, he equates appearance with the passions. If the reader learns the signs of passions, then it becomes easy to recognize someone for whom these are all-consuming. After all, he states, "the repetition of the passions engrave their signs so deeply that they resemble the original stamp of nature. Hence certainty (sic) may be deduced that the mind is addicted to such passions."[7] At this point in his *Essays on Physiognomy*, he clearly perceives this "addiction" as a positive force, relating it to the Biblical light of Christ. "If," he quotes from Luke, "thine *eye* (emphasis mine) be single, thy whole body shall be full of light."[8] Here, the "passion" is the love of God, and the addicted individual shines this love, like the rays from Karsch's eyes, onto others.

However, this quasi-mesmeric notion of evangelism can pertain, as poets and physicians of the era were quick to deduce, not only to light but also to dark, demonic forces. In, for instance, Lavater's drawing of a "melancholy madman" (Fig. 6.1), we see a similar "attention to one object," denoted in the "very outline of the eye." Here, the "concentrated attention" produces "madness."

Sunken cheeks, a large forehead, and protuberant eyes characterize a prototype later popularized by the work of Esquirol himself, who commissioned etchings of over two hundred patients at Salpêtriere (although, as Albert Boime points out, far fewer were actually published). Esquirol desired to render images of his patients in all stages of their disease, usually a form of monomania. By also analyzing the death mask and autopsy results, he could, he was certain, correctly "read" or diagnose the patient's condition. To validate his practice, his Medical Encyclopédie entry on monomania includes "before" and "after" pictures of patients he treated successfully, and detailed engravings of the ones he could not heal. In the latter category, he provides an etching named "monomania" (Fig. 6.2) and then proceeds to describe what the probing analytical eye can *see* in the illustration: "The physiognomy expresses physical pain, the fixity of ideas, and repressed desperation."[9]

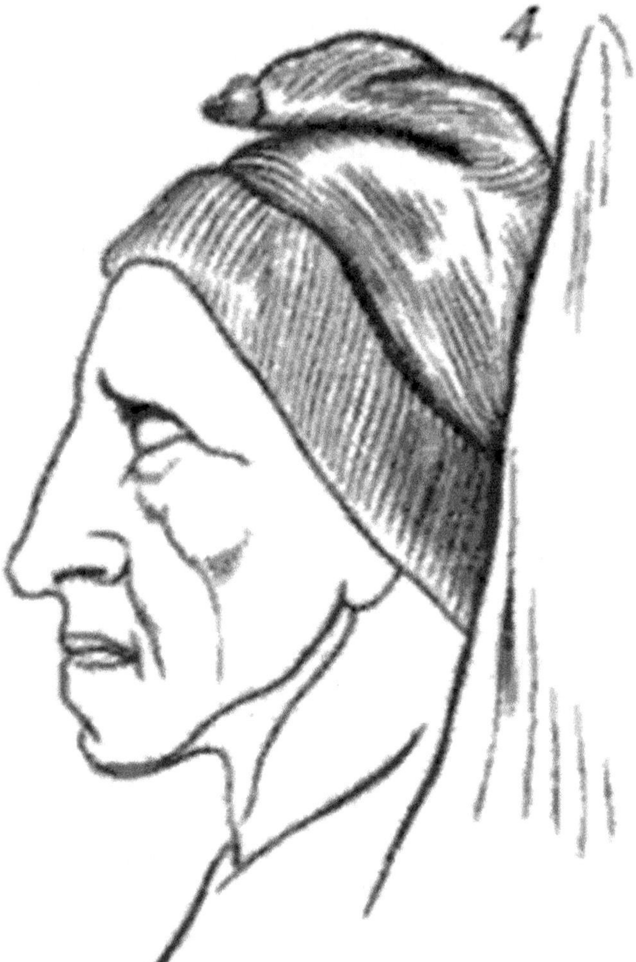

Fig. 6.1 Lavater, Johann Caspar. *Essays on Physiognomy*, vol. 1. London: John Murray, 1789–1798

Fig. 6.2 Etienne Esquirol, Des maladies mentales considerees sous les rapports medicale, hygienique et medico-legal, Planche VI, Monomanie (Courtesy of the National Library of Medicine, USA)

The "fixity of ideas" corresponds with monomania, and Esquirol's contention of "physical pain" reinforces his psychosomatic notion of illness. For Esquirol, the eyes are always large, the forehead expansive.

While this person does not look like what would earlier have been characterized as a "lunatic," a careful observer like Lavater or Esquirol can read the signs on his face, especially in his eyes.

Esquirol's disciple, Étienne-Jean Georget, also replicated this practice, but his portraits were even more difficult to read as portraits of the insane. Instead of using an etcher, usually less expensive and less prestigious, he commissioned the painter Theodore Géricault to provide ten portraits of the "insane" at the Salpêtrière. The woman in Fig. 6.3, for instance, was categorized as *La Monomane de L'Envie*.

The large forehead, sunken cheeks, and small and concentrated eyes resemble the description of Karsh's; also like Lavater's etching and unlike Esquirol's, Georget's eyes never look directly at the spectator, ostensibly

Fig. 6.3 Géricault, *La Monamanie de L'Envie*, 1819/1822. Musée de Beaux-Arts, Lyon

focusing instead on their fixed idea. These eyes are also red-rimmed, recalling Lavater's assertion that focus on a single (in this case poetic) idea could produce red eyes. Yet unlike Lavater or Esquirol, this woman is not pictured in restraints or asylum clothing, and we are left to trust Georget in his assessment.

Influenced by Lavater's studies in physiognomy, Gall and Spurzheim, in their studies of phrenology, had diagnosed a preoccupation with an idea as an enlarged "organ of ideality," located "above the temples"—like the broad forehead reported by Lavater. They reported this organ as commonly enlarged in poets and in artists, rendering them "enthusiasts."[10] Often, these ideas are equated with the mystical or magical; according to Gall and Spurzheim,

> if the part of the head, above the organ of ideality and a little backward from it, be very much developed, the persons are disposed to mysticism, to have visions, to see ghosts, demons and phantoms, and to believe in astrology, magic and sorcery.[11]

Gall and Spurzheim read ideality as a propensity toward imagination, one that could result in beautiful poetry, like Karsch's, or in these visions and "belief" in astrology or sorcery. The 1824 *Phrenological Journal and Miscellany*, which promoted Gall and Spurzheim's notions of phrenology, even contains comparisons of Locke, who has quite a small organ of ideality and a large organ of language, to Chaucer, who "wanders and luxuriates in the delightful wilds of poetry and fancy, and particularly in that rich field of poetical imagery, allegory."[12] Allegory, fancy, and imagination are, for the author here, crucial to creativity, to storytelling.[13]

Yet in Forster's *Sketch of the New Anatomy and Physiology of the Brain and Nervous System of Drs. Gall and Spurzheim* (Fig. 6.4), the facet of ideality that demands attention is not poetical imagery but the propensity, mentioned above, for seeing "visions, ghosts, demons, and phantoms."

Cruikshank represents the man as a lunatic (note the full moon outside), clutching desperately at the covers as a story told by a group of elderly people (bottom right) becomes, literally, an outfit without an inhabitant and, behind him, a ghost. In other words, the idea here has become a nightmare, a "death in life."

For Spurzheim and Gall, who were, after all, materialists, this was just an enlarged organ of ideality: it had no real relation to the group of smoking storytellers or to the "real world." However, philosophers

Fig. 6.4 Cruikshank, "Ideality," in Sketch of the New Anatomy and Physiology of the Brain and Nervous System of Drs. Gall and Spurzheim (London, 1815)

such as John Dennis and doctors like Thomas Beddoes believed that ideas themselves could, and did, become material realities. Adding smoke to the fire was David Hartley's theory of association, which posited that any idea that inspired a terror associated with an initial stimulus would recall that stimulus, causing it to reoccur mentally. If these ideas kept recurring, the fear lay in contemplating what would happen if perception became truth—if they became a reality. In this chapter, I will argue that ideas come to obsess characters in Romantic works like Samuel Taylor Coleridge's "Rime of the Ancient Mariner" and the narrators of multiple Edgar Allan Poe's works. These texts not only illustrate ideas that literally become realities but also posit that the "compulsion" to write, to tell stories, comes from just this type of ideation.

Part I: "The Fiends That Plague Thee Thus"—Coleridge's Ancient Mariner

"Metaphysics and psychology," Samuel Taylor Coleridge wrote in his *Biographia Literaria*, "have long been my hobby horse."[14] Coleridge's metaphor is well-chosen, and his *Biographia* remains, like a rocking horse, in between the physical and the metaphysical realm, particularly influenced by Kant, the "venerable sage of Königsberg." Thus it is no surprise that he was particularly interested in the idea as a Kantian "Thing-in-itself." This "thing-in-itself," Kant's *noumenon*, is not material, nor does it exist in the semiotic realm. While he philosophizes at length about the "thingness" of the Idea, Coleridge comes closest to a definition when he cites Plato, who

> adopted it as a technical term, and as the antithesis to eidolon, or sensuous image; the transient and perishable emblem, or mental word, of the idea. Ideas themselves [Plato] considered as mysterious powers, living, seminal, formative, and exempt from time.[15]

The Idea is, for Coleridge, neither a "sensual image"—one cannot perceive it merely through the senses—nor a word, which, after all, is a material signifier. Instead, Coleridge connects the Idea with magic, with mystery: it is "seminal," creative, "exempt from time." It is, like the "spirit" he connects with the "I AM" of self-consciousness, not enclosed within the material realm.

For this reason, physiognomy and phrenology were problematic for the poet. When, in the *Biographia*, he calls "the predominance of a popular philosophy, at once the counterfeit and the mortal enemy of all true and manly metaphysical research," he seems to be thinking of these forms of "popular" science.[16] In his 1806 *Notebook*, he writes this cryptic entry:

> Ideal = the subtle hieroglyphical *felt*-by-all though not without abstruse and difficult analysis detected and understood, consonance of the *physiognomic* total & substance (Stoff) with the obvious *Patho*gnomic/ herein equi-distanct from Opie-ism…[17]

The physiognomic "total and substance," which Coleridge equates with the material, is difficult to analyze, to read. As opposed to this, the "pathognomic" is "obvious," "*felt* by all." As opposed to an etching in Lavater's opus or a painting by Opie, who "superimposes passions on his characters," pathognomy refers to ideas in motion, and thus relates to Ideas in their living, formative, Platonic sense.[18] For similar reasons, Coleridge was ambivalent toward Spurzheim and Gall, specifically toward the ability to isolate tendencies in specific areas of the brain. For him, this, like Lavater's work, was too materialistic.[19]

Describing his poetic project in *Biographia Literaria*, Coleridge distinguishes his part in the writing of *Lyrical Ballads* from that of Wordsworth. While Wordsworth will focus on the natural world, Coleridge proposes that his

> endeavours should be directed to persons and characters supernatural, or at least romantic; yet so as to transfer from our inward nature a human interest and a semblance of truth sufficient to procure for these shadows of imagination that willing suspension of disbelief for the moment, which constitutes poetic faith.[20]

Coleridge uses "romantic" here to hearken back to medieval romance, lending an air of unreality—of historical asynchronicity—to his project; his mariner is "ancient," out of and apart from the movement of time. Yet he asks us, his readers, to suspend our disbelief, to lend "human interest" and, even more significantly, "truth" to what we would otherwise see as "shadows" or imaginary ghosts. What he means by "truth" is implied by his use of the word "faith"; he demands of his readers that, despite the supernatural, ahistorical nature of his tales, they take these flitting shadows, these dream-like ideas, as reality.

This, after all, is the purpose of literature as a whole, and works of fantasy and horror demand of us an even more faithful suspension of disbelief. Matthias Rudolf places this in a philosophical context when he argues that

> indeed the *Biographia Literar*ia parallels the attempts of Kant's successors (Fichte and Schelling…), as well as the early German Romantics around the Schlegel brothers, Novalis and Hölderlin in Jena, to complete Kant's critical system by positing literature and the literary aesthetic as the locus where the supersensible could be presented substantially, rather than merely analogically as Kant had insisted.[21]

Rather than presenting an analogy—the albatross is *like* a cross around my neck—literature can make the albatross a real source of penance.

Metaphor, like the fiery eye of the mesmerist, then works to take something from the noumenal realm and *transport* it to a piece of paper, or a recitation, in the tangible world. Conversely, an albatross can come to mean something inexpressible, that sublime Thing. Here, I am indebted to Gavin Budge's recent study concerning medicine and the "natural supernatural," in which he writes that, for Coleridge, metaphor is the process "by which matter is spiritualized."[22] Faced with sublime, supernatural images, the reader fancies them real, producing the requisite effect of horror.

In this way, literature becomes a vehicle for madness, at least according to Dennis.[23] In 1701, Dennis wrote that

> the warmer the Imagination is, the more present the things are to us, of which we draw the Images, and therefore when once the Imagination is so inflam'd as to get the better of the understanding, there is no difference between the Images and the things themselves; as we see, for example, in Fevers and Mad men.[24]

Dennis here uses the image of warmth, of expansion, in order to envision closing the space between imagination and what he calls "the understanding." The Images, the mental pictures, become the "things themselves," but he connects this to people in delirious "fevers" and "Mad men." This, then, is a good starting place from which to explore Coleridge's mariner, a character caught between the past and present, dreams and reality, "understanding" and the most "mad" act of all: irrationally killing the albatross.

Most readers and critics of the *Rime* cannot find an explanation for the mariner's killing of this bird of "good omen." While I agree that there is no rational explanation, I argue that the negatively sublime feelings precipitated by the storm and the mariner's isolation become contained in the figure of the albatross. In this way, idea itself—a noumenal feeling irreducible to words—occasions horrors and apparitions. This terrifying feeling is replaced by the non-egoistic love for the water snakes and, later, the larger community of mankind, but the mariner is fated to remain alone, attempting, like the poet himself, to translate the sublime feeling into words to his mesmerized listeners.

Almost from the very beginning, the poem overwhelms its readers with sublime imagery—the ice, the mist, the storm, and the very notion of traveling to the South Pole are significant to Coleridge's neo-Platonic view of the world. Discussing the difference between Ideas and Nature, the material world and perception, he writes that

> these Theses refer solely to one of the two Polar Sciences, namely, to that which commences with, and rigidly confines itself within, the subjective, leaving the objective (as far as it is exclusively objective) to natural philosophy, which is its opposite pole...the result of both the sciences, or their *equatorial point* (emphasis mine), would be the principle of a total and undivided philosophy.[25]

The ship, as Coleridge informs us, "passed the Line" and travels "towards the South Pole," becoming mired near the equator. What, then, if the mariner's vision, and its eventual resolution, represent a "total and undivided philosophy," one encompassing the magical as well as the material? According to Stanley Cavell, "It may be…that killing the bird is derivative from the ensuing drift into the cold country, along with the other events of that realm; derivative both in itself being a consequence of transgression rather than an original transgression on its own…"[26] What if this equatorial philosophy allots as much weight to feelings, to intuition, as it does to ideas encased in the semiotic realm?

Coleridge derided the pure materialism of Lavater and of Bell and Spurzheim. In 1796, he wrote that he knew "a *great many* Physicians." "They," he wrote, "imagine that in the whole system of things there is nothing but Gut and Body."[27] Yet his interest in pathognomy is relevant here. Especially in his 1798 version of *Rime*, he was influenced by Beddoes, who believed in what Paul Youngquist calls "mental medicalism." Much as the body, as Youngquist has elsewhere argued, informs the workings of the mind, the passions of the mind inform the body.[28] Yet for Coleridge, these passions not only caused disease but, in fact, altered visual images. As he makes clear in his later "Dejection: An Ode," a change in *feelings* corresponds with a change in perception, and

> …we receive but what we give
> And in our life alone does nature live.
> Ours is her wedding-garment, ours her shroud! (IV, 47–49)[29]

Imagination dresses "nature," the disembodied spirit of the "external" world.

"Dejection" also takes place during a storm—or, rather, in anticipation of one. Coleridge's narrator sees the outline of the old moon in the light refracted by the new one, recalling folk belief that "we shall have a deadly storm." The narrator anticipates it, wishing that

> …even now the gust were swelling,
> And the slant night-shower driving loud and fast!
> Those sounds which oft have raised me, while they awed,
> And sent my soul abroad,
> Might now perhaps their wonted impulse give,
> Might startle this dull pain, and make it move and live! (15–20)[30]

The sounds of the storm, "loud and fast," achieve a sublime effect as they "awe" his soul, elevating his thoughts, and bring him to life. This "life," for him, lies in poetic creativity, a rejuvenation of his "genial spirit."[31]

The mariner's tale in *Rime* also begins with a sort of anticipation: an eerie silence that forces the mind to substitute its own feelings for material realities. The vast ocean, the solitude, and *lack* of sensory input occasion the mariner's initially feverish feelings. In addition to having read many contemporary accounts of exploration, Coleridge would have been aware, from mythology as well as from literature, of the trope of the haunted sailor. In "On Popular Illusions," Ferriar summarizes Lavater's 1570 *De Spectris* about how "unwary sailors" were deceived by specters in "Norwegian seas," adding that "solitude and silence will always produce apparitions."[32] In a 1799 letter to his wife Sara from Göttingen, Coleridge writes about his own solitude as an "extinction of light in my mind." "I have thought," he writes, "of a man who should lose his companion in a desert of sand, where his weary Halloos drop down in the air without an echo. I am deeply convinced that if I were to remain a few years among objects for whom I had no affection I should wholly lose the powers of intellect."[33] As readers, we are to assume that the mariner, even in the midst of the other, unnamed sailors, also feels isolated, solitary, and is beginning to "lose [his] powers of intellect."

In *Rime*, a similarly sublime storm becomes conflated with, or perhaps associated with, the albatross quite early in the poem. Coleridge read widely in Greek and Latin and would have known that the name for the albatross, *Procellariiformes*, comes from the Latin word *procella* meaning "a violent wind" or "a storm."[34] By the 1834 edition, Coleridge had made this connection even more clear when he describes the blast as

> …tyrannous and strong
> He struck with his o'ertaking wings
> And chased us south along. (42–44)[35]

The storm is awesome and exhibits the elements (namely, here, power), of the sublime, but "he" is also described as possessing "o'ertaking wings," much like the albatross itself. While critics (and Coleridge's own gloss) read the albatross as a saving spirit from the storm, I argue that Coleridge's imagery encourages us to read them both as sublime elements that occasion powerful feelings and, later, poetic creativity.

This movement from perception to feeling reveals the influence of David Hartley's theory of associationism, explored in the introduction and Chapter 3. To reiterate, a sensation can produce an association, which can then produce a successive association (A → B → C). When associations derive from past associations, the effect becomes exponential.[36] Because, according to Hartley, every sensation produces a vibration of the mind, a complex series of associations revolving around the same object,

> affecting one and the same part of the brain, in nearly one and the same manner, must irritate it at last, so as to enter the limits of pain, and approach to the states peculiar to fear, anxiety, despondency, peevishness, jealousy, and the rest of the tribe of hypochondriacal passions.[37]

In *Rime*, we definitely see fear, anxiety, despondency, and a host of other, almost undefinable passions. These passions, these feelings, circle back upon themselves, both in terms of the imagery and, as Ewan Jones points out, in the structure of the poem.

In considering philosophy as connected to form, Jones looks at the work of tautology, arguing that "Spatial and ontological difference is blurred into the close-to-hand, the self-identical, the already-known."[38] I wish to expand on his argument: to connect Coleridge's interest in tautology, in supposedly meaningless repetition, to his philosophical concern with the repeated idea…and its manifestation in poetry. Here, I circle back to (pun intended) Chapter 4, where I explored Keats's use of repetition in *Isabella, or the Pot of Basil.* Keats, too, repetitively rhymes similar sounds and often, in ballad form, repeats lines of poetry almost verbatim. Coleridge also uses ballad form, allowing his readers (or listeners) to be lulled into a quasi-trance. He uses tautology knowingly, substituting words for others so close in meaning that the repetition becomes meaningless. In his own words, he defines "tautegory," a word he coined, as a technique that enables

> That Law of Passion which inducing in the mind an unusual activity [to seek] for means to waste its superfluity — in the highest & most lyric kind, in passionate repetition of sublime tautology (as in the Song of Debora). [At her feet he bowed, he fell, he lay down; at her feet he bowed, he fell; where he bowed there he fell down dead.][39]

When a feeling stimulates the mind to this extent, the remainder, the residual feeling, needs to exist somewhere; for Coleridge, this happens with repetition of tautology. In his example, from the Bible, "he bowed" and "he fell" are so powerful that they must be allowed an outlet—in fact "he fell" is replaced with the tautological "he fell down dead." In *Rime* itself, many words are repeated, most famously "water, water everywhere/ and not a drop to drink," in a way that magnifies their emotional appeal. The constant repetition acts on the audience, evoking our "passion" until the final, "circular" statement, "He loveth best, that prayeth best," a statement that, through repetition, achieves a meaningless, but affective state.[40]

Even before the mariner shoots the bird, he exists in such a circular state, in between waking and sleeping, where feelings become ideas which, then, become realities, and back again. The mist and the snow are clearly sublime, and he associates the noise of the ice cracking with the "noises in a swound," or a fainting fit. Later, the "swound" reappears when the ship begins to move, flinging "the blood into [his] head/ [He falls] into a swound" (159). These two fainting episodes, after which according to McDonald, noises seem louder and assault the senses, bookend the ship's inability to move, the crew's inability to talk. This lack of will, of volition, also characterizes the dream; Erasmus Darwin's *Zoonomia* characterized dreams as an utter absence of volition.[41] Dreams are important to this poem, which literally takes place in a fog, or a dream-like state: "Whiles all the night, through fog-smoke white/ Glimmered the white moon-shine" (75–76). It is this dreamscape that produces ideas that become realities: the "fiends" and spirits referenced throughout the poem.

These fiends appear as early as the prayer by the wedding guest that God will save him from the "fiends that plague thee thus" (78). It is instructive here to return to Coleridge's letters, where he defines his condition of "atonic gout," which he refers to as "the Fiend," as one in which "the smallest impulses quickly and regularly recurrent aggregate themselves and again a kind of visual magnitude with a correspondent intensity of general feeling."[42] These impulses attack Coleridge's stomach, producing, sympathetically, an "intensity of general feeling." As I have argued in the introduction to this book, Romantic-era medical journals witnessed debates between the stomach and the brain as the source of "madness." In his letters, Coleridge posits the former, and he ties his own intense feelings back to the mariner's with the image of the fiend. In this same letter, Coleridge connects his intense feelings with his dreams, which "are no Shadows with me; but the real, substantial miseries of Life."[43] As the mariner's feelings become more intense, so do the poem's dream-like images, many of which feature spirits or fiends. This becomes especially apparent in the 1817 gloss, which features the word "Spirit" twelve times.

These spirits function to take feelings, which have become ideas, and lend them material sensation. In his notebooks, Coleridge writes, in 1798, that "Dreams sometimes useful by giving to the well-grounded *fears & hopes* of the understanding the *feelings* of vivid sense."[44] Coleridge begins his notion of the mental process with feelings: with "fears and hopes." As David Vallins writes, "ideas are set in motion by an emotion which played no part in their production."[45] In other words, the emotion, the feeling, exists *before* the idea. Coleridge writes in his notebook that one should "Mix up Truth & Imagination, so that the Imag[ination] may spread its own indefiniteness over that which really happened, & Reality its sense of *substance & distinctness* to Imagination."[46] Here again, "Reality" is useful only insofar as it lends "substance and distinctness" to the imagination-tinged event.

Perceptions, then, can lead to other perceptions, removing the Hartleian need for an initial source of sensory input. In this arena, Coleridge was influenced by Tom Wedgwood, who conducted experiments for Humphry Davy. Specifically, he seemed interested in the idea of "double touch"—if the subject crossed his or her first and second fingers and felt an object, blindfolded, the brain would think that there were two objects there. When the experimenter removed the blindfold, there was, of course, only one.[47] Wedgwood used this experiment to prove that "Ideas are not merely associated with other ideas…but can be associated with perceptions themselves."[48] These, then, as Coleridge writes in his letters, are connected to other perceptions.

Perceptions stem from a variety of senses, and, as the poem proceeds, Coleridge uses both visual and aural images to add distinctness to an association of perceptions which can only be described as irrational or, perhaps, dream-like:

> About, about, in reel and rout
> The death-fires danced at night;
> The water, like a witch's oils
> Burnt green, and blue and white. (127–130)

This effect clearly evokes astonishment, as the fires "dance" in a reel and the water assumes its brilliant colors. Scholars have rightly connected this with the effects of the aurora borealis,[49] but the extreme sensory effect is, in and of itself, important to understanding the mental state of the mariner. Later, too, we have a repetition in Coleridge's description of the water snakes who, "blue, glossy green, and velvet black/ ...coil'd and swam" (271–272). The blue and green colors, often associated with the sea itself, become vivid, oily, glossy, and "velvet," assuming interesting, unusual textures.

Sounds, too, mesmerize the mariner, the wedding guest, and, eventually, the reader/listener. Recall the cracking ice, which, according to contemporary accounts, made a horribly loud, grating noise, or the sound of the crew's souls as they whiz by the mariner, "like the whiz of my Cross-bow" (215). And, of course, the sound of the poem itself would affect the wedding guest and, by extension, the readers. Through meter and alliteration, Coleridge allows the poem to formally express the aural sublime:

> The breezes blew, the white foam flew
> The furrow follow'd free:
> We were the first that ever burst
> Into that silent sea. (99–102)

This passage, directly following the shooting of the albatross, is important to the plot but also to our sense of awe. Here, the alliteration emphasizes the eeriness of the "silent sea" with its repetition of (strangely snake-like) "f" and "s" sounds. Sound, too, emphasizes Coleridge's sublime landscape, what Matthias Rudolf calls a "cognitive geography."[50]

While the 1798 edition stresses the physical geography of the poem, the 1834 edition is focused on the mind, specifically on the strength of ideas and beliefs. The edition opens with a long quotation, in Latin, from Thomas Burnet's *Archeologiae Philosophicae* (1692), which ultimately argued that the Fall from Eden was symbolic rather than literal...and resulted in Burnet's resignation from court. Yet Burnet seems to have a complicated relationship with the symbol, attesting to both its power (a symbol, for example a cross worn around someone's neck, can become the thing it purports to be), and its dangers. Because Coleridge includes sections from Burnet's text, I quote his selection at length:

> I can easily believe, that there are more invisible than visible Beings in the universe. But who shall tell us what family each belongs to, what their ranks and relationships are and what their respective distinguishing characters may be? What do they do? Where do they live? The human mind has always circled around a knowledge of these things without ever attaining it. I do not doubt that it is beneficial sometimes to contemplate in the mind, as in a picture, the image of a greater [grander] and better world; for if the mind [spirit/thoughts] grows used to the trivia of daily life, it may dwindle too much [may contract itself too much], and decline altogether into worthless thoughts. Meanwhile, however, we must be on the watch for the truth, keeping a sense of proportion so that we can tell what is certain from what is uncertain and day from night.[51]

Burnet struggles between an acceptance of invisible Beings, the thought of which expands the mind and keeps it from "worthless thoughts," and a need to place them into a logical hierarchy, locating their "family," "rank," and "relationship." Not entirely suspending his disbelief, Burnet wonders what they "do" and "where…they live," attempting, like many hierarchical religions, to turn belief into system.

Coleridge's *Rime* seems to imply that the necessity for a system, a coherent narrative, disrupts the noumenal strength of the Idea, trying to force it into a reality. One of the systems that Coleridge merely hints at is the extensive mythology behind Catholicism; while the subject of Coleridge and religion is too large in scope for this chapter, he does mention the Virgin Mary multiple times and, in the 1834 gloss, details the "invocation of a guardian saint."[52] The attempt to categorize (much like Gall and Spurzheim did with the brain) is mocked in the gloss, notably when Coleridge tells us that, when the spirit follows the ship, it is neither a departed soul nor an angel, "concerning whom the learned Jew, Josephus, and the Platonic Cosmopolitan, Michael Psellus, may be consulted."[53] According to Josephus's own "dream reports," he did see "evil spirits" or "phantasms," but Coleridge's reference here might be a veiled reference to the wandering Jew (Josephus was exiled from his homeland and attempted to expiate his guilt by writing Jewish history) or, more probably, a red herring. Michael Psellos, a Byzantine philosopher, did write a classification of demons, turning them into a veritable hierarchy, but both of these references are attempts at finding scholarly validation for supernatural events.

Yet it is not conventional beliefs that have power in this poem; rather, it is the power of the repeated, irrational idea. The albatross itself, as other critics have argued, is just a bird until the crew decides that the Mariner "kill'd the Bird/ That made the Breeze to blow" (91–92). In the next stanza, when the sun rises, the crew changes their thinking: "all averr'd, I had kill'd the Bird/ That brought the fog and mist" (150). Thoughts might be fickle, but ideas have power, and they become the "Spirit" that plagues the mariner. They also become manifested tangibly as the Albatross itself. Instead of the cross, a symbol that has become imbued with meaning, the Albatross, also an equally "real" symbol, is hung around the mariner's neck. This guilt, and the sublime feelings wrought by the mariner's environment, wreak havoc on him, bringing him to a state of agony. The combination of the storm, the sea, the solitude, and the omen of the Albatross prey on the mariner's mind and also manifest in his body. Again, Beddoes and Coleridge believed in the motion of mental medicalism, wherein one's psychological state caused one's physiological response.

Coleridge details the physiological response most clearly through the mariner's eye. In a poem about the spectacular, and about specters, the eye clearly holds some importance; physician John Haslam, known for his writings about mental illness, declared that "The perceptions of the Eye, under an attentive inspection, leave on the Sensorium a phantasm or Idea of the object, a vivid memorial of that which has been perceived..."[54] In another work, he connects these phantasms with the eyes: "as straining the muscles produces fatigue, stiffness, and tremor;—as ocula spectra intrude on the forced and protracted attention of the visual organs,—so confusion ensues, when thought is racked and goaded to exhaustion."[55] Erasmus Darwin's *Zoonomia* also treats ocular spectra, which are usually splotches of vivid color that appear when one gazes at the sun for too long. However, Darwin also cites an instance when Benvenuto Celini, an Italian artist, painted on a mountain with a "conjurer," performing ceremonies to raise the devil. On his

> return the morning to Rome, and looking up when the sun began to rise, they saw numerous devils run on the tops of the houses, as they passed along; so much were the spectra of their weakened eyes magnified by fear.[56]

The vivid colors and skewed perspective of the ocular spectrum are "magnified by fear." Eyes play a large role in Coleridge's poem, from the "glittering eye" (17, 220, 442, 497) of the mariner and the crew to the inhabitant of the specter ship who curses the mariner "with his eye" (153). The wedding guest tells him that that, "which comes out of thine eye, doth make/ My body and soul to be still" (364–365). The glittering eye controls others in a sort of hypnosis or trance, recalling Benjamin Rush's assertion that "a man deprived of his reason…is for the most part easily terrified, or composed, by the eye of a man who possesses his reason."[57] Coleridge subverts this notion of animal magnetism, however, by having the mariner, the one "deprived of his reason," control the wedding guest, who, by all accounts, still possesses his. Like Anna Karsch, the mariner manifests his "illness" through his very power to possess someone else. The passage below recalls Haslam's description of ocular exhaustion:

> I closed my lids, and kept them close,
> And the balls like pulses beat;
> For the sky and the sea, and the sea and the sky,
> Lay like a load on my weary eye. (240–244)

The eyeballs move in response to the emotions evoked by the "sky and sea" until the mariner can no longer, physiologically speaking, see. The tongues of the mariner and his crew also turn black, dry, and mute as their emotions become more and more unspeakable.

While Coleridge cannot name the feeling that instantiates this "death in life," he makes the solution somewhat clear. It would, based on opinions of doctors and philosophers alike, make sense that, if an idea can thus infect the mind, a different idea—here blessing the slimy water beasts—can help it to heal. Yet the mariner also, and still, feels compelled to tell his story repeatedly. This might, as critics have argued, return him to the social world, the world outside of the mind where an idea is only an idea. Yet the mariner is not, in any sense of the word, "cured" by his spontaneous prayer or even the story's repetition. The pilot, upon seeing him, "falls down in a fit," and the pilot's boy,

> Who now doth crazy go,
> Laughed loud and long, and all the while
> His eyes went to and fro. (597–599)

Clearly, the mariner is still possessed by his terror to the degree that he can communicate it to the pilot and to his boy, whose eyes express a similar feeling. The mariner's compulsion to tell his story illustrates that terror still has dominance over his mind:

> Since then, at an uncertain hour
> That agony returns
> And til my ghastly tale is told
> The heart within me burns. (1834, 582–585)

The hour is "uncertain," and his body responds physiologically—"the heart within me burns"—until he can relieve himself. Yet the telling of the tale only provides momentary relief.

The tale, the story, is, in effect, the only vehicle to translate the idea, the signified, into a word, a reality. What was a "personal" experience for the mariner becomes a "universal" one (insofar as it is told to others, told to the narrator, and eventually told to us). "One," McDonald argues "makes contact with the numinous in the artistic mode through mediums such as dreams, archetypes, rituals, and works of art; and, therefore, the meaning of the numinous in this mode is both ambiguously personal and universal at once."[58] The mariner asks the hermit to "shrieve" him, to hear his confession (OED). Thus the hermit is the first person to whom he recounts his tale, enacting a penance but, more importantly, communicating the power of his idea to someone else. The mariner has, as Coleridge puts it, a "strange" power of speech, a power of words to captivate, to enthrall, to leave the person a "sadder and a wiser man" (657). This is the power used by storytellers, poets, and all artists: the power to turn their perceptions, their ideas, into real words on a printed page or, in the case of visual artists, real images.

If the idea cannot be contained, if it is so powerful that it must be transferred, then the poet or author might be a vehicle, mesmerized by his ideas as much as he mesmerizes his readers and listeners. Like Coleridge's Aeolian Harp, the poet is inspired, in turn inspiring others. Yet this model of poetry, and of authorship in general, is a compulsive, painful one. Like Anna Karsch, whose eyes emanated poetic fire—a fire that, like the one encircling the scorpion, can mortally wound—the poet might rather not be subject to the fate of constantly, compulsively telling a story. And yet, telling, attempting to signify the otherwise overwhelming idea, is the only way to attain even momentary relief from the weight of the authorial albatross.

Part II: "Des Idees"—The Horror of Ideality in Edgar Allan Poe

While many sublime elements contribute to the ultimate horror of Coleridge's *The Ancient Mariner*, Edgar Allan Poe, heavily influenced by British Romantic writers, philosophers, and proto-psychologists, focuses his "penetrating gaze" on one idea: the idea of death. Death has been connected with the obscurity and terror of the sublime; while none of us know what happens to "us" after death, we, as Smith puts it, sympathize with the dead person. For him, it is inconceivable to

> be deprived of the light of the sun; to be shut out from life and conversation; to be laid in the cold grave; to be prey to corruption and the reptiles of the earth; to be no more thought of in this world, but to be obliterated, in a little time, from the affections, and almost from the memory, of their dearest friends and relations.[59]

While the dead person could not experience these feelings, this sympathetic approach to death brings up the fears associated with premature burial which, as Adam Bradford, James Hutchisson, and others have pointed out, was a real anxiety in early nineteenth-century America (and Europe).[60] What if the body "laid in the cold grave" was still living? Reptiles and rot could prey upon a body, living but helpless to call out to "dearest friends and relations."

In "Premature Burial" (1850), Poe's narrator uses Smith's sympathetic technique, addressing his audience in second person about the literal horror of what Coleridge had called "life-in-death." The narrator turns to tell the reader, with confidence, that "it may be asserted" that nothing can distress us more than the thought of burial before death:

> The unendurable oppression of the lungs—the stifling fumes of the damp earth—the clinging to the death garments—the rigid embrace of the narrow house—the blackness of the absolute Night—the silence like a sea that overwhelms—the unseen but palpable presence of the Conqueror Worm... with memory of dear friends who would fly to save us if but informed of our fate...[61]

Including his readers in this psychological speculation, Poe uses elements of the sublime, including smell ("stifling fumes"); darkness, which Burke associated with the sublime; silence and solitude that recall Coleridge's poem, "like a sea that overwhelms"; and power, represented here by the "Conqueror Worm." With the addition of the "narrow house," he also introduces a fear of confinement or entrapment, both sublime in their own ways.

While my focus will be not on biography, but on the philosophical and medical foundations of what Poe would have conceived of as "monomania," it is useful to mention that Poe also had reason to fear death—the early death of his parents, the death of his foster mother, and the premature death of his first love clearly resound in his literary works. And resound they do, both literally (most notably in his poetry) and figuratively in his many prose works featuring characters who either do not die or who come back to life. These characters are often framed as—or deliberately labeled as—"monomaniacal" (unlike Coleridge, Poe wrote after Esquirol had coined the term monomania).

Poe clearly had access to the ideas of physiognomy and phrenology (Lavater, Spurzheim, and Gall) elaborated earlier in this chapter. Benjamin Rush, lauded as America's first "psychiatrist," argues that a predisposition to madness is connected with dark hair and light eyes, a prototype that we see over and over again in Poe's works (and one that characterized Poe himself).[62] A *Philadelphia Saturday Museum* sketch of Poe's life, one that he almost certainly wrote, is a phrenological estimate of himself: "... his forehead is extremely broad, displaying prominently the organs of Ideality, Causality, Form, Constructiveness, and Comparison, with small Eventuality and Individuality."[63] In other words, Poe assessed himself phrenologically and found that he was given to ideation, to pondering cause and effect, but not to a sense of future consequences or, even more damning, a strong sense of "self."

Other psychological ideas also interested Poe; Rush had argued that madness originated in the "blood vessels of the brain," and that blood vessels "are, to a physician, what the meridian sun is to a mariner," a comparison that could not have been lost on either Poe or his contemporaries.[64] Rush, in turn, was greatly influenced by many of Coleridge's later contemporaries. Benjamin Franklin, who Poe knew of and read, had traveled to London and recommended Rush to Sir Alexander Dick, president of the Royal Society of Physicians.[65] In London, Rush stayed for the lectures of William Hunter (lecturer, obstetrician, and brother of John Hunter, anatomist). He attracted notables like Edmund Burke and Edward Gibbon and met Mark Akenside at Saint Thomas.[66] He also met

Joshua Reynolds, who invited him to dine with Samuel Johnson, Oliver Goldsmith, and other literary characters.[67]

Poe was also connected to Esquirol and French proto-psychologists through his friend Pliny Earle, the superintendent of New York's Bloomingdale Asylum, who also wrote a piece for the *Journal of Insanity* called "Poets of Insanity," detailing the way/s in which imagination could lead to poetry, madness, or, more commonly, both. For Earle, Rush, and others, "the ubiquitous mental illness called monomania, in which the patient becomes fixated on one particular idea to the point of delusion, is the medical correlative of what Emerson described as the soul-sickness stemming from the "divided or social state" of modern life."[68] As Lennard Davis has posited in *Obsession: A History*, the very mechanization of the industrial age was thought to drive people toward obsessive actions and thoughts.

Monomania was of particular interest to both nineteenth-century American medicine and law because it was the example *par excellence* of what Rush and proto-psychologist James Cowles Prichard termed "moral insanity." "Moral" insanity was a type of partial insanity that affected only a part of the brain. As Prichard writes, "The individual affected is, under ordinary circumstances, calm, and exhibits no symptom of that perturbation and constant excitement which are observed in raving madness."[69] Instead, the monomaniac's problem was with "volition": facing an impulse, like shooting an albatross, possessing a woman's teeth, or killing a man with a disturbing eye, the monomaniac cannot help but to act on it. Prichard expands upon this, explaining that what begins as a "phantom," an unassociated idea, eventually becomes "reality."[70] Differentiating himself from Pinel, Esquirol, and most continental proto-psychologists, Prichard held that monomania was the first step toward a total state of insanity: one that would end in "delirium" or "idiocy." Learning to read the signs—through art or literature, but most reliably through "empirical" means—could keep the partially insane from moving further along the spectrum.

Like Coleridge, Poe was fascinated by the maddening consequences of the repeated idea. He was influenced by Coleridge himself, namely the *Biographia Literaria*, which he somewhat replicates, or "purloins," as Alexander Schultz would have it, in his texts concerning composition and poetry.[71] Poe himself, in an 1840 review of Thomas Moore's "Alciphron," lists Coleridge as one of the pioneers of imagination and refers to three of his works: "Kubla Khan," "Rime of the Ancient

Mariner," and "Christabel."[72] While Poe does, as Schultz puts it, "purloin" some of Coleridge's already "purloined" ideas, he also evinces mixed feelings about the elder poet's interest in metaphysics:

> Of Coleridge I cannot speak but with reverence. His towering intellect! his gigantic power!...He has imprisoned his own conceptions by the barrier he has erected against those of others. It is lamentable to think that such a mind should be buried in metaphysics, and, like the Nyctanthes, waste its perfume upon the night alone.[73]

On one hand, Poe is in awe of Coleridge, seeing in him the "towering intellect" and "gigantic power" typical of the sublime. On the other, his interest in appealing to his audience's emotions—giving his reader a sustained, "supernal" response—forces him to lament Coleridge's inwardly focused texts. Like the Nyctanthes, flowers that only bloom at night, Coleridge is "buried" in metaphysics, almost buried alive by the solipsism of his own thoughts.

Here, then, we have an author who wrote for popular magazines and miscellanies, whose interest in the science of the mind influenced his own poetical theories, but who was also interested in the effects of the sublime. While he almost certainly did not read Kant—his *Eureka* mocks the "oneness" that the Kantian sublime ultimately ends in—his works illustrate an interest in the physiological sublime of Burke.[74] Unlike Burke, he does not separate the sublime and the beautiful; in fact, beauty, for Poe, contains elements of the sublime. Yet his interest in the repeated idea does recall Burke's link of repetition to the "madman." One could write a book about Poe and obsession, but I will focus here on two of his stories, "Berenice" (1835), and "The Tell-Tale Heart" (1843). Both of these stories feature what Gall and Spurzheim would call a diseased organ of ideality: an idea, or "phantom," as Prichard would have it, that eventually becomes a reality. In Poe's stories, this idea overwhelms the protagonist until it overtakes his volition, causing him to act on irrational impulse.

Egæus, the narrator of "Berenice," begins his tale by musing upon both misery and heredity; reminiscent of other Poe tales, namely "Fall of the House of Usher," he focuses his attention on family portraits, highlighting the fact that we have all, in some way, lived before our births. Rush had argued that monomania is hereditary, but Poe's Egæus points toward something even more macabre when he recollects that

> my earliest years are connected with that chamber...Herein was I born. But it is mere idleness to say that I had not lived before — that the soul has no previous existence. You deny it. Let us not argue the matter. Convinced myself I seek not to convince. There is, however, a remembrance of ærial forms — of spiritual and meaning eyes — of sounds musical yet sad — a remembrance which will not be excluded: a memory like a shadow, vague, variable, indefinite, unsteady — and like a shadow too, in the impossibility of my getting rid of it, while the sunlight of my reason shall exist.[75]

Anticipating the denial of the reader, the "you" addressed in this passage, Poe nevertheless begins this story by musing about "life in death," in this case the lives of Egaeus's ancestors as intermingled with his own. This theme will later be more prominent in "Ligeia" (1838), but it is noteworthy that a horror story about teeth begins with this musing on an "undefinable" memory, "musical yet sad," "like a shadow, vague, variable, indefinite, unsteady." All of these adjectives define something obscure, spectral, and sublime.

Linked with the notion of death, Poe introduces his idea of the sublime; in his *Poetic Principle*, he writes that "We are often made to feel, with a shivering delight, that from an earthly harp are stricken notes which cannot have been unfamiliar to the angels."[76] The "shivering delight" gained from reaching an elevated state is one that we have seen throughout this book, from Shelley's Victor Frankenstein to Coleridge's mariner. Also, like Baillie and Coleridge, Poe introduces the element of music, something Dennis Pahl has connected to Poe's sublime. Aural elements "often constitute the emotional power behind Poe's literary art, and at times Poe affords to sound an even greater priority than logical sense, as reflected in such works as 'The Bells,' 'Ulalume,' and 'The Raven'."[77] In all of these poems, Poe repeats various sounds and phrases until their sense becomes "incantatory" working to put the reader in a sublime state.[78]

Yet "Berenice" is not a poem, nor is its chief subject matter the notion of "musical" memories, so why begin the story in this way? I believe that the subject of this story is not really Berenice, or her teeth, but the repeated idea. As in Coleridge's *Mariner*, this is reinforced by Poe's focus on visions and dreams. As Egaeus's character unfolds, we learn that he lives inside his mind. "The realities of the world," he tells his reader, "affected me as visions, and as visions only, while the wild ideas of the land of dreams became, in turn, not the material of my every-day existence, but in very deed that existence utterly and solely in itself."[79] As Coleridge also wrote in his letters, the external appearances of the world become secondary to ideas presented through visions and dreams. In an 1839 article entitled "An Opinion on Dreams," Poe elaborates upon this, arguing that each individual contains three components: the body, the "mind," and the soul. For Poe, the mind connects the soul and the body. Although the body might sleep and the mind also might sleep,

> the soul never sleeps; which assertion may receive additional confirmation from the following argument; that were it only for one single moment to be unconscious of its existence, this would at once break in upon its eternal principle, as being a suspension of its own powers, and which cannot happen to eternity. It is the slumber of the mind and not the soul, therefore, which causes forgetfulness.[80]

In this story, "forgetfulness" is a prominent theme, not only for Egaeus—as we shall soon see—but also for Berenice, who suffers attacks of epilepsy.

Berenice's epilepsy is of interest here because it forces her "mind" to slumber. Thus, her "species" of the disorder results in "trance itself—trance very nearly resembling positive dissolution, and from which her manner of recovery was in most instances, startlingly abrupt."[81] Berenice's trances seem unrelated to the story's subsequent events, but they do reiterate the theme of visions and forgetfulness, as well as the sense of "dissolution" that evoke Poe's sense of the sublime. Biographically, Poe himself experienced this "dissolution," experiencing long periods of forgetfulness and personality change that Dr. Carl W. Bazil has attributed to seizures of "prolonged postictal states," states of altered consciousness after epileptic seizures.[82] In this type of state, the mind and the body were clearly volition-less, but what would it reveal about the sufferer's soul?

Poe's introduction concerning misery and heredity, his explication of Egaeus's character, and his mention of Berenice's epileptic states all contribute to the crux of this story: after Berenice, who Egaeus has married, begins to experience her seizures, Egaeus also becomes ill with "monomania." While his "mind" still functions in this state, it focuses its attention on seemingly insignificant objects. Once he "meditate[es]" on an object, the idea tied to it repeats; "the meditations were never pleasurable; and, at the termination of the reverie, the first cause, so far from being out of sight, had attained that supernaturally exaggerated interest which was the prevailing feature of the disease."[83] Echoing Hartley's notion of association, the "first cause," the primary sensation, occasions other ideas that only serve the strengthen the initial "trigger." Here, we see Poe echoing Rush, Prichard, and Esquirol's notion of "monomania," but the idea remains vague and inexpressible. Instead, we know that insignificant objects occasion what can only be called a terrifying sublimity.

The "object" on which Egaeus fixates is, interestingly in light of my chapter about erotomania, a part of Berenice's body: her teeth. The thought of the "white and ghastly spectrum of the teeth," cannot be "driven away" from the "disordered chamber" of his brain, perhaps his organ of ideality. The word "spectrum" also evokes the image of the rainbow presented at the beginning of the story: "MISERY is manifold. The wretchedness of earth is multiform. Overreaching the wide horizon like the rainbow, its hues are as various as the hues of that arch, as distinct too, yet as intimately blended."[84] Here, the spectrum of the rainbow, like the teeth, symbolizes misery and wretchedness. If this is the idea evoked by the object (who happens to be a living woman), then this idea follows Egaeus mercilessly. "Teeth!" he tells us, "they were here, and there, and everywhere," somewhat purloining Coleridge's line, "Water water everywhere/ and not a drop to drink." The teeth, like Lorenzo's head in Keats's poem, become a fetish object, completely disembodied from their possessor.

Also like Keats's Isabella, Poe's Egaeus exists in a world of his own making: a world inhabited by Berenice's teeth. He longs for them with a "phrenzied desire," and they become "the essence of [his] mental life."[85] The word "phrenzy" has often been used by the Romantics, but the second phrase gives us pause: is his imagination inhabited by teeth? If so, are all of his ideas of teeth? Poe complicates this notion of ideality even more when he compares a quotation from Marie Salle, "Que tous ses pas etaient des sentiments" [her every step was a sentiment] with how he feels about Berenice: "que toutes ses dents etaient des idees. Des idees!—ah" [that all of her teeth were ideas. Ideas!].[86] Here, Poe plays with the notion of ideation: if ideas can be perceived as realities, can "realities," like hard, enduring teeth, assume the essence of ideas?

Poe's masterful ending turns this around once more: when Egaeus reads a quotation from a poet, Ebn Zaiat, he takes an idea and turns it into a disturbing reality. After a long lapse of memory, similar to Berenice's lapses or even Poe's own, he awakens to the thought that he had "done a deed." He looks to a book that lies open next to him and reads the following sentence: "*Dicebant mihi sodales si sepulchrum amicæ visitarem* [[*visitarem*]] *curas meas aliquantulum fore levatas*," translated as "my companions told me I might find some little alleviation of my misery, in visiting the grave of my beloved."[87] When one thinks of "visiting the grave" of a "beloved" person, one assumes the visitant standing by the graveside, paying respects. Taken literally, however, Egaeus's "misery" is his desire for Berenice's teeth…and so the "alleviation" consists of taking them from her still-living body ("a body enshrouded, yet still breathing, still palpitating, still alive!") and placing them in a box together with "instruments of dental surgery."[88] Here, Egeaus's monomania manifests itself in a deranged sense of "ideality": one in which the commonplace idea becomes an all-too-disturbing reality.

One wonders about the implied audience of "Berenice": the "you" who might object to Egaeus's beliefs about the persistence of the soul. Much as the ancient mariner needs to keep retelling his story, Egaeus needs to write down his account. Echoing the concerns about death and immortality, this is, as Clayton Koelb points out, a sort of "revivification": "The hideous drama of revivification taking place in the narrative is doubly chilling because it is repeated, wittingly or not, willingly or not, and to varying degrees, by those to whom the narrative is directed."[89] In other words, the minute readers read this story, we form an image in our own minds: an "idea" of Berenice's defiled body that brings it to life, again and again. Koelb continues by linking ideality to writing: "The letters on the page live or die according to how they are seen by the shining orbs that look upon them."[90] Here, it is the reader who is compelled to read, to interpret, and to compulsively retell the story.

This sense of compulsion is even stronger in Poe's more famous "The Tell-Tale Heart," where it is not only the heart, but, more significantly, the narrator who cannot help but tell his tale. Here, we have a much clearer sense of audience, one that hearkens back, as many critics have argued, to the contemporary controversy of the "insanity defense." From working as a magazine editor, Poe knew of the cases involving attorney Peter A. Browne, who attempted to argue that crimes could occur as a result of insanity—without volition. The type of insanity he focused on was, significantly, partial insanity, or monomania. Although he argued that some might find his defense based on "new fangled doctrines," or "a *modern French* notion" which recalls Pinel and Esquirol, he firmly believed that these criminals were subject to "irresistible impulses."[91]

Undergirding this defense were the theories of Dr. Isaac Ray, America's leading nineteenth-century authority on medical jurisprudence. He grounded his knowledge on Gall and Spurzheim, explaining that moral faculties and intellectual faculties were, quite simply, located in different areas of the brain.[92] A person could maintain reason and be, biologically speaking, morally defective.

The beginning of "The Tell-Tale Heart" takes on a defensive tone as the narrator tells his reader (perhaps a member of law enforcement?) to "observe how healthily --how calmly I can tell you the whole story."[93] The use of the word "calm" evokes Prichard's notion, quoted earlier in this chapter, that "The individual affected [with monomania] is, under ordinary circumstances, calm, and exhibits no symptom of that perturbation and constant excitement which are observed in raving madness."[94] Of course, the narrator's idea that he is "healthy" leads us to believe the opposite, but we are immediately put in the position of judging, perhaps "shrieving" the narrator. This nameless narrator, like Egaeus, feels compelled to tell us the story of his obsession.

The eye—Karsch's eye, the mariner's eye, the protuberant eye of asylum sketches—has come to haunt this chapter, and so it is fitting that it haunts Poe's narrator. Again, the narrator details why one would feel compelled to judge him insane:

> Object there was none. Passion there was none. I loved the old man. He had never wronged me. He had never given me insult. For his gold I had no desire. I think it was his eye! yes, it was this! He had the eye of a vulture --a pale blue eye, with a film over it. Whenever it fell upon me, my blood ran cold; and so by degrees --very gradually --I made up my mind to take the life of the old man, and thus rid myself of the eye forever.[95]

Succinctly, in short sentences, he lists the reasons that his crime cannot be considered sane: there is no "object," no "passion," no mercenary desire. Instead, his eye resembles that of a "vulture." The film over the eye obscures it, making it foggy, unreadable; because vultures feed on dead carrion, this reinforces the connection with death. In order to "rid [himself]" of this chilling sense of sublimity, the narrator feels that he must, paradoxically, kill what he reads as an idea suggesting death.

As in "Berenice," this idea "haunted me day and night." Even though he formulates a plan, he cannot kill the old man unless his "Evil Eye" is open, with a ray of light shining on it. Although B. D. Tucker argues that "it does not seem to be superstition that preys upon the mind of the narrator," Poe's use of the superstitious term is too evocative to not be mentioned.[96] According to folklore scholars, the evil eye would cause "injurious effects" but, interestingly, without the possessor's consent or will. In "all cases," the evil eye was involuntary, often possessed by people who had no malicious intentions.[97] Poe would have known of this superstition, and the "involuntary" nature of the evil eye parallels the narrator's (legally assumed) involuntary monomania. Poe intends for us to link the two, as is clear in the death scene, when the narrator tells his auditor/reader that the old man's groan was

> not a groan of pain or of grief --oh, no! --it was the low stifled sound that arises from the bottom of the soul when overcharged with awe. I knew the sound well. Many a night, just at midnight, when all the world slept, it has welled up from my own bosom, deepening, with its dreadful echo, the terrors that distracted me.[98]

Our narrator connects to the old man on the basis of a sound that arises from a sublime state of the soul, "overcharged with awe." Later, he mentions "terrors that distracted me," adding the second component of the Burkean sublime. The sound, the notion of the "dreadful echo," and the alliteration of "stifled sound" all add to the passage's tone, evoking feelings of terror in the reader as well.

We have already briefly considered the incantatory nature of Poe's poetry; here, he plays with the ringing in his ears and the old man's heartbeat, each driving the narrator further into insanity. Writing about a suicidal, monomaniacal patient, Prichard mentions the "ringing or burring noise" in her head.[99] Already faced with a repeated, grating sound, the narrator now also begins to hear the beating of the old man's buried heart. Here again, Poe uses the sounds of his words, the order of his diction, to heighten the sublime effect:

> I talked more quickly — more vehemently; — but the noise steadily increased. I arose, and argued about trifles, in a high key and with violent gesticulations; — but the noise steadily increased. Why *would* they not be gone? I paced the floor to and fro, with heavy strides, as if excited to fury by the observations of the men; — but the noise steadily increased. Oh God! what *could* I do? I foamed — I raved — I swore! I swung the chair upon which I had sat, and grated it upon the boards; — but the noise arose over all and continually increased. It grew louder — louder —*louder!*[100]

The continued repetition of the "I"—"I talked," "I arose," "I paced,"—and the repetition of "the noise steadily increased" allows the story's readers to also experience the grating quality of constant repetition. His use of dashes adds to the manic quality of the passage until we come to the final "louder—louder—*louder!*"

When Poe's readers finish this story, they are to also feel the sublime effects of the old man's filmy evil eye, the continued ringing of the ears, and the constant, ever-louder beating of the old man's heart. Like the Ancient Mariner, the story's narrator must "tell" his account, both to the officers who seem to not suspect him at all, and to the readers of the *Pioneer*, the magazine in which it was published. Again, obsession results in art, and the readers' reaction to the story would—and has—resulted in its constant retellings. Yet Poe, unlike Coleridge, does not even attempt to place a religious, moral, or transcendent meaning on his sublime (In *Eureka*, he mocks Kant and other metaphysical thinkers who do this). In *Communities of Death*, Adam Bradford argues that Poe, through his use of horror, urged his readers to repulse the horrific idea and, in doing so, reach for something transcendent. I agree that Poe's works evince an anxiety about memorializing death but, much as the mariner never finds relief after telling his story, these "memorials" (the teeth, the bells, the raven, and the old man's heart) only serve to contribute to the reader's sense of the negative, traumatic sublime. In fact, I would argue that he subverts the notion of memorialization by "visiting" Berenice's grave but desecrating her living body, or killing the old man but hearing his (equally disembodied) beating heart.

Instead of "repulsing" the horrific idea, Poe seems to consider it essential to the quality attributed most to artists: the sense of ideality. Living in a world of ideas is, in fact, necessary to art, which seems to be the one form of relief from their constant presence; as in Coleridge's poem, both of Poe's narrators feel a need to defend their actions, tell their stories, and confess their crimes. These ideas also travel, whether from the mariner to the wedding guest to the poem's readers or from Poe's narrators to their auditors and to the many readers of circulating magazines. The eyes of the readers become mesmerized by these sublime ideas until they too exist in a world of ideality.

NOTES

1. Susanne Kord, "From Evil Eye to Poetic Eye: Witch Beliefs and Physiognomy in the Age of Enlightenment," in *Practicing Progress: The Promise and Limitations of Enlightenment: Festschrift for John A. McCarthy*, eds. Richard E. Schade and Dieter Sevin (Amsterdam: Rodopi, 2007), 46.
2. Quoted in Kord, 35.
3. Samuel Taylor Coleridge, *Biographia Literaria* (Public Domain Books, 2012), Kindle Edition, 229.
4. Bruce Mills, *Poe, Fuller, and the Mesmeric Arts* (Columbia: University of Missouri Press, 2006), 34.
5. Quoted in Mills, 38.
6. J. P. F. Deleuze, *Practical Instruction in Animal Magnetism*, trans. T. C. Hartshorn (London, 1850), 101.
7. Lavater, *Physiognomy*, 308.
8. Ibid., 308.
9. Albert Boime, "Portraying Monomaniacs to Service the Alienist's Monomania: Géricault and Georget," *The Oxford Art Journal* 14, no. 1 (1991): 82.
10. Johann Spurzheim, *The Physiognomical System of Drs. Gall and Spurzheim, Founded on an Anatomical and Physiological Examination of the Nervous System in General, and of the Brain in Particular; and Indicating the Dispositions and Manifestations of the Mind* (London, 1815), 346, accessed via Google Books.
11. Ibid., 346–347.
12. *The Phrenological Journal and Miscellany*, vol. 1 (Edinburgh, 1824), 513.
13. Scholars have also commented on Spurzheim and Gall's connections to the growing field of "racial science," a "science" intended to showcase the superiority of Europeans, namely Britons. See especially Stephen Tomlinson, *Head Masters: Phrenology, Secular Education, and Nineteenth-Century Social Thought* (Tuscaloosa, AL: University Alabama Press, 2005). The *Phrenological Journal* includes a list of skull sizes that compares the painter Raphael, with a 5 1/2 inch temple, to a "Hindoo" at 4 1/8 inches, and a "Negro," smallest at 3 7/8 inches. Clearly, these writers view ideality as a positive quality and do not seem to refer to the visions, magic, or astrological beliefs mentioned by Gall and Spurzheim themselves.
14. Coleridge, *Biographia Literaria*, 26.
15. Ibid., 244.
16. Ibid., 90.

17. Quoted in Nichola Deane, "Coleridge and JC Lavater's *Essays on Physiognomy*," *Notes and Queries* 49, no. 1 (2002): 29.
18. Julian Knox, "Coleridge and the Arts," in *Oxford Handbook of Samuel Taylor Coleridge*, ed. Frederick Burwick (Oxford: Oxford University Press, 2009), 627.
19. Richardson, *British Romanticism*, 3.
20. Coleridge, *Biographia Literaria*, 99.
21. Matthias Rudolf, "Unspeakable Discovery: Romanticism and the 'Rime of the Ancient Mariner'," *European Romantic Review* 24, no. 2 (2013): 185.
22. Gavin Budge, *Romanticism, Medicine, and the Natural Supernatural* (Basingstoke: Palgrave, 2013), 97.
23. For more about John Dennis, please see my introduction to this book.
24. John Dennis, *The Advancement and Reformation of Modern Poetry: A Critical Discourse.In Two Parts. … By Mr Dennis* (London: Printed for Rich. Parker, 1701), 33.
25. Coleridge, *Biographia Literaria*, 87.
26. Stanley Cavell, *In Quest of the Ordinary* (Chicago: University of Chicago Press, 1988), 57.
27. Samuel Taylor Coleridge, "Letter to Charles Lloyd," quoted in George Rousseau, "Coleridge's Dreaming Gut: Digestion, Genius, Hypochondria," in *Cultures of the Abdomen: Diet, Digestion, and Fat in the Modern World*, ed. C. Forth (New York: Palgrave, 2005), 117.
28. See Paul Youngquist, "Romantic Dietetics! Or, Eating Your Way to a New You," in *Cultures of Taste/Theories of Appetite*, ed. Timothy Morton (New York: Palgrave, 2004).
29. Coleridge, *Major Works*, 115.
30. Ibid., 114.
31. Coleridge, *Complete Works*, 115.
32. Quoted in Budge, *Romanticism, Medicine*, 76, 75.
33. Kathleen Raine, ed., *The Letters of Samuel Taylor Coleridge* (London: Grey Walls Press, 1950), 93.
34. A. F. Gotch, "Albatrosses, Fulmars, Shearwaters, and Petrels," in *Latin Names Explained: A Guide to the Scientific Classifications of Reptiles, Birds & Mammals* (New York: Facts on File, 1996), 190.
35. All line numbers for Coleridge's *Rime* are from the 1798 edition (Bedford St. Martin's, 2000), ed. Paul Fry.
36. Priestley, *Hartley's theory*, 16.
37. Ibid., 231.
38. Ewan James Jones, *Coleridge and the Philosophy of Poetic Form* (Cambridge: Cambridge University Press, 2014), 171.
39. Samuel Taylor Coleridge, *The Notebooks of Samuel Taylor Coleridge*, October–November 1811, 2 vols., ed. Kathleen Coburn (New York: Bollingen, 1957), 4113.

40. Jones, *Coleridge and the Philosophy*, 186.
41. Richardson, *British Romanticism*, 6.
42. 1803, Letter to Southey, 130. According to John Gardiner's 1793 *An Inquiry into the Nature, Cause, and Cure of the Gout and Some of the Diseases with Which It Is Connected*, "no disease is attended with a greater variety of nervous complaints" (67). The atonic gout, an "irregular" form said to afflict the elderly, and "the external parts of the head, brain, and with it the mind, are variously affected" (69).
43. Raine, *Letters*, 130.
44. Seamus Perry, ed., *Coleridge's Notebooks: A Selection* (Oxford: Oxford University Press, 2002), 6.
45. David Vallins, ed., *Coleridge's Writings. Vol. 5, On the Sublime* (Basingstoke: Palgrave Macmillan, 2003), 32.
46. Perry, *Notebooks*, 36.
47. Budge, *Romanticism, Medicine*, 108.
48. Quoted in Budge, 112.
49. See Dewey W. Hall, "Wordsworth and Emerson: Aurora Borealis and the Question of Influence," *Romanticism and Victorianism on the Net* 50 (2008).
50. Rudolf, "Unspeakable Discovery," 190.
51. Coleridge, *Rime*, 27.
52. Ibid., 55.
53. Ibid., 37.
54. John Haslam, *On the Nature of Thought, or the Act of Thinking* (London, 1835), 5, National Library of Medicine, USA.
55. John Haslam, *Sound Mind* (London, 1819), 125, National Library of Medicine, USA.
56. Erasmus Darwin, *Zoonomia*, vol. 1, xl.2.3 (E. Earle, 1818), 447, accessed via Google Books.
57. Rush, *Medical Inquiries*, 175.
58. Beth E. McDonald, *The Vampire as Numinous Experience: Spiritual Journeys with the Undead in British and American Literature* (Jefferson and London: McFarland, 2004), 59.
59. Adam Smith, *The Essential Adam Smith*, ed. Robert L. Heilbroner (New York: W. W. Norton, 1987), 68.
60. See Adam Bradford, *Communities of Death: Whitman, Poe, and the American Culture of Mourning* (Columbia: University of Missouri Press, 2014) and James M. Hutchisson, *Poe* (Jackson: University Press of Mississippi, 2005).
61. Edgar Allan, Poe, *Tales and Sketches*, vols. 1 and 2, ed. Thomas Ollive Mabbott (Chicago: University of Illinois Press, 1978), 204.

62. The use of "psychiatrist" here is only somewhat anachronistic. The term was coined in 1869, but the word "psychiatry" was already in use in 1828 as "the branch of medicine concerned with the causes, diagnosis, treatment, and prevention of mental illness" (*Oxford English Dictionary*). Rush, *Medical Inquiries*, 54, 55.
63. Michael J. Deas, "The *Saturday Museum* Woodcut," in *The Portraits and Daguerreotypes of Edgar Allan Poe* (1989), 15, Edgar Allan Poe Society of Baltimore, http://www.eapoe.org/papers/misc1921/deas102a.htm.
64. Rush, *Medical Inquiries*, 29.
65. David Freeman Hawke, *Benjamin Rush: Revolutionary Gadfly* (New York: Bobbs-Merrill Company, 1971), 51.
66. Ibid., 65, 67.
67. Ibid., 71.
68. Benjamin Reiss, *Theaters of Madness: Insane Asylums and Nineteenth-Century American Culture* (Chicago and London: University of Chicago Press, 2008), 126.
69. James Cowles Prichard, *A Treatise on Insanity and Other Disorders Affecting the Mind* (New York: Arno Press, 1835), 28.
70. Ibid., 28.
71. See Alexander Schultz, "Purloined Voices: Edgar Allen Poe Reading Samuel Taylor Coleridge." *Studies in Romanticism* 47 (Summer 2008).
72. Mills, *Poe, Fuller*, 64. Poe also pays homage to Coleridge in many of his stories, most notably "MS Found in a Bottle." In this story of a shipwreck and subsequent rescue by a ship of (geriatric) ghosts, Poe utilizes the sublimity of the sea in a Coleridgean way: he writes about the "unfathomable ocean," and, during the ship's upheaval, the narrator explains that they "gasped for breath at an elevation beyond the albatross—at times became dizzy with the velocity of our descent into some watery hell." While the narrator does not compulsively tell his story, he does write the story up until the moment of his demise. In Poe's biography, Hutchisson argues that it is the writing itself that keeps this narrator alive.
73. Edgar Allan Poe, "Letter to B——," in *Southern Literary Messenger* (July 1836), 501, Edgar Allan Poe Society of Baltimore, http://www.eapoe.org/works/essays/bletterb.htm.
74. Dennis Pahl, "Poe's Sublimity: The Role of Burkean Aesthetics," *The Edgar Allan Poe Review* 7, no. 2 (2006): 30.
75. Poe, *Tales and Sketches*, 209.
76. Edgar Allan Poe, "The Poetic Principle" (reprint), *Home Journal*, series for 1850, no. 36, whole number 238 (August 31, 1850), 1, cols. 1–6.
77. Dennis Pahl, "Sounding the Sublime: Poe, Burke, and the (Non) Sense of Language," *Poe Studies* 42 (2009): 45.
78. Ibid., 52.

79. Poe, *Tales and Sketches*, 210.
80. George E. Hatvary, "Poe's Possible Authorship of 'An Opinion on Dreams'," *Poe Studies-Old Series* 14, no. 2 (1981): 21.
81. Poe, *Tales and Sketches*, 211.
82. Carl W. Bazil, "Seizures in the Life and Works of Edgar Allan Poe," *Archives of Neurology* 56 (1999): 740.
83. Poe, *Tales and Sketches*, 212.
84. Ibid., 209.
85. Ibid., 212.
86. Translation from The Edgar Allan Poe Society of Baltimore, http://www.eapoe.org/works/tales/bernicea.htm.
87. Ibid.
88. Poe, *Tales and Sketches*, 219.
89. Clayton Koelb, *The Revivifying Word: Literature, Philosophy, and the Theory of Life in Europe's Romantic Age* (Rochester: Camden House, 2008), 177.
90. Ibid., 174.
91. John Cleman, "Irresistible Impulses: Edgar Allan Poe and the Insanity Defense," *American Literature* 63, no. 4 (1991): 627.
92. Ibid., 629.
93. Poe, *Tales and Sketches*, vol. 2, 792.
94. Prichard, *Treatise*, 28.
95. Poe, *Tales and Sketches*, vol. 2, 792.
96. B. D. Tucker, "'The Tell-Tale Heart' and the 'Evil Eye'," *The Southern Literary Journal* 13, no. 2 (1981): 93.
97. James Kirkland, "'The Tell-Tale Heart' as Evil Eye Event," *Southern Folklore* 56, no. 2(1999): 135–147.
98. Poe, *Tales and Sketches*, vol. 2, 794.
99. Prichard, *Treatise*, 71.
100. Poe, *Tales and Sketches*, vol. 2, 797.

Bibliography

Bazil, Carl W. "Seizures in the Life and Works of Edgar Allan Poe." *Archives of Neurology* 56 (1999): 740–743.

Boime, Albert. "Portraying Monomaniacs to Service the Alienist's Monomania: Géricault and Georget." *The Oxford Art Journal* 14, no. 1 (1991): 79–91.

Bradford, Adam. *Communities of Death: Whitman, Poe, and the American Culture of Mourning*. Columbia: University of Missouri Press, 2014.

Budge, Gavin. *Romanticism, Medicine, and the Natural Supernatural*. Basingstoke: Palgrave, 2013.

Cavell, Stanley. *In Quest of the Ordinary*. Chicago: University of Chicago Press, 1988.

Cleman, John. "Irresistible Impulses: Edgar Allan Poe and the Insanity Defense." *American Literature* 63, no. 4 (1991): 623–640.

Coleridge, Samuel Taylor. *Biographia Literaria*. Public Domain Books. Kindle Edition, 2012.

———. *Coleridge's Notebooks: A Selection*. Edited by Seamus Perry. Oxford: Oxford University Press, 2002.

———. *The Major Works*. Edited by H. J. Jackson. New York: Oxford University Press, 2008.

———. *The Notebooks of Samuel Taylor Coleridge*, October–November 1811, 2 vols. Edited by Kathleen Coburn. New York: Bollingen, 1957.

———. *The Rime of the Ancient Mariner*. Edited by Paul Fry. New York City, NY: Bedford St. Martin's, 2000.

Cruikshank, George. "Ideality." In *Sketch of the New Anatomy and Physiology of the Brain and Nervous System of Drs. Gall and Spurzheim*. London, 1815. Courtesy of the National Library of Medicine, USA.

Darwin, Erasmus. *Zoonomia*, vol. 1, xl.2.3. E. Earle, 1818. Google Books.

Deane, Nichola. "Coleridge and JC Lavater's *Essays on Physiognomy*." *Notes and Queries* 49, no. 1 (2002): 29.

Deas, Michael J. "The *Saturday Museum* Woodcut." In *The Portraits and Daguerreotypes of Edgar Allan Poe*. 1989, 15. Edgar Allan Poe Society of Baltimore. http://www.eapoe.org/papers/misc1921/deas102a.htm.

Deleuze, J. P. F. *Practical Instruction in Animal Magnetism*. Translated by T. C. Hartshorn. London, 1850.

Dennis, John. *The Advancement and Reformation of Modern Poetry: A Critical Discourse. In Two Parts. ... By Mr Dennis*. London: Printed for Rich. Parker, 1701. http://name.umdl.umich.edu/004890743.0001.000.

Gardiner, John. *An Inquiry into the Nature, Cause, and Cure of the Gout and Some of the Diseases with Which It Is Connected*. Edinburgh, 1793. Google Play.

Gotch, A. F. "Albatrosses, Fulmars, Shearwaters, and Petrels." In *Latin Names Explained: A Guide to the Scientific Classifications of Reptiles, Birds & Mammals*, 190. New York: Facts on File, 1996.

Haslam, John. *On the Nature of Thought, or the Act of Thinking*. London, 1835. National Library of Medicine, USA.

———. *Sound Mind*. London, 1819. National Library of Medicine, USA.

Hatvary, George E. "Poe's Possible Authorship of 'An Opinion on Dreams'." *Poe Studies-Old Series* 14, no. 2 (1981): 21.

Hawke, David Freeman. *Benjamin Rush: Revolutionary Gadfly*. New York: Bobbs-Merrill Company, 1971.

Hutchisson, James M. *Poe*. Jackson: University Press of Mississippi, 2005.

Jones, Ewan James. *Coleridge and the Philosophy of Poetic Form*. Cambridge: Cambridge University Press, 2014.

Kirkland, James. "'The Tell-Tale Heart' as Evil Eye Event." *Southern Folklore* 56, no. 2 (1999): 135–147.

Knox, Julian. "Coleridge and the Arts." In *Oxford Handbook of Samuel Taylor Coleridge*, edited by Frederick Burwick, 627. Oxford: Oxford University Press, 2009.

Koelb, Clayton. *The Revivifying Word: Literature, Philosophy, and the Theory of Life in Europe's Romantic Age*. Rochester: Camden House, 2008.

Kord, Susanne. "From Evil Eye to Poetic Eye: Witch Beliefs and Physiognomy in the Age of Enlightenment." In *Practicing Progress: The Promise and Limitations of Enlightenment: Festschrift for John A. McCarthy*, edited by Richard E. Schade and Dieter Sevin, 35–58. Amsterdam: Rodopi, 2007.

Lavater, Johann Caspar. *Essays on Physiognomy*, vol. 1. London: John Murray, 1789–1798. Courtesy of The Wellcome Library, London.

McDonald, Beth E. *The Vampire as Numinous Experience: Spiritual Journeys with the Undead in British and American Literature*. Jefferson and London: McFarland, 2004.

Mills, Bruce. *Poe, Fuller, and the Mesmeric Arts*. Columbia: University of Missouri Press, 2006.

Pahl, Dennis. "Poe's Sublimity: The Role of Burkean Aesthetics." *The Edgar Allan Poe Review* 7, no. 2 (2006): 30–49.

———. "Sounding the Sublime: Poe, Burke, and the (Non) Sense of Language." *Poe Studies* 42 (2009): 41–60.

Poe, Edgar Allan. "Letter to B——." In *Southern Literary Messenger*. July 1836, 501. Edgar Allan Poe Society of Baltimore. http://www.eapoe.org/works/essays/bletterb.htm.

———. *Tales and Sketches*, vols. 1 and 2. Edited by Thomas Ollive Mabbott. Chicago: University of Illinois Press, 1978.

———. "The Poetic Principle" (reprint). *Home Journal*, series for 1850, no. 36, whole number 238 (August 31, 1850): 1, cols. 1–6.

Prichard, James Cowles. *A Treatise on Insanity and Other Disorders Affecting the Mind*. New York: Arno Press, 1835.

Priestley, Joseph. *Hartley's Theory of the Human Mind, on the Principle of the Association of Ideas; with Essays Relating to the Subject of It*. London: J. Johnson, 1775.

Raine, Kathleen, ed. *The Letters of Samuel Taylor Coleridge*. London: Grey Walls Press, 1950.

Reiss, Benjamin. *Theaters of Madness: Insane Asylums and Nineteenth-Century American Culture*. Chicago and London: University of Chicago Press, 2008.

Richardson, Alan. *British Romanticism and the Science of the Mind*. Cambridge: Cambridge University Press, 2001.

Rousseau, George. "Coleridge's Dreaming Gut: Digestion, Genius, Hypochondria." In *Cultures of the Abdomen: Diet, Digestion, and Fat in the*

Modern World, edited by C. Forth, 117. New York and Basingstoke: Palgrave, 2005.

Rudolf, Matthias. "Unspeakable Discovery: Romanticism and the 'Rime of the Ancient Mariner'." *European Romantic Review* 24, no. 2 (2013): 185–210.

Rush, Benjamin. *Medical Inquiries and Observations Upon the Diseases of Mind*. Philadelphia, 1812.

Schultz, Alexander, "Purloined Voices: Edgar Allen Poe Reading Samuel Taylor Coleridge." *Studies in Romanticism* 47 (Summer 2008).

Smith, Adam. *The Essential Adam Smith*. Edited by Robert L. Heilbroner. New York and London: W. W. Norton, 1987.

Spurzheim, Johann. *The Physiognomical System of Drs. Gall and Spurzheim, Founded on an Anatomical and Physiological Examination of the Nervous System in General, and of the Brain in Particular; and Indicating the Dispositions and Manifestations of the Mind*. London, 1815. Google Books.

The Phrenological Journal and Miscellany, vol. 1. Edinburgh, 1824. Google Books.

Tucker, B. D. "'The Tell-Tale Heart' and the 'Evil Eye'." *The Southern Literary Journal* 13, no. 2 (1981): 92–98.

Vallins, David, ed. *Coleridge's Writings. Vol. 5, On the Sublime*. Basingstoke: Palgrave Macmillan, 2003.

Youngquist, Paul. "Romantic Dietetics! Or, Eating Your Way to a New You." In *Cultures of Taste/Theories of Appetite*, edited by Timothy Morton. New York and Basingstoke: Palgrave, 2004.

CHAPTER 7

Coda: From Scorpions to Spiders in A.S. Byatt's *Possession*

While intellectual monomania, erotomania and nymphomania, revolutiana, and ideality were fascinating Romantic constructs, they do seem (and, in many ways, are) products of a bygone era. As I have been arguing throughout this book, they reveal anxieties central to Romantic-era Britain and America, from the anxiety regarding the written word (and its gendered connotations), to anxieties regarding female sexual desire, war, and the imagination writ large. These anxieties, and the very human desire to ruminate and to repeat, were pathologized, constructed into the *disease* of obsession, in the Romantic era.

The disease of obsession looks very different today; specifically, our own pathologized form of obsession has been given a new label, obsessive compulsive disorder. While I do not view OCD as coequal with Romantic notions of obsession (and I find suspect scholarship that diagnoses literary characters with modern-day disorders), I do think it useful to briefly consider what we now pathologize: what we have constructed as our twenty-first-century American norms. I will then move on to argue that vestiges of the Romantic construction of obsession remain in our *popular* vocabulary of "obsession," one we can see in popular media like television, films, and print. As a case in point, I will end this coda with a close reading of A. S. Byatt's 1990 *Possession*.

K. Béres Rogers, *Creating Romantic Obsession*,
Palgrave Studies in Literature, Science and Medicine,
https://doi.org/10.1007/978-3-030-13988-9_7

Part I: "A Little OCD"

A cursory analysis of the discourse of the 2013 DSM V, the Diagnostic and Statistical Manual used by the American Psychiatric Association, quickly reveals that American psychiatry's "official" take on obsessive compulsive disorder has very little similarity to Romantic-era monomania. Obsessions are, in the DSM V, defined by (1) and (2):

1. Recurrent and persistent thoughts, urges, or impulses that are experienced, at some time during the disturbance, as intrusive and unwanted, and that in most individuals cause marked anxiety or distress.
2. The individual attempts to ignore or suppress such thoughts, urges, or images, or to neutralize them with some other thought or action (i.e., by performing a compulsion).[1]

Romantic-era authors and proto-psychologists do focus on "recurrent and persistent thoughts," as evidenced by Victor Frankenstein, Emma Courtney, and most of the characters in this book; we also see "urges and impulses" in the Romantic-era nosology of erotomania, nymphomania, revolutiana, and, of course, ideality (one can best describe the mariner's killing of the albatross or the murder in "The Tell-Tale Heart" as an impulsive act). Some monomaniacs experience these thoughts, urges, and impulses as "intrusive or unwanted," but many, like Darlowitz, Victor Frankenstein, or Count Basil, experience their obsessions as (at least initially) very much products of will.

Compulsions play very little, if any, role in Romantic obsession; perhaps we see what we would now call "compulsions" in the mariner's and Poe's narrators' need to recount their stories, but we see none of the DSM V's examples of compulsions: "hand washing, ordering, checking or mental acts (e.g., praying, counting, repeating words silently) that the individual feels driven to perform in response to an obsession or according to rules that must be applied rigidly."[2] This notion of "rigid" rules, prominent in memoirs of OCD like Amy Wilensky's 1999 *Passing for Normal*, is relatively absent in both proto-psychological and literary accounts of Romantic-era obsession. What *is*, however, present, is the time-consuming nature of obsession: the manner in which, like the scorpion that stings its own tail, the mind eventually begins to destroy itself. The DSM V states this clinically: "The obsessions or compulsions are time-consuming (e.g., take more than 1 hour per day) or cause clinically significant distress or impairment in social, occupational, or other important areas of functioning."[3] While what we determine as "important" areas of functioning are socially determined and constructed, the notion of "distress" and, simply, of time, is one that recurs in Romantic-era accounts.

As opposed to the clinical language of the DSM, the popular discourse of Obsessive Compulsive Disorder, relies, often, on humor and even condescension. In the movie *As Good as It Gets* and the television show *Glee*, the protagonists compulsively clean their food; in fact, both characters (Melvin Udall and Emma Pillsbury) wear gloves to avoid food-based contamination. The television show *Monk* also showcases a compulsion with cleanliness and order: the titular character counts and arranges repeatedly in order to achieve some semblance of control (which, of course, assists him in his detective duties).

The anxieties regarding the unspeakable are not completely absent: the more recent HBO show *Girls* (2011–2017) illustrates some more disturbing OCD compulsions, like "need[ing] to visualize a murder eight times, or masturbate eight times at night," and J. K. Rowlings's book *The Casual Vacancy* (2012) offers us a rare glimpse of a character who obsesses about the irrational thought that he killed his best friend.[4] This fear, a fear occasioned by a powerful thought, is much more present in our discourses of what we colloquially call "obsession."

Part II: Obsessed

When we colloquially exclaim that a person or character is "obsessed," we come far closer to the Romantic notion of the term. While no one today would diagnose someone with "vigilia," we do often speak of an excessive, overpowering curiosity: a curiosity that makes us, like Edgar Huntly or Caleb Williams, amateur psychoanalysts. We wonder why famous, successful people like Robin Williams or Kate Spade commit suicide. Like Edgar, who begins as an amateur proto-psychologist and then becomes himself obsessed with his curiosity about Clithero, we can attempt to understand a celebrity through social media and find ourselves bombarded, becoming obsessed. Spade herself, according to her sister, was "obsessed" with Williams's suicide; she kept watching the graphic, detailed footage of the suicide, "over and over. I think the plan was already in motion even as far back as then."[5] While most of our curiosity might stem from a human need for sympathy or reassurance, it can also come to possess us.

Our media also participates in our own version of the nineteenth-century philosophical debate concerning perception and reality, or "ideality." Does having an idea make it "real?" What, many have asked recently, is the relationship between "news" and storytelling? As anyone who has visited Facebook or Twitter knows, the need to tell a story can be compulsive, and the story is retold, or "shared," much as the ancient mariner shares his story with the wedding guest, who must keep retelling it. Movies like Tim Burton's 2003 *Big Fish* also comment on our need to tell, and retell, "fish tales," exceedingly unbelievable tales that, through their telling, become "real." Will Bloom, the son who listens to his father's seemingly unbelievable tales, says that "A man tells his stories so many times that he becomes the stories. They live on after him, and in that way he becomes immortal."[6] In many ways, the proto-psychological discussion about "ideality," the pathology that makes an idea seem like a reality, examines our intrinsic need to create, tell, and retell stories.

Nymphomania has also found (or, rather, never lost) its way in our vocabulary, leading to the figure of the somewhat threatening woman who revels in her sexual power. Lars von Trier's 2013 *Nymphomaniac* illustrates that we are still fascinated with women who own their sexual desire. The Romantic-era anxiety about a woman's agency, seen through Dacre's Apollonia, for instance, has only been intensified in the main character, Joe, who takes ownership of her sexuality and tells a therapy group that "I'm not like you. I am a nymphomaniac and I love myself for being one, but above all, I love my cunt and my filthy, dirty lust."[7] This is a far cry from the Romantic-era nymphomaniac, possessed by her body and socially disempowered; Joe here both craves the pleasure of orgasm and also uses sex as a way to gain control over her turbulent life.

Often, it is turbulence or chaos that provokes obsession, and this is nowhere more true than in depictions of war. Like the Romantics, we also tie the discourse of the sublime to war—again, war at a distance. Media representations like Kathryn Bigelow's 2008 *The Hurt Locker* emphasize the awe and sublimity of war, a sublimity that, according to James Der Derian, is "addictive." In fact, the first thing the viewer sees is a quotation to this effect: "The rush of battle is often a potent and lethal addiction, for war is a drug—Chris Hedges."[8] The quotation is immediately followed by sirens, horns, and shouts that put the viewer into sensory overload. Throughout the screenplay, written by Mark Boal, we see references to insanity, obsession, and the sublime. For instance, Boal describes one scene as "Bedlam…as the firing continues on all sides," and director Kathryn Bigelow does not disappoint with the auditory and visual components of the scene.[9] James, the protagonist who dismantled IEDs, is especially obsessed with the bombs themselves. "I think," he states, "it's interesting to hold something in your hands that could have killed any of us."[10] This obsession is clearly linked to the sublime, as the distance from something, here death, is what fuels his "interest," what he later calls the "morbid thrill" of a "bomb in his hands."[11]

From the beginning, James seems impervious to the emotional demands of war, locking up his feelings like the box of bomb parts he keeps to remind him of the instability of war…and life. When he does return home to his life in suburbia, one scene shows him wandering the sterile, packed grocery store, unable to make such a mundane decision. Unable to reintegrate into everyday life, he tells his infant son that there is only "one thing" he loves, and he re-enlists. Unlike Joanna Baillie in *Count Basil* or Robert Gleig in *The Subaltern*, Bigelow questions this desire to return to the sublimity of war, illustrating the dire costs through the "hurt locker" itself. The "good soldier," conditioned not to question, is not, she implicitly argues, the "good father" or the "good husband." Yet, here, the experience of sublimity squares with societal expectations, allowing James to exist, if not happily, with his obsession.

PART III: THE GOOD SCHOLAR: BYATT'S *POSSESSION*

In line with the "good soldier," the "good scholar," as A. S. Byatt, herself a literary scholar, illustrates in her 1990 novel, is characterized by what the Romantics would have termed intellectual monomania. *Possession* takes us back to the original meaning of "obsession": a possession by the devil. In Byatt's novel, it is a desire for knowledge, a curiosity, and also erotic desire that possess the main characters. Both scholarship and heterosexual desire are, in this novel, critiqued, treated as potentially pathological.

Byatt, herself a scholar of the Romantics and of women writers, critiques the curiosity for knowledge, the penchant for storing artifacts, and the 1990s obsession with theory that characterized and continues to inform academia. Roland, Byatt's protagonist, discovers a letter between the Victorian poet Randolph Henry Ash, based on Robert Barrett Browning, and an unknown lover, eventually discovered to be a fellow poet, Christabel LaMotte. The novel's plot, then, involves Roland and feminist scholar Maud as they uncover the correspondence and relationship between these two poets…and eventually develop a relationship of their own. Roland, whose name hearkens back to Browning's "Childe Roland to the Dark Tower Came," is, like Childe Roland, embarked on a perilous quest to a "dark tower." This tower, the resolution of LaMotte and Ash's relationship, threatens his academic success (he takes the letter from the archives and neglects to tell his thesis advisor, Dr. Blackadder).

While Roland's curiosity does threaten his career, it does not seem to detract from his essential selfhood. When he first reads the letter and begins to communicate with Maud, a LaMotte scholar, about its possible relevance, he is "urged on by some violent emotion of curiosity—not greed, curiosity, more fundamental even than sex, the desire for knowledge."[12] Byatt's diction indicates that, even though Roland's curiosity is "violent," it "urge[s] him on" instead of consuming him or, in this case, possessing him. It might be "more fundamental" than sex, but the equation here assumes that sex, greed, and curiosity can coexist. Later in the novel, Roland does become "possessed" by his quest, but never too perilously so. Talking to Blackadder about his deceit in taking the letter and pursuing the quest without academic support, he says that he "felt possessed. I had to know."[13] For a brief period of the text, he feels that Maud is able to pursue her research but that he, "had begun this—what should it be called—this investigation, and had lost everything…"[14] However, Byatt does not allow for this to be the resolution of the novel; instead, Roland's curiosity is rewarded with a number of prestigious, lucrative job offers. If Roland's counterpart is Randolph Henry Ash, then the latter is even less affected by his desire for knowledge, which can coexist with a variety of other preoccupations. Never in his letters does Ash complain about being possessed, obsessed, or at a loss due to his desire for knowledge.

This desire for knowledge takes a much more pathological turn with Byatt's female characters. Maud's name alludes to Alfred, Lord Tennyson's "Maud," a poem featuring a woman who has

> neither savor nor salt,
> But a cold and clear-cut face, as I found when her carriage past,
> All that I saw (for her eyes were downcast, not to be seen)
> Faultily faultless, icily regular, splendidly null,
> Dead perfection, no more; nothing more…[15]

Tennyson plays here with the senses of taste and warmth, describing Maud as a dish that is bland and has "neither savor or salt." Her face is "cold" and "icily" regular, echoing an adjective that Byatt also uses to describe her Maud. Although she is "perfection," she is "dead" perfection, unmoving, "faultily faultless" in her lack of variability, her lack of humanity. This sort of "dead perfection" is what Byatt's Maud attempts to achieve by focusing solely on academia, on viewing the world through a theoretical lens, and on growing her Women's Studies program.

Byatt's focus on feminism, centered around Maud and her some-time-lover, Leonora Stern, allows her to flip the Romantic-era category of "intellectual monomania," gendering the pathology female. Early in the novel, Maud tells Roland that she feels "faint with curiosity"; this reads remarkably differently than Roland's earlier "urge" for knowledge.[16] Curiosity and the quest for knowledge are, for Maud, indicative of a loss of self; she later exclaims that "I want to—to—follow the—path. I feel taken over by this…"[17] Like Dacre, Byatt uses em dashes to indicate a confusion, perhaps a loss of reason: one reiterated by Maud's feeling of being "taken over" by the "path" she follows. While Maud herself views this as a facet of academia—she says that "All scholars are a bit mad. All obsessions are dangerous. This one's got a bit out of hand"—the fact is that Maud's obsession threatens to destroy her very identity.[18]

Christabel, whose name hearkens back to Coleridge's poem regarding a threatening, distinctly lesbian-leaning serpent woman (similar to the poem, "Melusina," on which LaMotte works), founds her identity on her work, on the "life of the mind." Without words, without creativity, she is reduced to nothing; they "have been all my life, all my life—this need is like the Spider's need who carries before her a huge Burden of Silk which she must spin out…"[19] While the silk here is viewed as a "burden" that, perhaps like the ancient mariner's tale, must be somehow unloaded, it also bears mentioning that the spider spins silk to hunt, to capture prey, to survive. Without words, then, Christabel is reduced to someone who must be provided for, ostensibly by a man. Maud compares herself to Christabel when she says that she "feel[s] as [Christabel] did. I keep my defenses up because I must go on *doing my work*," but Maud's work seems to detract from instead of forming her identity.[20] As opposed to Maud, Christabel's work is directly threatened by another obsession: her obsession with Randolph Henry Ash.

As Kathleen Renk has convincingly argued, Byatt's novel pathologizes heterosexual desire by aligning Christabel's creativity with her neo-platonic lesbian relationship. This relationship with Blanche Glover (whose name connotes whiteness as opposed to the sooty quality of Randolph Henry Ash) allows her the freedom to spin her silk unencumbered.

Together, the two women can live the "Life of the Mind," and Blanche recalls in her diary that their coexistence, "weave[s] together the simple pleasures of daily life…and the higher pleasures of art and thought which we may now taste as we please."[21] This again recalls the image of the spider, "weaving" together the quotidian with the Platonic virtues of "art and thought." For Byatt, erotomania seems more of a threat in her characters' heterosexual relationships; as Renk remarks, the enchantment of erotic desire

> can bring debility in which the lover has no control and is possessed. Beyond this, Byatt also foregrounds another version of love that "mixes" eros and artistic enterprise and raises the lovers beyond mere selfish attachment.[22]

Even though both of her sets of heterosexual lovers are writers and/or scholars, their desire for one another becomes pathologized, akin to Dacre or Keats's erotomania.

While Randolph Ash is never, in Byatt's text, possessed by a pathological curiosity, his desire for Christabel LaMotte is described in exactly these terms. In one of his letters to Christabel, he claims that he has never "felt such a concentration of my whole Being—on one object, in one place, at one time…"[23] Like Maud's obsession with knowledge, this obsession consumes his "whole Being," focusing it all exclusively on Christabel. Ash even connects his desire for LaMotte with demonic possession, writing to his wife Ellen that "For the last year perhaps I have been in love with another woman. I could say it was a sort of madness. A possession, as by daemons. A kind of blinding."[24] Byatt here not only evokes the original meaning of obsession, demonic possession, but also connects the obsession back to the eyes. In this case, it is not the eyes that obsess but the eyes—or, rather, the ability to see—that is *possessed*. Later in the novel, the image of the eye is reiterated when LaMotte and Ash's son "recites the passage [from Rime] of the blessing of the snakes, and the vision of the glittering eye of the ocean cast up to the moon, most feelingly, and his own eyes are bright with it."[25] This is, after all, a child who has been conceived in an obsession, first with words and then with erotic desire: a child who can more than understand the magnetic, mesmeric power of poetry.

While Maud attempts to resist the lure of heterosexual desire (as opposed to her lesbian, academically productive relationship with Leonora Stern), it is Roland who is consumed by this particular "dark tower." In her attempt to "do her work," Maud defensively pulls her hair, a symbol of femininity, back into a headscarf, braiding it compulsively into "repeating patterns." Byatt describes her hair as "glossy with constricted life," and Roland feels "pity, for the rigorous constriction all that mass had undergone, to be so structured into repeating patterns."[26] Here, the "repeating patterns," the "constriction," symbolizes Maud's obsessive scholarship, her need to defend against competing forces. Maud does eventually let down her defenses and allow for Roland to distract her from academic obsessions, but Roland's obsession with Maud takes on a life of its own. In a self-conscious, postmodern rewording of LaMotte and Ash's romantic letters, he exclaims to Maud that he feels "total obsession, night and day. When I see you, you look *alive* and everything else—fades. All that."[27] While the "all that" attempts to treat Roland's obsession ironically, Byatt's em dash, here before the word "fades," illustrates his psychic weakness.

Byatt's novel, then, critiques academia and its constant deconstructionist urges, but it also reverses the Romantic-era gendering of intellectual monomania, which was ascribed to men's brains and to women's bodies; here, obsession is clearly located in Maud and Christabel's brains. To add to this, Byatt ascribes erotomania/nymphomania almost exclusively to her male characters. Her novel owes much to the Romantic-era pathologization of both intellectual pursuits and erotic desire, but it also updates this construction, ascribing women's obsessions to their brains and men's obsessions to their bodies.

Part IV: Conclusion

On one hand, Romantic-era conceptions about obsessive thinking, encapsulated in terms like "phrenzy," "melancholy," and, later, "monomania," clearly reflect the anxieties of the late eighteenth and early nineteenth centuries. Some of these constructions, like intellectual monomania, have mostly lost their power over us, although, as Byatt illustrates, they still have a life in academia. Others, like "ideality," exemplify a Romantic philosophical debate about perception and reality, one that still informs discussions of art and creativity today.

Often, constructions of obsession did, and still do, reflect anxieties about binary categories. At what point does obsession become a disease? A disability? How do we mark the boundary between the mentally healthy and the mentally ill? As Shayda Kafai writes,

> A mad border body exists in-between the fixed definitions of sanity and madness; this body is a duel inhabitant. I believe the mad border body reminds us, just as the mestiza and queer border body do, that identity categories are not given but constructed; identities are created in the act of edging, in the in-between living that dominant culture often scrutinizes and assumes invisible.[28]

All of this book's categories call into question the social construction of mental illness—at what point does "normal" desire for knowledge, sexual desire, interest in war, or a fascination with ideas morph into something pathological? The answer to this question, like most questions regarding the norm, involve the power structures undergirding the society in question. An obsession with war, for instance, allows people to re-enlist and fortify nations that survive based on their military power. On the other hand, an obsession with an idea can run the gamut from "mental illness" (an idea, like an old man's eye or the sublime, that seems superfluous) to what drives most authors: a desire to create, to give form to an idea. Yet these constructions often remain invisible, their edges unseen until, perhaps, we can put view them through the lens of history.

As scholars of disability studies have argued, the concept of the "norm" was not constructed until the 1840s, after the end of the traditionally circumscribed Romantic era. Adolphe Quetelet (1796–1847) used astronomy's "law of error," used to locate stars by averaging the "errors," to determine the concept of "l'homme moyen," the "average man." Moreover, this average man was a combination of the physically and the "morally," or we might say psychologically, average.[29] Yet the notion of the "norm" was being constructed before the word appeared in 1840. Studying Romantic-era disability, here obsession, allows us to view a time when these norms were coming into being, made and remade based on social anxieties. If we now assume "invisible" the slippages of the dominant border body, we can see these slippages by viewing a time period before categories like obsession were crystallized. I am, by far, not the first to make this argument for the importance of studying Romantic-era "disability"; Fuson Wang, for instance, argues that the era "represents a transitional moment between Enlightenment yearning for universal humanism and the Victorian codification of social mores; it sits between two restrictive movements to classify the human against the inhuman and the normal against the abnormal."[30] Other scholars like Kevis Goodman ask important questions about reading medical texts in a time before codification; examining the earlier pathologization of nostalgia, Goodman argues that, like many of Esquirol's categories, we can look to medical history and literature to view certain cultural anxieties that have changed or no longer exist.[31] Emily Stanback, in her 2016 *The Wordsworth-Coleridge Circle and the Aesthetics of Disability*, argues that the diversity and complexity of "medicine" during the Romantic era allowed for a multiplicity of interpretations of what she calls "nonnormative" embodiment.[32] She goes on to rightly argue that this rich complexity was interdisciplinary or even pre-disciplinary, infusing many of our now-rigid nosological categories.

Viewing these Romantic slippages then, through the lenses of literature, science, medicine, and philosophy, allows for us to perhaps see them more clearly today. One might wonder why an insatiable quest for knowledge, most often characterized as workaholism, now seems to be such a positive trait. Conversely, most pathologized obsession today concerns the "what if" scenarios perpetuated by an often obsessively sensationalized media. If Romantic anxieties were mirrored and proliferated by the era's rapidly expanding media, our anxieties are similarly showcased by television, movies, the internet, and social media platforms. Fears about sexuality, about violence, are both magnified by their constant representations in the media; yet, when people themselves begin to ruminate about these very fears, they become "mentally ill." We both bombard our citizens with violent and sexual images and simultaneously tell them that thinking about these images is "bad" or, even, "dirty."

One very common form of obsession that illustrates our own anxieties, in this case about motherhood, is postpartum OCD. A blogger writes that "Our society puts so much pressure on mothers and for new mothers the stress of this pressure is often unbearable."[33] The fact that these irrational ideas carry so much power for new mothers is indicative of the anxiety that motherhood carries with it. Joanna Limburg brings us into this anxiety by forcing us to sit with her intrusive thoughts:

> when certain images came into my mind, say of my stamping on the baby's neck, or dashing his brains out against the wall, or gouging out one of his beautiful blue eyes, or pushing his buggy under a bus, or pressing a pillow into his face, or holding him under the bathwater until he drowned, or throwing him out of his bedroom window, or stabbing him, or dousing him in boiling water, or any number of other terrible things, I knew with certainty that these were evil thoughts, and that I was an evil mother, capable of the most evil things.[34]

Here, the "images" in her mind, in her imagination, overpower her, coming, like Frankenstein's creature, unbidden. Her colloquial "say" belies the power of these images, all connected with "or" that keep us reading, unable to stop ourselves much as Limburg is unable to stop her thoughts. While obsession relies on uncertainty and obscurity, she writes that she knew "with certainty," that she is an "evil mother," using the word three times. Here, the religious valence of her diction also squares with earlier notions of obsession as possession by "evil." A person dealing with post-partum OCD has very few places to turn for "positive" or sympathetic representations; in addition to the image of the "good mother," we see, over and over again, the "evil" mother who, like Susan Smith, drowns her children in an extreme, unusual manifestation of PPD.

The point I wish to make here, and throughout this book, is not that these images are not extremely painful, and not that OCD is not "real." Rather, it *is* real, as are our mixed messages concerning violence and sexuality, the fears we all have of overstepping our socially prescribed bounds. It is as real as the cult of the "good mother" that leaves new mothers fearing that they will somehow break a social taboo, become (contrary to their own inclination) "evil." At a time when we conceive of psychology as indisputable fact, a diagnosis as a sentence, it is helpful to reconceive that sentence as not inflexible, ending with a period, but constantly changing, socially constructed. All of us have, or might have, in a different time, had, scorpions in our minds.

Notes

1. Donald W. Black and John E. Grant, eds., *DSM-5 Guidebook: The Essential Companion to the Diagnostic and Statistical Manual of Mental Disorders* (American Psychiatric Association, 2014), 149.
2. Black and Grant, 148.
3. Ibid.
4. Fletcher Wortman, "'*Girls* Gets OCD," *Psychology Today*, March 13, 2013, https://www.psychologytoday.com/us/blog/triggered/201303/girls-gets-ocd-0.
5. Ewan Palmer, "Kate Spade Was Obsessed with Coverage of Robin Williams' Suicide, Sister Claims," *Newsweek*, July 20, 2018, https://www.newsweek.com/kate-spade-was-obsessed-coverage-robin-williams-death-sister-claims-963809.
6. *Big Fish*, directed by Tim Burton (Sony Pictures, 2004).

7. *Nymphomaniac*, directed by Lars Von Trier (Zentropa Entertainments, 2013).
8. *The Hurt Locker*, directed by Kathryn Bigelow, *Scripts on the Net* (Warner Bros., 2008), 1.
9. Ibid., 59.
10. Ibid., 74.
11. Ibid., 78.
12. A. S. Byatt, *Possession* (Vintage International, 1990), 92.
13. Ibid., 527.
14. Ibid., 474.
15. Alfred, Lord Tennyson, "Maud," in *Maud, and Other Poems* (CreateSpace Independent Publishing Platforms, 2015), 10.
16. Byatt, 120.
17. Ibid., 258.
18. Ibid., 360.
19. Ibid., 198.
20. Ibid., 549.
21. Ibid., 225, 51.
22. Kathleen Renk, "Erotic Possession, the 'Phantasm,' and Platonic Love in Two Neo-Victorian Novels," *Critique: Studies in Contemporary Fiction* 56, no. 5 (2015): 576–585.
23. Byatt, *Possession,* 210.
24. Ibid., 492.
25. Ibid., 546.
26. Ibid., 295.
27. Ibid., 550.
28. Quoted in Patricia Friedrich, *Literary Disability Studies: The Literary and Linguistic Construction of Obsessive-Compulsive Disorder: No Ordinary Doubt* (Basingstoke: Palgrave Macmillan, 2015), 92, ProQuest ebrary.
29. Davis, "Disability, Normality," 3.
30. Fuson Wang, "The Historicist Turn of Romantic-Era Disability Studies, or Frankenstein in the Dark," *Literature Compass* 14, no. 7 (2017): e12400.
31. Kevis Goodman, "'Uncertain Disease': Nostalgia, Pathologies of Motion, Practices of Reading," *Studies in Romanticism* 49, no. 2 (2010): 197–227.
32. Emily B. Stanback, *The Wordsworth-Coleridge Circle and the Aesthetics of Disability* (Palgrave Macmillan, 2016), 43.
33. Wide Lawns, "The Vines in My Mind—My Struggle with Postpartum OCD," March 31, 2011, http://widelawns.blogspot.com/2011/03/vines-in-my-mind-my-struggle-with.html.
34. Joanna Limburg, *The Woman Who Thought Too Much* (London: Atlantic Books, 2010), 265.

Bibliography

Big Fish. Directed by Tim Burton. Sony Pictures, 2004.

Black, Donald W., and John E. Grant, eds. *DSM-5 Guidebook: The Essential Companion to the Diagnostic and Statistical Manual of Mental Disorders*. Arlington, VA: American Psychiatric Association, 2014.

Byatt, A. S. *Possession*. New York: Vintage International, 1990.

Davis, Lennard. "Introduction: Disability, Normality, and Power." In *The Disability Studies Reader*, edited by Lennard J. Davis, 3. New York: Routledge, 2017.

Der Derian, James. "Now We Are All Avatars." *Millenium: Journal of International Studies* 39, no. 1 (2010): 181–186.

Friedrich, Patricia. *Literary Disability Studies: The Literary and Linguistic Construction of Obsessive-Compulsive Disorder: No Ordinary Doubt*. Basingstoke: Palgrave Macmillan, 2015. ProQuest ebrary.

Goodman, Kevis. "'Uncertain Disease': Nostalgia, Pathologies of Motion, Practices of Reading." *Studies in Romanticism* 49, no. 2 (2010): 197–227.

Limburg, Joanna. *The Woman Who Thought Too Much*. London: Atlantic Books, 2010.

Nymphomaniac. Directed by Lars Von Trier. Zentropa Entertainments, 2013.

Palmer, Ewan. "Kate Spade Was Obsessed with Coverage of Robin Williams' Suicide, Sister Claims." *Newsweek*. Last updated July 20, 2018. https://www.newsweek.com/kate-spade-was-obsessed-coverage-robin-williams-death-sister-claims-963809.

Renk, Kathleen. "Erotic Possession, the 'Phantasm,' and Platonic Love in Two Neo-Victorian Novels." *Critique: Studies in Contemporary Fiction* 56, no. 5 (2015): 576–585.

Rowling, J. K. *The Casual Vacancy*. New York and London: Little Brown, 2012.

Stanback, Emily B. *The Wordsworth-Coleridge Circle and the Aesthetics of Disability*. London, UK: Palgrave Macmillan, 2016.

Tennyson, Alfred. "Maud." In *Maud, and Other Poems*. Scotts Valley, CA: CreateSpace Independent Publishing Platforms, 2015.

The Hurt Locker. Directed by Kathryn Bigelow. *Scripts on the Net*. Warner Bros., 2008.

Wang, Fuson. "The Historicist Turn of Romantic-Era Disability Studies, or Frankenstein in the Dark." *Literature Compass* 14, no. 7 (2017): e12400.

Wide Lawns. "The Vines in My Mind—My Struggle with Postpartum OCD." Last updated March 31, 2011. http://widelawns.blogspot.com/2011/03/vines-in-my-mind-my-struggle-with.html.

Wilensky, Amy. *Passing for Normal: A Memoir of Compulsion*. New York: Broadway Books, 2010.

Wortman, Fletcher. "'Girls' Gets OCD." *Psychology Today*. Last updated March 13, 2013. https://www.psychologytoday.com/us/blog/triggered/201303/girls-gets-ocd-0.

Index

K. Béres Rogers, *Creating Romantic Obsession*, Palgrave Studies in Literature, Science and Medicine, https://doi.org/10.1007/978-3-030-13988-9

CPSIA information can be obtained
at www.ICGtesting.com
Printed in the USA
LVHW051739110419
613834LV00010B/311/P